Simeon Eben Baldwin

Modern political Institutions

Simeon Eben Baldwin

Modern political Institutions

ISBN/EAN: 9783337078416

Printed in Europe, USA, Canada, Australia, Japan

Cover: Foto ©ninafisch / pixelio.de

More available books at **www.hansebooks.com**

Modern Political Institutions

By

Simeon E. Baldwin, LL.D.

President of the American Social Science Association
formerly President of the American Bar Association and of
the New Haven Colony Historical Society

Boston
Little, Brown, and Company
1898

Copyright, 1898,
By SIMEON E. BALDWIN.

All rights reserved.

University Press:
JOHN WILSON AND SON, CAMBRIDGE, U.S.A.

TO

WILLIAM KNEELAND TOWNSEND, D.C.L.

DISTRICT JUDGE FOR THE DISTRICT OF CONNECTICUT,
PHELPS PROFESSOR OF LAW IN THE YALE LAW SCHOOL,

ONCE MY PUPIL,
LONG MY ASSOCIATE,
ALWAYS MY FRIEND,

THIS WORK IS DEDICATED.

CONTENTS.

Chapter		Page
I.	Introduction	1
II.	The Centenary of Modern Government	6
III.	The First Century's Changes in our State Constitutions	45
IV.	Absolute Power, an American Institution	80
V.	The Exemption of the Accused from Examination in Criminal Proceedings	117
VI.	Freedom of Incorporation	141
VII.	American Jurisprudence	239
VIII.	The Decadence of the Legal Fiction	266
IX.	The Recognition of Habitual Criminals as a Class to be Treated by Itself	290
X.	The Defence by the State of Suits Attacking Testamentary Charities	316
XI.	Salaries for Members of the Legislature	322
XII.	Permanent Courts of International Arbitration	341
XIII.	The Monroe Doctrine in 1898	359
Index		369

Modern Political Institutions

CHAPTER I

INTRODUCTION

MODERN history, as that term is commonly used, may be said to date from the first publication of printed books. Modern politics can hardly be said to have begun to shape themselves until after the Protestant Reformation, nor to have assumed anything like definite and settled form before the middle of the eighteenth century. Modern political institutions are of still later growth. Political history is the tree from which they branch. Many a shoot is put forth in the spring-time of a nation, to wither and perish. The work of natural selection is nowhere so unremitting and remorseless as in the development of processes of government. The Puritans and the Commonwealth brought no lack of new political theories before the people of England and of New England. Many were tried, but few chosen. The French philosophers of the eighteenth century did as much for their countrymen, and the revolution, which they brought on, winnowed their work, and scattered most of it to the winds. Their seeds of socialism were blown over Europe, and have found perhaps the most friendly soil among the Germans, but from the counter spirit of imperialism with which they must contend, what root they have taken there is for the most part of a sentimental and personal, rather than a practical and national description. And where any new principle of legislation or jurisprudence has been fairly adopted by any nation, it cannot assume an institutional character until the generation by which it was adopted has passed away.

Political institutions rest on popular assent. They must have been tested by long use, and not found wanting. They must seem part of the natural order of things to those whom they affect; and nothing seems natural to any man into which, as part of his earliest surroundings, he was not born and bred. Such there are, native to the nineteenth century. It came into existence when they were already established, and it accepted them, if not without a question, yet at least with the presumption in their favor. It has added to them others, akin in character, and to the second and third generation of men which it has produced, these too have been familiar and cherished from earliest childhood.

It is of institutions of our own time, institutions which became such by the recognition and approval of our own century, or are contending for that of the twentieth, that this volume is designed to speak. And what, taking the term in this sense, are the chief among modern political institutions?

Any answer that can be given must be largely a matter of individual opinion. I shall venture to state them, as they appear to me, in the order of their importance.

INTRODUCTION

The foundation of all government on the consent of a majority of the people.

Religious liberty.

The written constitution as the supreme law.

The protection by law of the individual against the State.

The protection by law of the individual against himself.

The combination of political absolutism with democracy.

The secret ballot.

Simpler and surer methods of legal procedure.

Freedom of incorporation under general laws.

Minority representation in office.

The regulation of succession to the dead in the interest of the State.

International arbitration.

To these I would add, for the United States, the Monroe Doctrine.

Political institutions come unheralded and unnamed. They defy close classification. It is hard even to define what manner of thing they are.[1] A law may

---

[1] One may be warned against the attempt by the definition of a legal institution recently essayed by a scholarly writer on the law of Corporations, in the following words : —

"The term legal institutions connotes a body of legal rules in their manifestation in legal relations between persons of whom certain correlated conditions of fact are predicable." (Taylor on Corporations, § 24.)

The hardest things to define are, happily, those which are so well understood that definition is unnecessary, except as a scholastic exercise. I once spent towards half a day with two friends in discussing the proper definition of "a stone." We failed to frame any that could pretend to exactitude, but nevertheless, in common with everybody

serve as their starting-point, but it can be nothing more. That only can be called an institution which has fastened itself upon the community, and sunk its hold deep into the heart and life of the people. No institution can be called great which has not thus become a part of the political conceptions and existence of more lands than one. In the brief list which has been given, there may be some which have less right to recognition than others that will occur to the thoughtful reader. There are some which loom up more boldly before the American than they may before the European. I believe, however, none have been included which do not fairly belong to the domain of the universal in modern state-craft. Each but the last has already been transplanted far, and each is of a kind to root in any soil.

Of the dozen which have been named, there are several of which little will be said. These are the best and most familiar. They speak for themselves; and more consideration has seemed due to those which appear open to just criticism, or are the growth of comparatively recent years.

Several of the chapters which follow treat of institutions which I had made, in previous years, the subject of public addresses, and my views are often expressed in the language employed on those occasions. I am sensible that such words may have a warmth of tone that seems less suited to the printed page than to the platform, but my apology must be that I feel warmly, now, as I did then, what to

else we all knew very well when to use the word, and what was the appearance of its subject.

Americans is the national importance of the theme. Unity of social policy, uniformity of statute law and judicial procedure, solidarity of national beliefs,— these are what the people of the United States must put before themselves as the ideals to be striven for. Their ultimate fulfilment has been made possible by the civil war that swept away forever what had made till then the great difference between the Northern and the Southern States, and brought in the new nation. It is hard not to be declamatory when one speaks in earnest, with such aims in view.

CHAPTER II

THE CENTENARY OF MODERN GOVERNMENT [1]

1789-1889

THE closing quarter of the nineteenth century came crowded with great anniversaries. A long series of American centennials ended with that of the voyage which first really added the new world to the old. England in 1888 commemorated the peaceful revolution which set William of Orange on her throne, and France a year later was on fire with the recollections of the fiercer struggle that re-created her institutions.

But among all these centennial years that of 1889 stood out the first, because it had more than a national significance. It closed the centenary of modern government.

Modern languages, modern literature, with its spirit of free inquiry, modern civilization and discovery, bringing in powers and necessities unknown before, had all given their new life to society before Europe began to demand political freedom. It was the incapacity of a highly civilized society, merely as such, to satisfy the human soul, that drove men to a new

---

[1] In preparing this chapter, free use has been made of the annual address before the American Bar Association delivered by the author at its meeting in Chicago, August 29, 1889.

opening for their energies in public life and in the public good. James Wilson, in the Convention by which Pennsylvania ratified our national Constitution, declared that the science of government seemed yet to be almost in its state of infancy. It was not because mankind were unfamiliar with the different forms governments may assume, or the different ends they may serve. It was known that they might be constituted simply for the good of the governed and by their consent. We had had free constitutional commonwealths on our own soil since the days of the Puritans, the sturdy outgrowth of the life of a liberty-loving people. But those colonial republics, such as Connecticut and Rhode Island, had nothing in them of the nation. If, for a few years, they claimed a kind of autonomy, it was soon gladly exchanged for a chartered dependence on the British crown.

In Europe there had been democracies and republics through half the history of the human race, but which of them deserved the name or earned the place of a constitutional government? England, if any. England had tried and executed one king, and had driven another from her throne a hundred years before the Federal Constitution was adopted; but England was still a monarchy, supported by an hereditary aristocracy and a corruptible and corrupted Commons, and limited by nothing stronger than traditions, as they might be interpreted by judges appointed by the crown.

Frederick Robertson said, fifty years ago, that he would close his Bible forever if he did not look for better times for England — times when merit should find its level; when worth should be interpreted by what a man is, and not by what he has, nor by what his relations have been.

The Declaration of Independence brought in such times to America. If for the next quarter of a century there lingered too much deference for distinctions of birth, if for the last quarter of a century there has been growing up a new power of property to give the rich too much of public consideration, these tendencies, at most, have been too slight to affect the main current of American life. It has swept on towards a true liberty, equality, fraternity; truer than has ever yet come to the great nation where first those words were linked together, — because she sought them by the path of destruction. She was driven by a sad history to seek them there. But to American soil they had been borne by friendly hands a century before. "The Mayflower" brought with her more than her company of Pilgrims.

> "Laws, Freedom, Truth, and Faith in God
> Came with those exiles o'er the waves."

And the spirit of Puritanism was nobler than Puritanism. They "builded better than they knew." It may be that the spirit of New England Puritanism was nobler than the spirit of Puritanism in the land they left. It looks so, as we review the history of their century, and see England turn so sharply from the austere simplicity of the Commonwealth to the gay license that came in with Charles the Second. No such revulsion of public feeling marked the return of the Stuarts in the American colonies. No man here had been acting a part. Institutions had been founded on ideas, not on military successes or political triumphs. Those ideas, no doubt, fell short of the ideals of the Americans of those days, as they fall short of ours; but their direction was right. They heralded the approach of modern government. For the first beginnings of its actual, its acted life, we look to America; for the first beginnings of its philosophy, we look to France.

France was to the statesmen of our Revolution what Greece in her days of greatness was to early Rome, the source of intellectual and political inspiration. They looked to England for precedents, to France for principles. The same year [1] had given to the world the studies of Pothier and D'Aguesseau in Roman law, and of Montesquieu on the spirit of laws in general. In the youth of Jefferson and Adams, of Madison and Hamilton, Montesquieu's definitions of jurisprudence, his rule for the threefold division of power, his limitation of republican government to small States, were the talk of the day.

France and America were both preparing, though they hardly knew it, to put these philosophies to a test.

The two countries had before them, each, a very different task. Both were to reform their political institutions. But France had also to reform, to re-adjust, to re-constitute, the relations of her people to each other.

The States General was a gathering of classes around a sovereign. King, nobles, clergy, commons

[1] 1748.

met to work some unknown, yet inevitable change in their mutual attitude. The law might thenceforth make all commons, all sovereigns; but generations must pass before such a law could be a living thing. When a society is re-constructed from turret to foundation-stone, by some fiat of legislation, make it what you will, and it remains still but a castle in the air, till long years have made men used to their new conditions. Then first will liberty, if it was gained, become a real possession, because then only will it be known for what it is.

No such issue lay before the American people when our States General — the representatives of their thirteen free commonwealths — met at Philadelphia in 1787. There were no hereditary privileges to attack, no absolute power to check, no classes to harmonize.

It was two years later that the people of France, represented in a National Assembly, published their memorable Declaration of the Rights of Man.

The States General, out of which that Assembly sprang, had been convoked for the first time for a century and a half. There is something majestic in the gathering of such a body, to be called into existence only at vast and unknown intervals, on some great emergency of State. So men felt, whatever their religious faith, when the Church of Rome brought together, in 1870, at the Vatican, the first council of her prelates throughout the world that had met since that assembled at Trent three hundred years before, to stay the progress of the Protestant Reformation. So it was when the delegates of the American people, for the first and last time met in convention in 1787, to frame a Constitution that would perpetuate their union. Such an assembly, with its far-reaching powers, untried by use, may precipitate or it may prevent a revolution.

When President Harrison, in 1889, stood in New York, on the spot where, under his great predecessor, the first true government of the United States began, to celebrate the close of its first century, no memories were recalled but those of peace. But when, a week later, President Carnot, at Versailles, met the legislature of the French Republic to commemorate the anniversary of the opening of the States General, no one could forget the reign of terror that had so soon followed the reign of despotism. The States General had met in the beginning of the seventeenth century. They met next at the end of the eighteenth. During that long stretch of time France had had no government but the king. While Virginia was forming her House of Burgesses that brought representative government into America; while the Puritans were constituting Christian commonwealths in New England; while all the English colonies on this continent were alike learning the true maxims of civil liberty; while the leaders of our Revolution were growing into statesmen by slow experience, — Frenchmen could know the principles of politics only by study of books, or by observation in foreign lands. We cannot wonder, then, that France, in 1789, felt that as for her civil institutions she had nothing to preserve; that all were bad, and that to abolish all was her first duty.

In his commemorative address, on the occasion I have just named, President Carnot declared that this meeting of the States General created a new era in history, and founded modern society.

It is a bold claim for any people to make that by one national event they have changed the current of human history. It has been made by Americans for the social compact signed upon the "Mayflower;" for the early Constitution of Connecticut; for the Declaration of Independence; for the formation of the Federal Constitution. But the real, unsolved problem of government, in 1789, was to make and keep a great people free; not any infant colony of Plymouth or Connecticut; nor any petty republic of Attica or San Marino; not even any cluster of States, bound together while fighting for independence; but a great people, spread over a great territory.

The United States of 1789 rested on a Constitution framed two years before, subversive and destructive of an earlier Constitution agreed to as perpetual; and of our thirteen States two had deliberately refused to accept the second. To the National Assembly of France, as to the ministry of Great Britain, it seemed, in 1789, that the American experiment had already failed.

But modern government was not to be compassed in a day. For one thing it needed a revival of that spirit of national patriotism that had been dead or sleeping since the days of the Roman republic.

Patriotism had been the keystone of virtue to the ancient world. It had glorified with immortality the pass of Thermopylæ, and made men deem a few sprigs of laurel or a street procession the most precious thing in life. But from the day that Brutus trampled on human love, for love of country, to the day when the dagger of political assassination reappeared in Europe, in the hands of a woman, and Charlotte Corday slew one of the new Cæsars of new-born France, the very word "patriotism" had gone out of the speech of men, and almost out of the thought of poets. Loyalty had usurped its place: the bond to law, not to country; to your king, your feudal lord, not to your fellow-citizens; to the Church universal, perhaps, not to the altars of your own community.

"Patriotism," said Johnson, after the American Revolution had done its work, "is the last refuge of a scoundrel." "Patriotism," wrote Lessing a few years before, "is, at the highest, a heroic weakness which I am very glad to be without." The world had been without it since the first century of the Christian era. It fell at Rome when free government fell. It found no help in the Christian Church. That had for its purpose the submission of all nations to a common faith, and it strove for a thousand years to achieve it by subordinating civil to ecclesiastical authority. The spirit of individualism arose in protest, and put manhood before citizenship. The middle ages rolled away; the Renaissance was followed by the Reformation; the Stuarts yielded to the Commonwealth, the Commonwealth to the Stuarts; the new world was peopled with European colonies; and still the life of modern society was unconceived.

The light broke when French philosophers asserted that correlation of forces in political power by which a true socialism complements a true individualism;

by which the authority, which must always be administered by a few, shall be constituted and controlled by the many; by which, as Mill has said, "the importance of the masses becomes constantly greater; that of individuals, less."

France has made the "Ideas of Eighty-nine" a familiar phrase, but they were only the acted expression of ideas struck out on the same soil a generation before. And modern government has risen out of them but slowly into form. The key with which the spirit of our time unlocks all mysteries, the law of evolution, life-giving and life-lifting, has done its work. In institutions, as in animated nature, there is the struggle for existence, and the survival of those fittest to survive.

And what, as we review the century, has been achieved, what retained, and what discarded? How has socialism been blended with individualism? What new ends have been proposed for legislation; what new immunities secured; what new chapter of liberty opened?

We must answer, first, that modern government does not concern itself only with the material well-being of the community. *Magna Charta* is no more its measure than is the Decalogue the measure of Christianity. The right to personal security, to property, to trial by one's peers, to tax one's self, — to establish these was the ultimate end of ancient government. Modern government retains them all, but adds: the right of equality before the law, and in the law; the duty in civil matters to ignore distinctions of religion; the duty of spreading education, information, intelligence at public cost; the right of labor to protection, at the expense of capital, and in the interest of humanity.

If I were to say which of these things was in the highest sense the fruit of our own century, I should name religious liberty.

Nowhere, until the last part of the eighteenth century, had the State been kept totally separate from the institutions of religion. The original beginning of human society, in the family, the clan, the tribe, made the patriarch also the priest. The household gods were peculiar to the household; the national gods to the nation. Religion was a part of patriotism. Rulers might change; kings might give place to republican magistrates; but the national deities, the national worship, would remain the same. *Pro aris et pro focis* was the watchword of war.

Christianity came, and found the world subject to this law. But the spirit of Christianity was universal, catholic, not national. Its kingdom was not of this world. As, however, its doctrines spread, and as some of them began to be but half understood by those who taught them, government turned to it for aid. It became a part of the imperial system. When that fell, it conquered the conquerors, and for fourteen hundred years was the stay of every civilized government in Europe and America.

The religious liberty for which the Puritans crossed the sea was simply liberty to make their form of religion the law of a new community. Rhode Island, with her utmost toleration, allowed no Roman

Catholic in public office until long after the Declaration of Independence.[1] In Protestant Europe, as in Catholic Europe, the union of Church and State remained unbroken. Men had risen up against the tyranny of ecclesiastical power; men had pulled kings from their thrones and set up others, or set up none. The same struggle against unjust government had sometimes been shared by those who attacked the Church and those who attacked the State. The same leaders might indeed attack both, but they seldom attacked or questioned the union of both. In England the Puritans fought against episcopal, the Republicans against royal tyranny; but both were ready to bind the Commonwealth to another form of national religion.

A State church had, no doubt, been long the scorn of atheists and indifferentists; but it endured until religion itself rose to the level of rejecting it; until Christianity came to see and teach that there are two worlds about us: the world we live in knowingly, — the world of time, the world of the body and the mind; and the world we live in unknowingly, — the world of eternity, the world of the spirit; that governments belong only to the world of the present, with no larger life than it can give; that they are less than the men they govern, and when they have sought to give laws to the human spirit have opposed themselves to the order of the universe.

Modern government began when the State withdrew from its long alliance with Christianity.

[1] 1783.

It was a natural epoch in the history of individualism. Family, patriarchal, tribal governments, had rested on a family, patriarchal, tribal religion. The teachers of Christianity had sought to make one family of all nations, under the Church of Rome, and had failed in the attempt. The Protestant Reformation had — so far as governments were concerned — done little except to put the power of the Church into the hands of the civil magistracy. But, so far as individual men were concerned, it had declared a new right of private judgment in matters of religion. And, however kings and legislators may have endeavored to reconcile this right with religious establishments at the common cost, the struggle has been a hopeless one.

Nor need I say that religion has nowhere suffered by being left to itself. In Leipsic, for instance, where a certain form of religious establishment exists, with a population of nearly 200,000, there are now but six churches in which Sunday services are regularly held. In no American city of that size would there be found less than a hundred; and it is on American soil that disestablishment had its earliest and has struck its deepest roots.

Virginia, in 1786, in a statute drafted by Jefferson, proclaimed it " to be a natural right of mankind that religious opinions shall never affect civil capacities, and that no man can be compelled to support any religious worship." This declaration, soon translated into French and Italian, was circulated widely in southern Europe. Madison had defended it in the legislature with his accustomed vigor. The question, he said, had been stated by the opponents of the bill, as if it were, "Is religion necessary?" But the true question was, "Are establishments necessary for religion?"

Next came the Ordinance of 1787, to lay the foundations of government for the vast territory out of which sprang the commonwealths surrounding the great lakes. It has not the ring, upon this point, of the statute of Virginia, but it does declare that no person shall ever be molested on account of his mode of worship or religious sentiments, so long as he keeps the public peace.

That same summer the convention that framed our Constitution was sitting with closed doors in Philadelphia. Its work was, no doubt, in the main, a rearrangement of existing materials. It took American institutions and put them in a new order and combination. But it did more.

Every delegate came from a State where some civil distinctions had always flowed from religious distinctions. There was probably not more than one who would not have considered himself an adherent of the Christian faith. The leaders were familiar with the political philosophy of antiquity, and with that of their own day; with Montesquieu and with Adam Smith. They found an unbroken current of authority in favor of uniting civil and religious institutions, to some extent, in every government. And yet at the call of the youngest of them, Charles Pinckney of South Carolina, fresh from his law studies in the Inner Temple, they were ready to take this great step forward, by forever prohibiting all religious tests for office or public trust, under the United States. He made the proposition a month after the enactment of the Ordinance of 1787. The committee of detail to which it was referred took no notice of the suggestion in their report; but Pinckney secured its adoption as an amendment, and it stands as the close of the last Article but one.

In advocating the ratification of the Constitution in the South Carolina convention, a year later, he insisted on this feature as all-important. There was, he said, but one great government in Europe which provided for the security of private rights, and that withheld from part of its subjects the equal enjoyment of their religious liberties. Avoiding this error, we were to "be the first perfectly free people the world had ever seen."[1]

At this time, we must not forget, and for forty years later, the Test Act and Corporation Act of England excluded all men from office who were not members of the Church of England. Most of our own States retained some religious test as a qualification for the higher offices, and religious establishments were not forbidden in any, and expressly provided for in the Constitutions of six.[2]

This opening of public trusts to all men, on an equal footing, found warm support from the leaders of the clergy, even in New England, where their influence was strongest. Fifteen ministers were members of the Massachusetts convention, and all but one voted for the ratification of the Constitution.

[1] 4 Elliott's Debates, 319.
[2] Delaware, Georgia, Maryland, Massachusetts, New Hampshire and South Carolina.

"Many," said one of them, the Rev. Isaac Backus, with reference to this abolition of religious tests, "appear too much concerned about it, but nothing is more evident, both in reason and the Holy Scriptures, than that religion is ever a matter between God and individuals. . . . The imposing of religious tests hath been the greatest engine of tyranny in the world."[1]

"God alone," said Rev. Phillips Payson, in the same body, "is the God of the conscience; and consequently attempts to erect human tribunals for the consciences of men are impious encroachments on the prerogatives of God."[2]

The provision against religious tests for office left Congress still free to set up a religious establishment. One may well fall without the other. Such has been the slow course of English history. But when the sons of New England Puritans, New York Churchmen, Pennsylvania Quakers, Maryland Catholics, Virginia Cavaliers, Huguenot Carolinians, came together to join their independent commonwealths in a national life, they could not fail to see that church unity was impossible. The very fact that so many of our States had had a State religion was the strongest argument why the Union should have none.

New Hampshire, where Roman Catholics were debarred from office until 1877, was the first to propose[3] a further guaranty of religious liberty as an amendment to the Constitution. Virginia and New York

---

[1] 2 Elliott's Debates, 148. [2] *Ibid.*, 120. [3] June 21, 1788.

acted promptly in the same direction, and it was for want of this, among other provisions, that North Carolina refused to ratify the Constitution at all. At the first session of the first Congress, such an amendment was proposed to the States. It was set third in a list of twelve, preceded by one to regulate the number of representatives in the lower house, and another to prevent Congress from increasing the pay of its members after their election. The States impatiently swept both of these away, and so put at the head of the ten which they ratified the provision against church establishments and church domination, — fitly placed first, because the most important, the most novel of all.

The National Assembly of France was also moving towards the same end, and there, too, the mass of the clergy were at first with the reformers. Progress in Europe has been naturally slower than with us, for there was more to surrender. The support of the nation has often been accorded to different churches, on equal terms. There has been disestablishment in one part of a country, and not in another. But it is safe to say that in no country of Christendom is any church connected with the government in the same close way in which it was throughout the course of ancient society.

And this again has thrown new functions on the State.

The Church, in former days, had the general charge of education. It collected the scholars, it supplied the teachers, it paid them, it regulated their work, and saw that its own doctrines and discipline were made a part of all instruction. But when it could no longer draw from the public treasury, or when the State went one step further and deprived it of its accumulated possessions, this duty of education became a public one. The more ignorant the people, the firmer the government, when that government exists for others' benefit. But give the people real power, and they must be taught how to use it, if you would not have it used to their destruction.

I do not forget that public education had been the child of New England from the days of the Puritans. But only in this century has it become national, and, we may say, universal in free governments.

It was the French Constitution of 1791 that really introduced it as a feature of modern government on a great scale; and Germany adopted the principle of compulsory education when it was, even here, but a half-tried experiment.

That the ideal State should rest on a basis of public instruction is indeed no idea of modern times. When Plato sketched his plan of the republic of the future, he set it on that foundation. It was the hope of Harrington, — the early practice of Massachusetts and Connecticut. It was for our age to extend it to great nations, at the cost of millions; to bring it even into Oriental government, so that in Japan to-day there are 30,000 public schools, nearly 200 colleges, and two great universities, all largely supported from the imperial treasury.

But this transfer of a great prerogative from the

Church to the people has its inevitable dangers. If there is a national peril towards which we are now drifting, it lies in this direction. It is the question of the right and duty of the State as to education in matters of religion.

It is the law of many of our States that every child must be educated to a certain point, either at a public school or under private instruction. The Roman Catholic Church has always believed that religion, and the religion which it holds itself, is a necessary part of all true education. It has, during the last twenty years, taken formal issue with the American public-school system and organized a system of its own, of parochial schools. Whether this policy be right or wrong, there should be, surely, the fullest liberty to pursue it. Laws have been recently proposed in more than one of the States to forbid the use of any text-book in a private school not examined and approved by some public authority, and even to make it penal to use influence upon a father to induce him to take his children out of a public school. If such laws ever come to be enacted, it would be indeed a sign that the principles of American liberty are losing ground.

The State church was never without a State university, and it was a fitting thing that the hand which drew the Declaration of Independence was also that which sketched the plan for the first great State university in America. The epitaph of Jefferson, written by himself, names but three events in a long life of public service, and they epitomize the history of American liberty. "HERE," say the solemn words, —

"HERE LIES BURIED

THOMAS JEFFERSON,

AUTHOR OF THE DECLARATION OF AMERICAN INDEPENDENCE,
OF THE STATUTE OF VIRGINIA FOR RELIGIOUS FREEDOM,
AND FATHER OF THE UNIVERSITY OF VIRGINIA."

The influence of an established church, also, in literature was always a controlling one. The great libraries, from which all good books grow, were founded and maintained by its revenues. Modern government has inherited this function, and the public library, free to all, and open to every author, from vast collections like the British Museum to the bookcase in the country schoolhouse, is the great gift of the age towards a larger national life.

The State church was a great bureau of registration, tracing out, where it was strongest, by its entries of baptisms, marriages, and funerals, the course of every individual life. The place of this is now everywhere supplied by a system of public record offices.

In thus separating from any political union with the Church, the State does not cease to regard it as a natural ally. And, in token of this, an exemption from taxation of property held for religious uses of any kind is almost universally conceded, the equivalent, of course, of a large annual grant from the treasury. Government seeks no longer from the Church the aid of any divine sanction for constituted authority, but it still recognizes religion as the best teacher of morals, and therefore the best friend of public order among a free people.

The exclusion of the Church, with its paternal authority and paternal bounty, from a voice in government, has contributed greatly towards the development of that State socialism which no civilized country is now wholly without.

It begins with giving free schools, free libraries, perhaps free universities; but it does not stop there. It establishes parks, museums, galleries of art; builds railroads, and controls them; inspects the tenement house; lays paved sidewalks in every village. It arranges this vast system of national and international mails, by which two cents takes a letter from Boston to San Francisco, and five cents carries it to Tokio or Australia. It regulates the hours of labor, the age of labor. It throws new duties on the employer. In Germany, where State socialism goes farthest, it forces the laborer to insure himself, out of his wages, against the chance of future want, as we have long compelled our seamen to insure in the same way against sickness or disability, by payments to the Marine Hospital Fund.

But while State socialism means more in one country than another, modern government has one universal characteristic, — popular representation in the legislature, based on a wide and constantly widening grant of suffrage.

There were hardly any of our American States, a hundred years ago, which did not demand that the elector should be a tax-payer. There are hardly any now that do require it. England has reached almost the same result. Germany, France, and Greece have gone beyond it, and made suffrage universal. Every citizen is incorporated into the German Empire by taking him, through a public education and military service, up to the ballot-box, on equal terms.

The republic is but one form of modern government, but this republican principle of a broad suffrage is at work in all. Its inevitable tendency is towards the universal abolition of class distinctions, — a tendency stronger, of course, in proportion to the freedom and equality already gained.

It was this that forced negro suffrage upon the South at the close of the Civil War. There were weighty reasons against thus pushing the freedman at once into the ranks of the electors. He belonged to a race that has known little of political power, and done nothing to prove its fitness to enjoy it, and he had been reared in ignorance and dependence. But negro suffrage was an American idea. It prevented the formation of a new social class. Laws had already been passed in several of the Southern States — " apprentice laws " — which would soon have formed one, had a class of freedmen survived the war.

The negro has often used the suffrage ignorantly, selfishly, unwisely. Many another has done the same. But when he received the gift and passed into the great circle of American citizenship, the last class less than citizens was abolished, I hope forever, from American statute-books. Nor was it, as an indication of political development, to be compared in significance to the movements in a similar direction in England, beginning with the Reform Bill of 1832, and ending with the vote, in 1889, of the House of Commons, when 160 members declared themselves in favor of abolishing all hereditary seats in the House of Lords, and the government could muster but about 200 to defeat the motion.

The grant of suffrage to women is now becoming common in municipal elections. It has been tried in those of a more public character. If I were to forecast the future I should say that whether modern government in Europe is to tend towards republicanism or towards monarchy will depend in no small degree upon its treatment of this question.

Goethe has declared that women love order rather than freedom. If the number of voters is doubled by their admission to it, the stability of settled dynasties and the glitter of courts may find a new support against any movement towards the rough changes of republican administration.

Modern government makes the ballot more and more the instrument of suffrage, even in legislatures. The change in this has been almost revolutionary.

In England, landlords seeking to control their tenants, employers seeking to control those in their service, established interests seeking to prevent reform, and sentimentalists relying on the dignity of manhood, had combined to exclude it from her institutions. Even in the Municipal Corporations Act of

1835, the ballot in municipal elections was made an open one, with the name of the voter who cast it written upon each.

Our own colonies passed into independence under the influence of the same ideas. Down to 1787 the State of New York had always elected the members of its legislature by acclamation, and its first Constitution permitted a change to election by ballot simply as something worthy of a "fair experiment"[1] and subject to a return to the old system, if the legislature should decide that the experiment was unsuccessful.

But no free nation has ever adopted the ballot and then discarded it, unless she was ready to discard her freedom. The ends of modern government demand it in its completest form. It was for remote Australia to revive this form, after the lapse of two thousand years, and give the world again the secret ballot as Cicero knew it, when he described it as the *vindex tacitæ libertatis*. The Roman ballot, under the Gabinian law, was furnished by the State, and bore the names of all who were in nomination, the elector marking by a point that of the candidate whom he preferred. The interplay of national influences, so characteristic of the age, was never more conspicuous than in the re-introduction of this plan in modern use. Successful in Australia, England, under the lead of Gladstone, did not disdain to follow one of her youngest children in extending it to Parliamentary elections, and our own States have adopted it in rapid succession.

[1] Poore's Charters and Constitutions, ii. 1333.

Modern government is coming to put a new limitation on the suffrage, — that the majority shall not govern.

Minority representation in office is the invention of the last half of the century, both as regards elections by districts of inhabitants of the district, as distinguished from voting for a general ticket, and as regards voting for less than the number to be elected.

Thirty years ago this latter plan was adopted by the British Parliament for the elections to the House of Commons from some of the larger constituencies, and a few years later the cumulative vote became a part of the elective system of Illinois for members of its legislature, and was adopted by Pennsylvania for the government of her private corporations. In our municipal corporations, one or the other of these methods is rapidly becoming the rule for the election of all official boards.

But with all these changes in the range and mode of suffrage, the power that goes with it, as distinguished from the numbers by whom it is shared, has not risen to the height anticipated in the "ideas of '89," as these were formulated then in the Constitution of the French Republic. Sovereignty, they said, belonged to the people. It was one and indivisible, imprescriptible and inalienable. One generation could not bind succeeding generations to its laws.[1]

Jefferson's private correspondence shows that he brought back from France these conceptions of the

[1] Constitution of 1793, Articles 25 and 28.

rights of the people, but they found no place in his political action or in the institutions of America.

On the contrary, it is the corner-stone of modern government that there shall be obligations created or preserved by an organic law which no popular majority and no legislative majority can overcome, except through forms and delays prescribed by that law for its own defence. It is this that makes the modern republic — that has made the United States and every State that is associated to compose them — possible. And it is itself made possible by an American device.

The history of all republics before ours had been that either of weakness or of certain lapse into the hands of tyrants. It was for us to show that supreme and ultimate power could be so intrusted to a few men that they would have slight temptation to abuse it, and that its exercise would seldom cause political disturbance, or even attract so much as the notice of the community.

The problem was to make the legislative power, whether exercised by popular or parliamentary vote, subject to some superior authority, and still leave it free to represent the public will. The American solution is through the judiciary, but it does not consist in simply writing down that will in the form of a Constitution and comparing every statute with it.

The justiciary of Aragon once had the power of annulling laws which he deemed contrary to the fundamental principles of the monarchy. But he could exercise it of his own motion, as an abstract political question; and the power was found too great to be tolerated. The modern plan of making the political question dependent on the issues of some private litigation, to be decided like any other contested matter incidental to the suit, seems illogical and unsystematic; but it does not offend by any show of authority; it takes the initiative from the court and gives it to any private citizen; it secures respect without seeming to command it.

A Rhode Island court, in 1786, first brought this function of the judiciary distinctly into action, in determining the construction of her charter, and the Circuit Courts of the United States exercised it without hesitation, in reference to an early Act of Congress, five years later,[1] so that when, in *Marbury* v. *Madison*,[2] it was first applied by the Supreme Court, it had already come to be recognized as a necessary part of our American institutions.[3]

The threefold division of the powers of government, insisted on by Montesquieu, is expressed in most modern Constitutions. In monarchies they seek to hold the power of the executive in check by increasing that of the legislature. In republics, they seek to hold the legislative power in check by strengthening the executive.

With us, this confidence in the executive power is not any traditional inheritance from colonial days. The veto of the colonial governors, when they had one, was rarely used except in opposition to the

[1] Hayburn's Case, 2 Dallas, 410.   [2] 1 Cranch, 137.
[3] This subject has been treated of with great fulness and learning in a posthumous essay by Brinton Coxe, on Judicial Power and Unconstitutional Legislation. Phila., 1893.

popular will and the popular interests. In the early State Constitutions, it was rejected, with one solitary exception, — that of Massachusetts. It is now found in all but six.

We have adopted it because experience — and experience is the result of many experiments — has taught us to believe in a strong executive, provided it is a good one, and because we find it easier to watch one man than an assembly of men.

We adopted it in the face of the course of the mother-country, which had turned so sharply in another direction. The Puritans left England before she came to be governed by a ministry, responsible to her legislature. Americans saw her change, in the hundred years that followed the accession of William and Mary, her whole system of administration. The executive was deprived of its veto; the upper house of Parliament crowded back into insignificance; the leader of the House of Commons had become the real king.

All this the new States of America saw, but they still, even while, at first, following England in abolishing the veto power, agreed in rejecting the device of a parliamentary ministry, and deliberately preferred to leave the responsibility of administration unchecked in the hands of their governors.

The Federal Constitution followed in the same lines. The President has his cabinet, but they are nothing in power, — men of his choosing, the agents and assistants of his will, with no seat in Congress, and no fear of it.

The veto, that English kings retain only in name,

has been with us often the best safeguard of the people, and was never more powerful for good than it is to-day. The legislature itself has come often to rely on the executive, and not in vain, to defeat bills which it has not the courage to reject, or the patience to examine. At a recent session of that of our greatest State, two-thirds of the bills enacted were passed within the last ten days; thus leaving it wholly in the hands of the Governor to say, after the adjournment, whether they should become laws or not.

We are not afraid of the executive, because we have guarded ourselves against any act of his that might oppress us by something stronger than *Magna Charta*. We have made him powerful because history has proved, even our own, that the executive power is often the best protection against the tyranny of majorities.

Nor does modern government in any way tend to lessen the personal dignity and weight of the executive. It recognizes the strong impulse of the human mind to respect and reverence for authority, as represented in whatever individual is the titular head of the nation. The public interest in every incident in the daily life of the President of the United States, or of Queen Victoria, means something. It is what has kept alive so many monarchies in the past, which existed only as an incumbrance on society. The personal equation in government is a constant force, the more powerful because unmoved by reason, uncontrolled by law.

We recognize the sentiment of hero-worship, but

we see its limits. Our governments guard against the hero, and against the unwisdom of his worshippers, by laws and institutions that are insensible to enthusiasm.

Carlyle may still preach to this generation that national well-being depends, not on any merit of laws or institutions, but on human goodness and human greatness. The century listens to him with respect, but not with faith. It would have men good, if it can; but it would have good laws, because it can. The people may stand for many bad men, many foolish men, many headstrong men; but the machinery of modern government keeps them in check. Marcus Aurelius was one of the best rulers that mankind has ever had, but the machinery of ancient government allowed him — in all ignorance and honesty of purpose — to persecute and tread down the new religion that had come to transform the earth. The laws of New England, rather than the Puritans, were guilty, when women were hanged as witches at Salem.

For another feature of modern government, we may look back to a Roman origin. The difficulty of combining a strong central administration for an immense territory with due provision for the good government of every part, Rome met by the organization of municipal corporations to regulate local interests. The dark ages, the institutions of feudalism, the strengthening of monarchical power, swept municipal autonomy out of existence. This century has restored it with new guaranties against corruption, or abuse of power, and broadened it from the walled town to the village, the school-district, the county, colony, province and State.

To these local agencies, more and more, matters of local regulation are being confided, and Home Rule has become the watchword of free government.

One quarter of our population is now centred in our cities. A hundred years ago there was no city in the Union which numbered 40,000 inhabitants. How many States are now without one? And how, except in this way, could such great gatherings of freemen be kept in order?

The combination of local home rule with a central authority to direct inter-communication between the several communities, and determine all questions of foreign relations, is the best form that modern constitutions assume.

It was a daring experiment to attempt it here in 1789, and the hazard grew when the Louisiana purchase came, a few years later. It is not too much to say that only the mechanical inventions of the century have preserved its political ideals. The steamboat, the railroad, the telegraph, the newspaper dashed from electrotypes by the cylinder press, have in quick succession brought the broadest territories into close communication with their centres.

In some respects they have reversed the practical working of our own Constitution, as men anticipated it. The electoral colleges, for instance, meeting on the same day in every State, might now agree by telegraph on common candidates; but, on the other hand, modern facilities of travel have made those national conventions possible the power of which has made the presidential electors but empty names. The capital, which many fancied, from the length of the journey to it, would become the ordinary residence of senators, if not of representatives, the seat of an intriguing oligarchy, is the home now of no one but the President, a handful of judges, and the department clerks. The centre of affairs for every office-holder remains the community from which he comes.

The rule of local laws for local interests, enacted under such limitations as may be prescribed by some central authority, has smoothed the way for another innovation of transcendent importance: that all laws must be general, applicable to all men, and all interests, in similar positions. To this, modern society is driven by its rule of equality. The world was not much given to legislation before the days of the French Revolution. All the statutes of Rome, in the days of her greatness, were not more in number than one of our larger States is now accustomed to enact in every decade. There is but one remedy to be applied: the universal prohibition of special legislation where a general law will secure the end. And this is possible only by granting extended powers of local administration to local governments.

The evils of over-legislation in this country, however, are by no means proportioned to its amount. Much of it is, at worst, but useless. Americans do not often legislate except to meet some practical necessity, real or imagined. There is little speculative or theoretical statute law, such as marked the entry of

France into the field of modern government. This makes our statute-books unsymmetrical, but it makes them safe. Nor are our Constitutions as open to this charge as our ordinary legislative acts. We have not forgotten that there are laws so deeply rooted in the society out of which they spring that they execute themselves. We know that these are the best laws, and that the modern Constitution does best when it is their simplest expression.

Another characteristic of modern government is its support from journalism. It may be fairly said that it could not exist and could not have existed without it, less from the direct influence which it exerts than from the publicity and close scrutiny of official action which it secures.

Until a hundred years ago, legislatures, the world over, sat, practically, with closed doors. Journalism during this century has demanded that they be thrown open, and has thus put the people bodily into the legislative assembly. Secrecy has been lost, and safety gained, — safety, for no law is so bad as the ill-considered law, and no law can be well considered that has not been fully discussed in public, by the men whose interests it concerns.

Here, I think, has been the great work of the newspaper in politics. It has turned on the electric light.

Its direct influence on the masses of the people may be easily overrated. It acts on the politicians more than on the community at large. It distributes offices, and brings men into power, but it is often forced to think and act too quickly, perhaps too selfishly, to be in touch with the real movements of public opinion.

Newspaper discussion of questions of State is, no doubt, often flippant, and sometimes shows a desire to say something striking rather than to say something true. In a government like Germany, but half modernized, the newspaper, too, is but half modernized. When Bismarck in 1889 brought into the Reichstag a bill to visit editors of socialistic journals, who denied the right of private property, with three years' imprisonment, it was because he wished no schemes of socialism but his own; and his law showed what Germany lacks, a Constitution which makes socialism, in the evil sense, impossible, and leaves it a harmless theory, the more harmless when the most discussed.

Modern government is becoming more and more a government by party. But parties represent less than they once did. As class lines fade out, and class interests no longer exist to be protected; as public education lifts the mass of the community to a more intelligent and, therefore, more candid view of political questions; as the general tone of morals is strengthened, as strengthened it is by all these influences, — parties come to have no policy but to get into power, or to keep in it, for the sake of place and patronage. Practical politics is thus becoming the art of managing and supporting nominations; and our American system of primary nominating assemblies, by which the voter has two opportunities of power, one at the caucus and one at the polls, seems likely to spread wherever popular election is found, and to find equal protection from law.

It often proves a means of undue minority representation. The nominees ordinarily gain their positions by a slender majority of their own party, and are opposed by the whole of the other. Where parties are nearly equal in numbers, their election, therefore, is really contrary to the will of the majority of the people, though a sense of party obligation may give them the votes of that majority.

And, on the other hand, this exposing every candidate for office to the gantlet of two votes, one of his political associates, and one of the whole people, is no slight guaranty that men notoriously unfit will be either set aside in the caucus or rejected at the polls.

As some barrier to the demands of party, those governments where it is strongest have taken care that their lesser functions shall be performed by those who have some special fitness and training for it. This training may be done by the government or by a private education, but in either case some public examination is the test of its success. Offices are no longer sold, or given. That "public office is a public trust," all governments are coming to acknowledge.

The principles of modern government make new nations conservative, and unsettle old ones.

In no country in the world is property as secure as it is with us. The guaranties of our Constitution have intrenched it against public as well as private attack. The British Parliament, during the last half-century, has destroyed vested rights, broken up titles, seized private property for private use, in a way that to an American seems almost revolutionary. Such legislation is the attempt of an old government to adjust itself to new conditions of society, by the use of powers that belonged to its old conditions. It is putting new wine into old bottles. It benefits one class and spreads a feeling of insecurity through all.

It was the want of guaranties against acts like these that kept the ratification of our Federal Constitution so long in doubt. Its framers guarded the people against unequal or unjust legislation by the States, but as against the United States they only preserved the writ of *habeas corpus*, ensured trial by jury in prosecutions for crime, forbade an increase of penalty after the commission of the act, and defined the nature and consequences of treason.

The contrast is marked between these scanty securities against the unknown powers of the new government they were creating, and the warm declaration of the Rights of Man that, at about the same time, came from the National Assembly of France. But the ideas of '89 in America, were not the ideas of '89 in France. They were then, where we were in '76, thirteen years before, proclaiming the universal rights of mankind. They had not reached the consideration of the particular rights and privileges best suited to the condition of their own people. Or, if they had reached it, they were not ready for it.

Our Constitution, therefore, has a cold and unshapen look as compared with those which France struck off in rapid succession in the closing years of the eighteenth century. This was one of the most telling arguments of those who opposed its ratification.

"In this Constitution," said Thomas Tredwell, in the New York convention of 1788, "we have departed widely from the principles and political faith of '76, when the spirit of liberty ran high, and danger put a curb on ambition. Here we find no security for the rights of individuals, no security for the existence of our State governments; here is no Bill of Rights, no proper restriction of power; our lives, our property, and our consciences are left wholly at the mercy of the legislature, and the powers of the judiciary may be extended to any degree short of almighty."[1]

And, in truth, the people everywhere, with a truer instinct than their leaders, saw with surprise that the Bill of Rights which they had framed into every State Constitution, was wanting here. They gave a hesitating assent to the new scheme, but recommended, in language that meant command, that the omission should be supplied, and supplied at once. Congress obeyed, and the first ten amendments placed the personal rights of the American citizen on higher ground than those then or now belonging to any other people.

But with all this there is no permanence in modern government. In its fundamental principles there is; in the proper adaptation of them to the needs of each

[1] 2 Elliott's Debates, p. 401.

particular community, there is not, and there never can be.

For this very reason it cannot fasten on the East — on Asia or Africa — until untold generations have passed away. Its instability is radically foreign to their national ideas. They can tolerate revolutions of dynasties, but not of laws.

Japan has signalized the opening years of the second century of modern government by the promulgation of a written Constitution. But it emanates from a single hand, which retains still the ultimate sovereignty, as an hereditary and irrevocable right, and forbids any future extension or alteration of its provisions, unless on the proposition of the crown.

The first centenary of modern government is closed. When the second is attained, this country, with a population now exceeding that of any European power but Russia, may not improbably have one as large as all of them combined. It will have had new perils to meet, a larger life to live, a greater work to do.

Carlyle has said that the true bible for every nation is its own history. If so it be, the last books must be better, wiser, truer, than the first. There must be a new testament built upon the old — with its broader, freer, higher life. And such, thank God, is to us, thus far, our bible of American history.

We have taken up the ideas of '89 and advanced them. We have taken religious freedom from the national Constitution, and put it into our State Constitutions also. We have widened suffrage, improved its methods, set guards to the power of the majority. We have advanced and extended public education. We have been loyal to our institutions, faithful to our laws, — each of us, as he understood them; and when men differed, and hesitated in their allegiance between State and nation, by the strong hand of war the will of the nation was lifted into acknowledged and unchallenged supremacy. It cost much: years of angry debate, years of fierce war, hundreds of thousands of lives and thousands of millions of money; but it has been done, and there are few to-day who, if they could, would have the result reversed.

We have carried human charity — in its widest sense — farther than it was ever pushed in any age or land before. We have struck hands with other nations in honest and successful efforts to make the whole world better. The slave-trade has fallen by our aid. International arbitration, in the place of war, has had its noblest illustrations in the last thirty years of American history. The right of choosing one's own sovereign — of voluntary expatriation — we have made, throughout the earth, free to every man who has once left his native land. The project of a code of general laws, common to all nations, once the mere dream of poets, has been put in form by an American,[1] to whose labors in jurisprudence the world is debtor, and is now under serious discussion by the jurists of every civilized country.

[1] David Dudley Field.

Washington, in his inaugural address, a hundred years ago, declared that "the destiny of the republican model of government" was "justly considered as deeply and perhaps finally staked on the experiment intrusted to the hands of the American people." We have fulfilled the solemn trust, and we have done more. In leading the way towards good republican government, we have, almost unconsciously, led the way too toward all that is best in modern government of every name. The great kingdom to which we once belonged is the better because we struck for independence, and has been glad to copy both from our public and our private law. The influence of our institutions is felt in every country where men read and think, and our own continent has been transformed by them into a great sisterhood of free governments, each resting on the consent of its people and planned only to promote their welfare.

CHAPTER III

THE FIRST CENTURY'S CHANGES IN OUR STATE CONSTITUTIONS.[1]

1779–1879

THE earlier Constitutions of our American States were generally quite similar in character. Their aim was to express the fundamental principles of civil liberty in language so explicit that no public officer could ever pretend to misunderstand them, and to distribute all, rather than to withhold any, of the powers of government.

The department most trusted was the legislative, and the main declarations of rights were meant to guard against any abuse of power by the executive and the judiciary.

Nor may we forget that civil liberty in 1776 did not mean what we understand by it to-day. The prevailing lines of thought were aristocratic. Few denied the right to hold men in slavery; fewer still supposed it to be either right or politic that every American citizen should have a vote.

The first Constitutions were hastily put together; sometimes by a revolutionary convention or congress; sometimes by the ordinary legislative assem-

---

[1] In the preparation of this chapter free use has been made of a paper read by the author before the American Social Science Association at Saratoga, September 11, 1879.

bly. The Declaration of Independence found the "old thirteen" colonies at work, as John Adams wrote a friend, erecting governments "as fast as children build cob-houses." Most of them were not much more substantial. They lacked the necessary evidence of popular assent. Two which South Carolina framed before 1779, one by a provincial congress, and one by the General Assembly, were afterwards judicially declared by the Supreme Court of that State to have no more force than any ordinary statute. If any of these so-called Constitutions of first impression, not directly authorized or ratified by popular vote, had greater strength or endurance, it is because they were accepted by general acquiescence, — so general that it might fairly be deemed universal.

Massachusetts and Rhode Island alone submitted theirs to the people for approval, each in 1778, and in each case approval was refused. Both States thereupon proceeded to provide for the assemblage of orderly constitutional conventions, and the work of these bodies was ratified in due course. The earliest true Constitutions, — Constitutions proceeding immediately from the ultimate depositary of sovereign power — were those of Massachusetts, adopted in 1780 and still in force, and of New Hampshire, adopted in 1784 and replaced by a better six years later.

Connecticut and Rhode Island, with the aid of declaratory statutes, maintained their colonial form of government, almost unchanged, until far into the next century.

The earlier Constitutions were made for a homogeneous people, mainly Protestants, few of whom were without property, or in want of remunerative employment. In the more Southern States, particularly in Pennsylvania, Maryland, Virginia, and South Carolina, there were some men whose fortunes would be deemed large even at the present day, and in all a considerable deference was paid to family position and professional rank.

Under the influence of these conditions, suffrage was generally, and office often, limited to certain classes of property holders, and as to the latter some religious test was also imposed.

These restrictions have been gradually disappearing, though four States still require the voter to be a taxpayer, five exclude atheists from public office, and it was not until 1877 that New Hampshire admitted any but Protestants to her legislature.

There were few amendments to any of our Constitutions during the first quarter of a century. Maryland was the first to act in this direction, by one adopted in 1792, to exclude members of Congress from State office and even from voting for State senators.

The only methods originally pursued for making an amendment were (as in Maryland) by a vote of two successive legislatures, or by calling a constitutional convention. In 1818, an important divergence from this policy was initiated by Connecticut, which in that year framed her first (and still only) Constitution. It was largely copied from that adopted by Mississippi the year before, but instead of following her by allowing the legislature, if changes were needed, to call a constitutional convention, provided that amendments proposed by the House of Representatives and agreed to by the succeeding legislature should become part of the Constitution, if ratified by the direct vote of the people at the polls.

This was simply an adherence to the ancient custom of the commonwealth in its colonial days. Its government had been originally constituted by an agreement between the first planters known as the "Fundamental Orders" of January 14, 1638–9.[1] These forbade the immediate re-election of the governor for a second term. In consequence of this, it became the custom to elect the governor of one year to be the deputy governor for the next, and *vice versa*. As the first term of Gov. John Winthrop, Jr., however, neared its close, the General Assembly proposed to the freemen of the colony to remove this restriction on re-eligibility, and ordered the secretary to insert the proposition in his next warrant for the choice of representatives, and to call for a popular vote upon it. This was accordingly had, and resulted in carrying the amendment, restoring for the future a "liberty of free choice yearly."[2]

This early action of the freemen of Connecticut was the origin of the modern *referendum*, rather than, as Borgeaud in his work on American Constitutions[3] has it, the Constitution of 1818 itself.

---

[1] Printed in Colonial Records of Connecticut, i., 20.

[2] Papers of the New Haven Colony Historical Society, vol. v., p. 182.

[3] *L'Établissement et la Révision des Constitutions aux États-Unis d'Amérique*. The passage is quoted in Thayer's "Cases on Constitutional Law," 221.

The Swiss put this method of legislation, in 1874, to a use quite foreign to its original conception, in making it applicable to any law which 30,000 citizens or eight cantons might disapprove. The maxim *Vox populi, vox Dei* justifies taking the popular verdict on those questions only which are of universal interest and prime importance, questions as to which every man's mind is or ought to be made up before they are brought forward for decision by his vote. A people who feel themselves uninformed as to the merits of any measure presented to them for final action will generally vote it down. Such has been the result in practice of the Swiss *referendum*.[1] Laws of the merest detail have been subjected to its operation; among others one granting a salary of $2,000 for a secretary of legation at Washington.[2] The rules of political as well as of dramatic art pronounce against resort on any but grand occasions to the ultimate tribunal of popular sovereignty.

"*Nec deus intersit nisi dignus vindice nodus.*"

Until the Civil War, there were few substantial changes in our principles of constitutional law, other than those already noted. Such as there were tended to lessen the legislative power, by transferring it to the people or imposing absolute prohibitions against its exercise in certain directions. Internal improvements became a fruitful source of action in the latter direction; so did the grant of special charters, or special privileges. The term of office of the governor

---

[1] Moses, on "Federal Government in Switzerland," 119.
[2] Winchester, on "The Swiss Republic," 167.

was prolonged in several States, and his election was generally, and that of the judges often, left to a popular vote. Executive councils and councils of revision or censorship, one after another disappeared.

The new Constitutions or amendments to Constitutions that were adopted were largely intended to secure improvements of an administrative nature. There were new schemes for the composition of the legislature, and the arrangement of electoral districts. The ballot grew in favor. Better provision was made for public education.

And now comes that which breaks the history of the United States sharply in two. The "irresistible conflict" between two philosophies of humanity, two groups of States, reached its final issue.

The Civil War struck slavery out of American government; and the tendency, which had been strengthening for half a century, to make suffrage universal was forced upon the country, irresistibly, by the fourteenth and fifteenth amendments to the Constitution of the United States.

But the war did more. It created a new order of ideas in the business world. The thousand new activities and enterprises that a few years then whirled into life; the sudden rise of great fortunes; the necessary concentration of vast capitals, public and private; the elevation of speculators and adventurers of every sort to the command of millions of money, massed together in the service of corporations; and, with all, that kind of dizzy glare and false coloring by which social ideas are always confused and distorted when a land accustomed to laws is given over to the rule of arms,—all these brought new men and new dangers to the front.

Statutes struggled against them in vain; and the people soon saw that nothing less than radical changes in their civil Constitutions could meet the evil. They were made, and it is to the aim and character of these that we must look for the great alterations thus far made in our system of governmental law.

The first century of American life under Constitutions framed by sovereign States began with the ratification by the people of Massachusetts of the work of their constitutional convention of 1779. The first Constitution of the United States, the Articles of Confederation, though framed by the Continental Congress in 1778, was not ratified until 1781. Massachusetts was the pioneer in re-constituting a political sovereignty by the free consent, formally expressed, of the people from whom it proceeded, and for whose benefit it was to be exercised. Her Constitution is the Alpha and the Omega of constitutional law for the age which produced it,—the only one produced in the eighteenth century which has lived through the nineteenth.

During the fifteen years between 1779 and 1794 ten State Constitutions were adopted: during the fifteen years between 1864 and 1879, thirty-seven. In no intermediate period of the same length had anything approaching the latter number been reached.

The first century of our constitutional existence closed, therefore, at a period of exceptional activity.

This was the work of the politics of the war.

During its progress some of the seceding States, when wholly or partly reoccupied by the national forces, formed temporary Constitutions to meet the exigencies of the times. On the restoration of peace and the adoption of the reconstruction policy, which forced negro suffrage upon the South, other frames of government were required by the party in power, and were wrung from the people as the price of representation in Congress. But, this representation once obtained, several of these States felt that they had fettered themselves too closely, and copied with unnecessary fidelity their Northern models. These, therefore, abrogated their "Reconstruction" Constitutions, and formed others, better suited to their tastes — perhaps to their institutions.

In this way Alabama, Arkansas, Georgia, and Texas each during this period lived under four different forms of government; and most of the other Southern States under three.

Each of these changing Constitutions, however, has naturally had a considerable influence in shaping its successor. North Carolina, for instance, began the Preamble to her Reconstruction Constitution of 1868 thus: "We, the people of the State of North Carolina, grateful to Almighty God, the Sovereign Ruler of nations, for the preservation of the American Union, and the existence of our civil, political, and religious liberties;" and went on to declare "That this State shall ever remain a member of the American Union; that the people thereof are a part of the American nation; that there is no right on the part of the State to secede." Six years later, when in full and unchallenged possession of every right of Statehood, she adopted a new Constitution, but the Preamble and the Declaration of Rights followed to the letter the same language, dictated as it was under circumstances so different.

The special features of these Constitutions of the " reconstructed States," in immediate relation to the war or the negro race, have lost their interest, by reason of the fourteenth and fifteenth amendments to the Constitution of the United States, and the passing out of existence of the Southern freedmen as a separate class. But they dealt also with the whole field of politics, and in common with those adopted during the same years at the North present for consideration certain social forces unconnected with the current politics (as we generally use that term) of the day, which before the close of its first century had stamped themselves deeply on American law and life.

I have said that, in our earlier history, the legislative department was that in which the people put most trust. It was of the people that our Colonial Assemblies were composed; though their governors and judges might be appointed by the crown or raised to office and kept there by the influence of wealth, family, or education, — all greater powers by far in American politics a hundred years ago than now. And it was the inroads of the British ministry upon the peculiar privileges of these Assemblies, I need not say, that brought about the Revolution.

But this generous trust, reposed by our early Constitutions in the State legislatures, was abused. The watch kept over them in colonial days by royal governors, Boards of Trade, and proprietary interests, was withdrawn, and the jealousy which overthrew these had supplied nothing adequate to fill their place. Reckless mismanagement of the public finances, particularly in the West and Southwest, soon followed, — mismanagement of which the consequences were often not developed for many years. State Banks were chartered, and their bills made receivable for taxes. State bonds were issued, and the proceeds sunk in public works, yielding no return. Special privileges were granted to the friends of the leaders of the party in power: trading monopolies; exemptions from taxation; power to corporate organizations to contract on a mere semblance of capital; statutes designed — under the guise of some general object — to affect a particular lawsuit pending in court. Appointments to office became more and more engrossed by the legislature, and offices themselves were needlessly multiplied. Municipal corporations were given unnecessary powers of expenditure, and encouraged to lend their credit to canal or railroad enterprises, which were only called for by a spirit of speculation. It seemed as if almost any legislation had only to be asked, to be granted.

A day of reckoning came. The disasters culminating in the panic of 1837 gave a shock to American credit abroad from which it has never yet fully recovered, but were not enough to wake our own people to a sense of their real danger. The few constitutional changes that it produced were a palliative rather than a preventive. It took another panic, twenty years later, and, more than this, the reaction since the Civil War, to show us and all of us where that danger lay, — that it was indeed in the very ark of the covenant; that those we had most trusted were to be trusted the least.

It brought on at last a new order of things. In the Constitutions and constitutional amendments soberly framed during the last decade of the century under review, we see a wide departure from the theories of government so long and so unquestioningly accepted among us.

The powers of the Executive are enlarged; he is given the power to pardon crimes, which was before intrusted to the sympathies of a mass-meeting (for a legislative assembly, put to this use, deserves no better name). He is allowed to veto one or more items in an appropriation bill, and yet allow the rest to become a law. He is given the appointing power as to important offices, and is, perhaps, himself elected for two or four years instead of one.

The terms of office of the judges have been lengthened; their jurisdiction extended, perhaps to pardons, perhaps to claims against the State, or to advising as to the validity of contemplated legislation; and any claim of judicial power by the legislature, as for instance, over divorces, or contested elections, or testamentary succession, cut off.

But while in general the judiciary has been strengthened, there has been no hesitation in checking its authority wherever it seemed to have borne too hardly on the liberty of the individual. Thus a disposition is shown to limit the power of attachment for contempt; and Louisiana (1879) provides, in favor of witnesses, for the protection of "confidential communications made to medical men by their patients." The ancient provision in our original Constitutions, that justice shall be administered "without sale, denial, or delay," has been found, in some States, to need a practical exposition of its meaning. In Georgia (1877) the Supreme Court is required to dispose of every case by the second term, and if the plaintiff in error be not prepared for argument at the first term ("unless prevented by Providential cause"), the judgment below is to stand affirmed. California (1879) requires from her judges every quarter, before their salaries can be paid, an affidavit that no case which has been submitted to them for over ninety days remains undecided.

Inroads upon the jury system have commenced. Colorado (1876) gives power to the legislature to abolish grand juries and to reduce the panel, in civil causes, to any number less than twelve. Texas (1876) diminishes the grand jury to twelve, of which nine are a quorum; and allows nine jurors in civil causes, and in prosecutions for misdemeanors, to return a verdict. California (1879) also allows verdicts of nine jurors in civil causes. Georgia (1877) refuses a jury trial "in all civil cases founded on unconditional contracts in writing, where an issuable defence is not filed, under oath or affirmation;" requires two verdicts from different juries, on two successive trials, as the condition of a divorce; and allows juries of five in the minor courts. North

Carolina (1876), though repeating her declaration of a hundred years before, in her original Constitution, that "in all controversies at law respecting property, the ancient mode of trial by jury is one of the best securities of the rights of the people, and ought to remain sacred and inviolable," proceeds to declare that "the distinctions between actions at law and suits in equity, and the forms of all such actions and suits, shall be abolished." This simplification of judicial process, while a thing highly desirable in itself, must, thus accomplished, make it far from easy in cases involving equitable rights to determine with precision whether a trial by jury may be demanded, and it will become less easy with every year, as the lapse of time obscures the recollection of the formal procedure, under the common law.

While most of these changes indicate greater trust in the wisdom and discretion of the judiciary, the legislative department has been the subject of universal attack. The chief design of most that was done in constitution-making for the last ten or twenty years of the century under consideration was to reduce the field of statute law, and withhold from it every subject which it is not necessary to concede.

Special legislation, as to any matters which a general law can fairly and reasonably cover, was prohibited. The Pennsylvania Constitution of 1873 may be taken as a type of most of the newer ones in this regard. It specifies about thirty classes of subjects as to which it forbids the passage of any "local or special law." Among them we find: regulating the affairs of municipalities, or chartering any particular one;

changing the descent of property; regulating judicial proceedings; remitting penalties; exempting from taxation; regulating labor; and chartering private corporations. And when local or special laws are necessary, the parties applying for them must give public notice, first, to all adversely interested.

Another provision commonly found is that "no senator or representative shall, during the time for which he shall have been elected, be appointed to any civil office under this commonwealth." This strikes at the root of what few can have failed to observe to be a very dangerous kind of favoritism. Where a legislature appoints to office, it seldom fails to have among its own members applicants for every place, and a natural feeling of fellowship speaks powerfully in their favor. It is hard, also, to deny your vote to a man whose vote you may want for some measure to-morrow. In this way, where the legislature appoints the judiciary, men from among its own members will often go upon the bench, who would never have been thought of for the position, had they been in private life.

Fourteen States originally gave the appointment of the judges to the legislature. All but four of these (Connecticut, Rhode Island, South Carolina, and Virginia) became satisfied that this method is a dangerous one, and discarded it; and a Constitutional amendment to the same effect, emanating from the State Bar Association of Connecticut, was approved by its General Assembly in 1879, and ratified by the people in 1880.[1]

[1] It placed the power of nomination in the hands of the Governor.

Where to place the power thus taken from the legislature has proved one of the most puzzling questions in American politics; but the general drift has been towards popular elections. Twenty-four States followed this mode in 1879, only eleven of which originally adopted it. Thirteen States, at first, gave the appointing power to the Governor, either alone or with the concurrence of a council or other advisory body: nine States, only, then vested it in that manner. A Constitutional amendment proposed by the New York Legislature, in 1873, to return to this plan — the original mode in that State — was defeated by a popular vote of nearly three to one.

The feeling seems to be, not that the people can choose more wisely than the legislature, but that they will choose more honestly. A few years before the change of system in Connecticut, a letter was incautiously dropped in the street, in Hartford, which had been sent by one member of the General Assembly to another. The person addressed was an active friend of a certain candidate for judicial honors, and the writer was desirous of the place of State Prison director. Without any circumlocution he wrote: "If you will support me for State Prison director, I will vote for your man for Judge of the Superior Court." Such bargains ought to be, not merely disgraceful, but impossible.

It is easier to circumscribe the appointing than the removing power. An amendment to the New Hampshire Constitution, prohibiting any removal from office for political reasons only, was sanctioned by the legislature, but defeated before the people, in 1877, receiving a little less than the two-thirds vote required for its ratification.

A seat in the Senate of the United States has, since the Civil War, acquired new dignity, with the steady increase of the powers conceded to the general government. Once thought inferior in position to the governor of his State, a senator now occupies a place of far greater consideration. The composition of the legislature which is to choose one is a subject of special interest on that account. At every stage in the nomination and election of its members the friends of the leading senatorial candidates take an active part.

Nebraska in 1875 initiated a movement which has since found more appropriate expression in a proposition to amend the Constitution of the United States by transferring the election of senators from the legislature to the people. The Nebraska plan was by an amendment of her own Constitution, authorizing a law to the effect that at the State election next preceding the expiration of the term of any United States Senator, "the electors may, by ballot, express their preference for some person for the office of United States Senator." Such a vote would, of course, be preceded by a nomination by each party at a State convention, — a nomination which, if confirmed by the electors, the majority in the legislature could not venture to disregard.[1]

[1] Mr. Schouler, in his "Constitutional Studies" (p. 108, note), calls attention to the fact that this has already been practically tried, with success, more than once in Illinois.

Changes have been found necessary in the mode of transacting legislative business.

The right to call for the yeas and nays has been extended. In Pennsylvania they can be demanded by any two members in either House.

Great trouble had arisen from the passage of bills which had been so altered by insidious amendments, after leaving the committee, as to destroy their original purpose, — perhaps to accomplish the contrary, while the title might remain unchanged, and, like false colors, serve only to mislead. This has been met by provisions that no bill shall be so altered on its passage as to change its purpose; nor voted upon until printed as amended; nor unless read, at length, three times on as many different days; and that the vote on every amendment, and on the bill itself, must be taken by yeas and nays, and the result show a majority of all the members of each House, present and absent, in its favor; also that no bill, except general appropriation bills, shall contain more than one subject, which shall be clearly expressed in its title.

The vote upon every measure must, of course, largely be governed by the statements of the chairman of the committee, or other member, having it in charge. But it seems to have been found prudent to trust to what he says no more than is necessary to secure the prompt transaction of business. If the title of the bill truly describes its only purpose, the most ignorant member may at least know the nature of the subject under consideration; and, where the bill is one of amendment, he is aided by another of these new safeguards, — that so much of the old law as is amended shall be printed, at length, as it will read in its amended form.

The most dangerous bills are generally hurried through at the close of the session, when there is no time to discuss or even to examine them. To meet this difficulty, Arkansas provided in her Constitution of 1874 that " no new bills shall be introduced into either House during the last three days of the session."

Corruption in elections has become almost as familiar in some parts of our country as it once was in England. It was formerly enough for the members of the legislature to swear fidelity to the Constitutions of the State and the United States. By 1879 our Constitutions began to exact a further oath that they had not paid or promised anything for their election, and that they would not directly or indirectly receive anything to influence or recompense their official acts. Violation of this oath is perjury, — that is, a State prison offence.

Back pay and extra compensation of every sort are generally forbidden. Congress in 1873 gave a useful object-lesson on that subject.

State aid or gratuities, except for military services or pensions; loans of public credit; municipal subscriptions or guarantees to private enterprises or local improvements; grants to religious organizations, — all these are to be known no more.

Great Britain has found it necessary to guard against profuse expenditures and grants by her colonial legislatures by measures yet more stringent. In the Union Act creating the Dominion of Canada (1867) it is provided that " it shall not be lawful for the House of Commons to adopt or pass any vote, resolution, address or bill for the appropriation of any part of the public revenue, or of any tax or impost, to any purpose that has not been first recommended to that House by message of the Governor General at the same session."

The Constitution of Louisiana of 1879 prohibits the contracting of any State indebtedness, " except for the purpose of repelling invasion, or for the suppression of insurrection."

In the last (and sixth) Georgia Constitution (1877) " lobbying is declared to be a crime." No definition of the offence is attempted, and I fear that none was necessary.

Corporations necessarily form the greatest subject of legislation, for they represent, probably, four-fifths of the wealth and industry of the country, apart from lands occupied as homesteads.

When the first State Constitution was adopted, there was probably not one business corporation with a moneyed capital in the whole country. At the present time there must be fifty thousand. Their general character of perpetuity, and the limited liability of their stockholders in case of insolvency, fit them well for the demands of American life. But the energy and persistence with which they concentrate power, in the prosecution of new enterprises, are no less irresistible when directed to the attainment of any legislation, in which they may find their profit. Their directors and presidents fill our senates, and their stockholders and employees are prominent in the lower house. Unless the Constitution sets up some barrier, there are few favors which organizations so powerful can seek in vain. But almost all corporations of the same class, or business character, can be conducted under the same rules. Instead of a special charter for every railroad — three-fourths of which must be a mere repetition of provisions found in every other — the modern Constitution makes imperative the adoption of the plan of general railroad laws, under which any set of men, with the necessary capital to build a new road, may obtain the authority to go forward with the work. The same is true of banks; of insurance companies; of manufacturing concerns. Let the legislature thus lay down a few general limitations, as to the amount of capital, the powers that may not be exercised, the transfer of shares, inspection by State officials, and annual returns, and a thousand corporations may organize themselves in a year, without burdening the statute books with useless charters, or besieging the State house with requests for special privileges or concessions.

In constituting the capital of these associations, watered stock, and stock issued for gratuities, or otherwise than for actual value, are by many of the later Constitutions made void. The consolidation of rival railroads or canals is forbidden. Railroad rings are prohibited; so are free passes.

The right of legislatures to prescribe the maximum charges for freight and passenger rates on railroads, affirmed by the Supreme Court of the United States in the "Granger Cases,"[1] has been made a duty in several of the States. The Constitution of California (1879) went a step farther, in assuming to prescribe what servants and agents corporations might, or rather might not, employ. It laid down an absolute prohibition against their use of Chinese labor. This — though designed as an attack upon the employed rather than the employer — was rested on the police power, and had it not been for the Fourteenth Amendment to the Constitution of the United States, would perhaps have been defensible, in the absence of any treaty obligations to the contrary, on the same grounds as the granger railroad laws.

Corporations are mere creatures of the legislative power, with such rights and franchises only as the legislature may choose to concede, and these — if their charters are drawn in the usual form — revocable at pleasure. They are not citizens of the State, or of the United States, so far as respects the constitutional guarantees of the privileges and immunities of citizens of either government. We have long been familiar with laws forbidding the employment of

---

[1] Munn v. Illinois, 94 United States Reports, 113; Chicago, Burlington, and Quincy R. R. Co. v. Iowa, *ibid.* 155. This right has since been declared to be limited by the duty of the State to respect vested rights and the obligation of contracts, so far that it cannot impair the security of railroad creditors by reducing rates below a point at which the road can fairly earn the interest on its obligations. Reagan v. Farmers' Loan and Trust Co., 154 United States Reports, 362.

children, under a certain age, in mills. Why not, California asked, as well extend the exercise of the police or regulative powers of the State so as to exclude laborers of a certain race or country? The courts, however, pronounced against this provision as a denial of that equal protection of the laws which the Fourteenth Amendment guaranteed to every person within the jurisdiction of a State, as well as an infringement of the Burlingame treaty.[1] The results aimed at by California have since been largely accomplished through Congressional legislation.

The precedents of the English common law allowed no compensation to be recovered from one who had, either wilfully or negligently, been the cause of another's death. For this — so contrary to the dictates of common-sense, and to the maxims of most other civilized and uncivilized nations — the only reason to be given was that human life was beyond price, and could not be measured by money. The frequent losses of life by railway and steamboat accidents early led to statutes, both in England and America, giving a right to compensation, in favor of the family of the deceased. The corporations most interested could not prevent the passage of such Acts, but they did succeed, generally, in limiting the right of recovery to $5,000. In most of our States, therefore, it has been cheaper to kill a man outright than merely to maim him. A Massachusetts physician, whose professional prospects were ruined by a railway accident, which left him a paralytic, recovered $39,000 dam-

[1] *In re* Parrott, 1 Federal Reporter, 481.

ages from the Eastern Railroad. Had he died from the shock, I presume they would have escaped with $5,000. The Constitution of Pennsylvania forbids any law fixing the limit of compensation in actions for any personal injury.[1]

No charters had been more abused — particularly in the Southwest — than those of banks. Texas, in her Constitution of 1876, — willing, apparently, to leave this business to be regulated exclusively by the United States, — declares that " No corporate body shall hereafter be created, renewed, or extended, with banking or discounting privileges." New Jersey, a year before, had provided that no bank charter should be passed, or amended, except by a vote of three-fifths of all the members elected, in each house; and that none should be granted for more than twenty years. Two States, which had suffered much from failing banks, Missouri (1875) and Louisiana (1879), made it a crime for any bank officer to receive deposits or negotiate loans with knowledge that the institution was insolvent. California makes stockholders in every corporation liable to its creditors to an amount proportioned to the stock owned by each, and gives a remedy against the directors for all embezzlements by officers or agents of their appointment.

We all know how frequently corporations are organized to do business in another State; and as a general rule, the farther they go from home, the less

[1] That of New York adopted twenty years later contained a similar provision.

capital they carry, and the less morality as well. Most of the mining companies in Colorado and Nevada are chartered in New York and New England. Their capital is a mining right, valued at a million or two, and worth, probably, less than nothing, because it involves quite an outlay to find out that it is worthless. Such a corporation, organized in New York, to do business in Connecticut, was finally wound up there by bankruptcy proceedings. It had a capital of $250,000, all paid in, on paper; but when the truth came out, it appeared that an irresponsible man had given his own note for $500 for a license to dig for barytes on a certain farm, for 99 years, subject to a royalty of so much a ton for all he got out, and that the stock was issued to the maker of the note, as the price of a transfer of this lease or license, the corporation assuming the payment of the note upon itself, and selling enough of its own stock, to outside parties, to meet it. As such corporations cannot be sued, ordinarily, out of the State which charters them, our new Constitutions provide for suing them in the State where they do business.

Most of our Constitutions have referred to the subject of taxation with some such general declaration, only, as that taxes should be equal and uniform.

California was, I believe, the first to declare in terms that all property must be taxed, and to attempt to describe in detail the items of which property may consist. This was the cause of much of the opposition to the ratification of her Constitution, but I fail to see how these provisions go farther than the statutes on this subject under which many of our States have been governed for centuries. It may be unwise to elevate such a rule of administration — disapproved by so many economists — beyond the reach of legislative amendment or repeal, but it is not communism.

In one respect we see an apparent increase of legislative power, or dignity. The sessions of the legislature are generally made biennial, thus doubling the terms of office of its members. There are but ten of the States which have not moved in this direction. But the controlling object of this change is to lessen legislation, by taking away half its opportunities. Though the representatives are elected for two years, they are paid for but one year's work, and are not likely to do more at their own expense.

As to the right of suffrage, a few attempts were made, within the last twenty years or so of the century under review, to create restrictions in the way of education, or tax-paying. Pennsylvania, Massachusetts, Tennessee, and Georgia, required every voter to be a tax-payer. A similar measure was submitted to the people in Maine in 1878, but failed of adoption. Rhode Island, which had always denied suffrage to foreign-born citizens of the United States, unless they owned real estate to the value of $134, refused in 1871, by an emphatic vote, to change its policy. Massachusetts denies a vote to those who cannot read and write; Connecticut to those who cannot read.

Female suffrage in school elections, coupled with the right to hold office on school boards, was authorized in Minnesota in 1875. Pennsylvania, in 1873, made women eligible to any office of control or management respecting schools, but did not give them the right to vote. Colorado, in 1876, authorized the submission to the people, for their ratification, of a law conceding to women the right to vote (but not to hold office) at all elections, on the same terms as men. The law was accordingly framed in 1877, but was rejected by a large majority.

A few of the older Constitutions excluded Roman Catholics and infidels from public office. New Hampshire was the last to retain this religious test, and abolished it in 1877.

The great object of all laws and Constitutions is to guard the weak and protect minorities.

In the regulation of private corporations, several of the more recent Constitutions provide that any stockholder may cumulate his votes in the election of directors; that is, if he has ten votes to give, and there are five directors to be elected, he may give ten to each of five candidates, or fifty to one candidate, or twenty-five each to two candidates.

Illinois extended this principle to her State elections for representatives in the legislature. Every district sends three, and every elector may cumulate or divide his three votes at his pleasure. In practical operation, the scheme is charged with this defect: that the best men get the fewest votes, because every one thinks that they are sure of a majority without his aid; while the more ignorant voter, unfamiliar with processes of calculation, is likely to be, more than ever, the mere tool of the party managers. Its friends, however, claim [I think with reason] that, on the whole, it results in the nomination of better candidates, as well as in a fair representation of the represented.

The old way was to give the legislature almost unlimited power as to the canvass of elections. It has been found, however, too partisan a body for the task, and the tendency now is to leave such questions to the courts, and to ensure an honest investigation there by numbering the ballots, and placing on each the name of the man who casts it. This is, in substance, the mode adopted by the English election bill of 1872.

The impress of Northern sentiments on the Southern mind, as to matters wholly aside from politics or sectional differences, we find strongly marked in several of the recent Constitutions.

The time is not far distant when the custom of duelling was a general social law in the Southern States. But in every one of them it was by 1879 restrained by a Constitutional provision.

Louisiana in that year, which, so late as 1864, provided in her Constitution for licenses to lottery-dealers and gambling-houses, after prohibiting lotteries subsequently to 1895, proceeded to say, with much of the old Puritanic commingling of the notions of crimes and sins, " Gambling is declared to be a vice, and the General Assembly may enact laws for its suppression."

Public schools, at public expense, is another Northern and New England institution which planted itself in all the Southern Constitutions soon after the war, less perhaps as a measure of expediency, or right, than of necessity, in view of the extension of suffrage. Georgia (1877) expressly confined her common-school instruction to " the elementary branches of an English education only."

North Carolina, in 1876, provided that a law might be made compelling every child between six and eighteen, unless otherwise educated, to go to a public school for at least sixteen months. Similar legislation was long ago obtained in some of the Eastern States, without the aid of any constitutional provision.

State universities are becoming more common. Texas (1876) provided that " The legislature shall, as soon as practicable, establish, organize, and provide for the maintenance, support and direction of a University of the first-class," and that they " shall also, when deemed practicable, establish and provide for the maintenance of a college or branch University for the instruction of the colored youths of the State." Georgia provided for State aid to the University of Georgia, and also to some one college or university for persons of color. Louisiana (1879) directed grants to her State University to the extent of not over $10,000 a year, and required the establishment of a university for persons of color, and an annual appropriation of not less than $5,000 nor over $10,000, for its maintenance.

We see in our recent Constitutions a general tendency in favor of the debtor class. In many of them imprisonment for debt is expressly abolished, except under circumstances of fraud. In many, the legislature is enjoined to pass "liberal" homestead and exemption laws, or else these exemptions are expressly defined and granted.

So far as such provisions take away the remedy of a creditor to collect pre-existing debts, the Supreme Court has told us that they are void; but as to future debts, contracted after their adoption, the exemptions are effectual. There are economists who claim that society should afford no remedy for the collection of debts, leaving men to give credit at their own risk. In this way, it is argued, trade will be healthy and unforced; rogues must work, because no one will trust them; prices will be uniform, because the profit need include no margin for bad debts; and commercial panics will be unknown. The exemption laws of some of our Southern and Western States, which secure to an insolvent debtor his farm and stock, his furniture and library, free from any claim of creditors, will go far to demonstrate the truth or falsity of these positions.

Texas gave unlimited protection to every wage-earner, by the provision in her Constitution of 1876 that "No current wages for personal service shall ever be subject to garnishment."

Forbidding taxation by municipalities, or even by the State, beyond a certain *per centum*, is another bulwark for debtors which has found place in several of the recent Constitutions. Too often it is but an indirect way of commencing or enforcing the policy of repudiation, which now disgraces the records of so many of our States. Louisiana, in 1874, by a constitutional amendment, sanctioning a legislative Act, refunded her debt, by a compulsory process, into new consolidated seven per cent bonds, for sixty per cent of the amount of the old ones; and declared the new issue to be a valid contract "which the State shall by no means and in no wise impair;" and that to secure the levy and collection of the taxes required to meet the interest and principal, "the judicial power shall be exercised when necessary;" and that these taxes should be annually assessed and collected, and the payments made, without any further legislative appropriation. But in July, 1879, the Constitutional Convention framed an ordinance, declaring — as if the State were the creditor instead of the debtor — that the interest on these scaled bonds shall "be and is hereby fixed at two per cent. per annum for five years from the first of January, 1880; three per cent. per annum for fifteen years, and four per cent. per annum thereafter;" and "that the coupons of said consolidated bonds falling due on the first day of January, 1880, be and the same is hereby remitted, and any interest tax collected to meet said coupons is hereby transferred to defray the expenses of the State government."

The rash incurring of municipal indebtedness received a check in Texas, in 1876, by resort to a means quite opposed to the usual course of modern government. The Constitution adopted in that year provides that while all qualified electors of city or town can vote for all municipal officers, " in all elections to determine expenditure of money, or assumption of debt, those only shall be qualified to vote who pay taxes on property in said city or incorporated town, *provided* that no poll tax for the payment of debts thus incurred shall be levied upon the persons debarred from voting in relation thereto." New York, two years later, rejected a similar proposition, recommended by a commission of marked ability, appointed to frame a general law for the government of cities.[1]

The prohibition of the liquor saloon, which had been decreed by statute with varying success before the war, by several States, was reinforced by the Constitution of Georgia in 1877, as regards sales within two miles of any voting precinct on the day of any public election.

The same State (1877) protected marriage by making it the condition of a divorce that the petitioner must obtain a verdict from a jury in his favor at two different terms of court.

As literary productions, many of the more recent Constitutions compare unfavorably with their predecessors.

They are more wordy. They often descend into what seems a pettiness of detail. Some are so hastily thrown together as to be absolutely slovenly. In Louisiana, for instance, — a State whose jurists have always been noted for the elegance of their taste and

[1] Hitchcock, on American State Constitutions, 28.

scholarship, — we find an entire article repeated and re-enacted, word for word, as part of a later one.

Occasionally we meet a section which for its grandiloquence of expression might have been suggested by the Hon. Elijah Pogram. Vices of style, however, are a pardonable fault in the legislation of a country where the administration is not responsible for the form of statutes. They deface the laws of the United States to an extent unequalled by anything to be found in all our State Constitutions put together. The Civil Rights Bill, enacted by Congress in 1875, for instance, commenced with a preamble, declaring that it is "the appropriate object of legislation to enact great, fundamental principles, into law," precisely the thing which, I should rather say, is the last object of legislative enactment in a free government, because they are, of themselves the highest law, and the very touchstones by which we test the validity of every statute. One of them, indeed, proved fatal to this very Act.[1]

Texas, as has been said already, has lived to wear out three Constitutions and take on a fourth. The first (of 1845) covers sixteen of the large pages of Poore's "Charters and Constitutions"; the second (of 1866) takes a page more; the third (of 1868) extends over twenty-two pages; and that adopted in 1876 occupies thirty-two.

The Colorado Constitution of the same year was nearly as long.

Both these States illustrate in their work the in-

---

[1] It was declared invalid by the Supreme Court of the United States, in the Civil Rights Cases, 109 United States Reports, 3.

creasing tendency to descend to the details of government, and tie the hands of the legislature at every point where danger can be anticipated from the misuse of power. Missouri, until 1855, had imposed but three express restrictions upon the law-making authority. By 1875 she had created thirty-three.[1]

There is a point beyond which it is unreasonable and unsafe to carry this jealous supervision of future legislatures. The great principles of human action vary little, but their application to the affairs of daily life changes at a thousand points with every generation and every decade. Unquestionably there are many superfluous pages in the long drawn out Constitutions of modern date, like those of Texas, Colorado, and Georgia; and there are in them many articles worse than superfluous.

The rule of Georgia, for instance, that costs in her Supreme Court shall not exceed ten dollars until otherwise provided by law, and that a poor man may appeal to it without liability to costs at all, has so flooded it with petty cases that there is scant opportunity to hear argument on any, or for that full consultation in all before judgment, by which justice is commonly best served.

The demagogue has, of late years, too often found his way into the constitutional convention. We have been more fortunate in escaping the influence of the political theorist and *doctrinaire*.

Here and there, but rarely, we observe his hand. Thus, in Alabama, in 1867, the legislature was

[1] Hitchcock, on American State Constitutions, 35.

directed to frame "a penal code, founded on principles of reformation." In her Constitution of 1875 this section disappeared.

This is but one of several instances, which a comparison of these two instruments discloses, of that vacillating spirit which grew with the century, and not infrequently led the constitutional convention of one year to adopt what a similar body in another, not very distant, would discard. In the Declaration of Rights in the Alabama Constitutions both of 1865 and 1867, the State was made liable to suit in her own courts: in that of 1875 it was provided that she should never be made defendant in any court of law or equity. The last Constitution also prohibited forever the imposition of any educational qualification for suffrage. A few years later public sentiment changed upon this point, and it seems probable that before long Alabama will range herself, on this point, with Mississippi and South Carolina, Massachusetts and Connecticut.

It is a redeeming feature of our American Constitutions that they deal so little in theoretical and unsettled questions of polity or jurisprudence. We can afford to experiment in our statute laws. If faulty in operation, they are easily repealed or amended. But our Constitutions should present no principles on which men, of the same generation at least, can honestly differ in opinion; none which are within the reach of ordinary change.

Such was certainly their original scope and frame. The many recent amendments of which I have spoken are the witness of a new epoch. The times have changed, and Constitutions have changed with them. But, as we compare the modifications thus introduced in our plans of internal government with those of the other great powers of Christendom during the century, we shall not find ourselves the greatest innovators. Rather may we take an honest pride in observing how few steps we have found it necessary to retrace, and how the good sense and good morals of our people have, on the whole, been adequate to keep in check every new tendency to corruption or injustice.

CHAPTER IV

ABSOLUTE POWER, AN AMERICAN INSTITUTION [1]

THE form of every government and the powers which it may exercise must rest either on the will of the governing authority or the consent of those who are its subjects. Political absolutism may be built up on either of these foundations. It exists whenever those who are governed are for the time under the dominion of a power which they cannot control, and which knows no limits but those of personal discretion.

The United States of America were created by the consent of the people of the United States. They were not to be, however, the only subjects of the nationality which they thus constituted. They had the power to make, and they did make, subjects also out of certain States, previously sovereign, independent, and self-governing. The people of each State, acting in concert with the people of all the rest, transferred to the United States part of its former sovereignty, and put it so far under the power of the new nation.

This power was limited by the Constitution of the United States, for the time being, to certain matters

---

[1] In discussing this topic, free use has been made of addresses delivered by the author before the Georgia State Bar Association, at Warm Springs, Georgia, July 1, 1897, and the American Social Science Association, at Saratoga, N. Y., Aug. 30, 1897.

particularly stated. But there was also a provision for further amendments of that instrument, by which the range and scope of federal power might be at any time enlarged. It could never be extended to depriving a State of its equal representation in the Senate, nor for twenty years could it be exercised to suppress the slave trade.[1] It could never destroy all the States, because without the States the United States could not exist. It probably could never be a warrant for dividing or consolidating any of the States, without their consent.[2] It may also be assumed that the objects of the Constitution could not be varied from those stated in its preamble.

But aside from these restrictions, what is there that an amendment of the Constitution could not effect?

Such an amendment can be made at the instance of two-thirds of both houses of Congress, when ratified by the legislatures of three-fourths of the States; and however obnoxious it may be to the interests of the rest, it will be as to all alike the supreme law of the land. It will be this because the people of the United States in 1788 consented that what was then done by their unanimous assent (manifested by the concurring votes of their appointed organs, the constitutional conventions in each State) might afterwards, at any time and from time to time, be altered at the will of two-thirds of Congress and three-fourths of the State legislatures. They freely put themselves under the absolute control of these depositaries of the amending power; for to them had been univer-

[1] Constitution of the United States, Art. V.
[2] *Ibid.*, Art. IV., Sec. 3.

sally and forever granted the right to speak for the whole people of the United States. Thenceforth that people had only two full, self-acting representatives in their system of government, who were directly responsible to them and all of them. One was the constitutional convention, to which the people of every State would send their delegates, for the purpose of proposing amendments. This was to be convoked only on the application of the legislatures of two-thirds of the States. The other was the President of the United States.

There is no part of the legislation of his country that is not of interest to the American, but he is most of all concerned with that which is institutional in character, or has become institutional by the progress of events. Whatever in human government has attained a foothold where it seems to belong, and from which it can be dislodged by no ordinary change, has by that fact alone a title to regard.

Laws may be passed and repealed in quick succession; individuals may rise to positions of commanding influence, only to be swept off in a moment into political oblivion by a sudden turn of party tide; the rules of science, the inductions of philosophy, accepted for ages, may, as some new door of Nature's laboratory is unlocked, shrivel into ashes before the issuing flame; but in every land, civilized or barbaric, where a strong race has long made its home, there will be certain institutions of civil society, that have grown up to slow maturity, so rooted in the soil that they form part of the nation's life and make its his-

AN AMERICAN INSTITUTION

tory. Such an institution a century of use has brought into being for Americans, — an expression of republican principles in the form of absolute power.

Among the constitutional governments now existing in the world, the United States rank as the oldest but one. It is, indeed, fairly open to question if our place is not the first. Great Britain, since our Constitution was adopted, by her union with Ireland and the introduction of a hundred Irish members into her House of Commons, followed by the Reform Bill and the recent Franchise Acts, has essentially changed the character of that body, and transformed a monarchy into a representative democracy; while the new name of Empress of India given to her titular sovereign seems but to mark the abandonment of her ancient colonial policy, — too mild for an oriental race, too rigorous for the great English-speaking dominions that have risen up under her flag to gain for themselves, one after another, substantial autonomy.

The United States are the offspring of a long-past age. A hundred years, it is true, have scarcely passed since the eighteenth century came to its end, but no hundred years in the history of the world has ever before hurried it along so far over new paths and into unknown fields. The French Revolution and the first empire were the bridge between two periods that nothing less than the remaking of European society, the recasting of European politics, could have brought so near.

But back to this eighteenth century must we go to

learn the forces, the national ideas, the political theories, under the domination of which the Constitution of the United States was framed and adopted. There is something in that instrument that gave it coherence and vitality; something on which we have built up institutions that are real, traditions that are imperious, a national life that is organic, a national history of which no civilized man is wholly ignorant, a national power that is respected on every sea. What is it that has brought us on so far, and given us an undisputed place among the great powers of the world? Is it a broad land and a free people, equal laws and universal education? Yes; but how are those laws administered? How are the forces of this great government that rules from sea to sea across a continent directed and applied? How, and by whom?

I think it may be fairly said that of the leading powers of the world, two, only, in our time, represent the principle of political absolutism, and enforce it by one man's hand. They are Russia and the United States.

The Czar of Russia, indeed, stands for Russia in a broader sense than that in which we can say that the President of the United States stands for them. The people of the United States have not put all their power in the keeping of all or any of their temporary rulers. They are the sleeping giant, that sleeping or waking is a giant still. Their word is still the ultimate rule of conduct—their written word. But when they gave their assent to the Constitution of the United States, they created in it the office of a king, without the name.

AN AMERICAN INSTITUTION

They set the key also, by this act, for our State governments and municipal governments.

The royal prerogative of pardon, which belongs to the President without limits, except in cases of impeachment, has been given to one after another of the governors of our States. Their appointing power is like his; their veto power is like his. Of the statutes passed in 1897 by the legislature of New York, nearly one-third — in all, over five hundred — failed of effect for want of the Governor's approval.

In city governments the authority of the mayor has been continually increased. He is held personally responsible for a fair and honest administration of municipal affairs, and each department under him is coming to be under the direction, not of some non-partisan board, but of one man, removable at the mayor's will, and taking his instructions from him.

But it is in the federal government that political absolutism is most deeply seated. Absolutism naturally follows centralization, and that belongs especially to the nation.

In form, at least, there is less of national character in our executive than in our judicial department. The judges of the United States have no relation to the States, except that the Senate of the States must confirm their nominations. The President, on the other hand, is chosen by the votes of local electors, appointed by each State for itself, and meeting separately in distant capitals. Three of these electoral votes are forever secured to the smallest State, so that a President may be — as, in the case of Hayes, a President was — elected by a majority in the electoral colleges, when the opposing candidate received the approval of a majority of the whole people. So, again, should the electoral colleges fail to make a choice, the States come together to take their place, like so many sovereign powers in an imperial diet; each casting in the House of Representatives an equal vote.

But, once elected, the President, during half the year, is the United States more truly than ever Louis XIV. was France.

Our people had tried, during the Revolution and after the Revolution, the experiment of a confederacy without an executive head. They knew the evils of a weak administration, and they were determined to have an energetic one. They were ready to pay the price by submitting to a system of personal government.

Had there not been, in 1787, a person at hand, to whom all eyes were turned with unfaltering trust, it is more than doubtful whether the Constitution, as thus framed, could have been ratified. Had they fully understood the great powers with which it invested the President, it is certain that it never would have been.

Hamilton and Madison, in the *Federalist*, minimized these powers to conciliate popular support. It was in truth impossible to predict beforehand what they were to prove. Pinckney, at the close of the convention, spoke of the new President as an officer of "contemptible weakness and dependence." Jefferson, on the other hand, wrote from Paris that he seemed "a bad edition of a Polish king," and would contrive to hold his power by successive re-elections for life. Between these views time was to decide.

A constitutional government is not constructed in a day. A constitution may be; but it is born into the world a helpless babe, to be nurtured and re-created by its environment and associations. Constitutions do not make history. History makes them. They may, indeed, be constructed in a day, but they cannot be construed in a day. The men who put such a document together do not know, cannot know, the meaning of their own work. It is what it comes to be. It is what later generations make it.

Plato tells us in his "Republic" that governments must change with every change in the character of those who constitute the political society, and in their relative conditions of life.

If we think of the United States as they were in 1787, occupying a narrow strip of the Atlantic seacoast; engaged only in agriculture; with no city larger than Utica or Savannah now is; with capital still so far in the hands of individuals that there were probably less than twenty business corporations in the whole country; with mails carried through half the States on horseback and at irregular intervals, if at all, — all must agree that the President of such a people could not, except in name, be the same as the President of the United States of to-day.

There were two theories of the executive before the convention of 1787.

Sherman insisted that the executive magistracy was

really nothing more than an institution for carrying the will of the legislature into effect, and therefore that it should be confided to one or more officials, as experience might dictate, appointed by that body and removable by that body.

Madison contended for the other view, that the executive was a representative of the people, rather than of their legislators.

During the century that has passed since then England, following the principle preferred by Sherman, has reduced her sovereign to a mere representative of the legislative will; and we, following the principle preferred by Madison, have raised our executive to the position of an elective king, chosen by the people, and responsible only to them, — a king who, for a four-years term, rules in his own right.

One of the most significant debates in the convention of 1787 was that over the proposition to surround the President with an executive council. Had it been carried, and his will thus subjected in any measure to cabinet control, the very foundation of our government would have been changed. It is the absolute supremacy of the President within his sphere of executive action, responsible to his own judgment and to no other man's, that has been the mainspring of our political system. Custom and convenience have brought the heads of departments together, in the presence of the President, at stated meetings, for consultation, and, when he asks it, for advice. We call them members of the Cabinet; but they have, as such, no standing before the law. No sultan in the presence of his divan is as uncontrolled and absolute as the President of the United States at a Cabinet meeting. Others may talk; he, only, acts.

It was an observation of Sir Henry Maine, that the success of the United States " has been so great that men have almost forgotten that if the whole of the known experiments of mankind in government be looked at together, there has been no form of government so unsuccessful as the republican."[1] It was unsuccessful because it was always inefficient in emergencies; because it had no political centre; because no free people had been intelligent enough to know that a strong and stable government is the best government, provided it is first kept within narrow bounds, and then administered in the public interest.

The first step towards strengthening the executive power was taken by the first Congress in its decision in favor of the right of the President to dismiss his subordinates at will. The *Federalist* had adopted the other view. The argument that if confirmation by the Senate were necessary to appointment it must also be necessary to removal, was logical; but in politics practical considerations are often stronger than logical ones. The President is invested with the whole executive power of the United States. He is to be held responsible to the people for his executive action. Justice then demands that he should have no agent in his service who has lost his confidence; no man on whose judgment he must rely, yet whose judgment he distrusts. That this is his absolute right may now be considered as settled law.[2]

[1] Popular Government, p. 202.
[2] Parsons *v.* The United States, 167 United States Reports, 324.

In the form of constitution adopted by the Southern Confederacy in March, 1861, the President's power of removal was essentially restricted. It should have been; for the guiding principle of that short-lived government was to secure at every point where it was practicable the sovereignty of each State, and to yield as little as possible to the confederate authority.

During the administration of Washington came another step in the development of the Constitution, in the act on his part which nearly precipitated us into a war with France. The President, by the Constitution, is to receive public ministers. It follows, said the first President, that I can refuse to receive them, or, if I find reason to be dissatisfied with them, can request their recall. Genet was recalled, at his request, and the beginning thus established of a long line of diplomatic precedent, which has made the voice of the President, as to foreign nations, the only recognized expression of the sovereign will of the United States.

Federal taxation was no more popular under Washington than it is under McKinley. It became necessary for the government to show its teeth, and in 1792 was passed the first national militia law. In case the execution of the laws of the United States should be opposed in any State by combinations too powerful to be suppressed by the courts or marshals, it was made lawful for the President to call out the militia of the State, and should they refuse to act and Congress not be in session, the militia of other States, in such numbers as he might think necessary. It was also provided that every able-bodied white male citizen, between eighteen and forty-five, with few exemptions, should be enrolled in the militia, and that the President should appoint an adjutant-general in each State to act as such, subject to the orders of the Governor. It was by virtue of these acts that Washington found the means to put down the Whiskey Rebellion in Pennsylvania; and while the general policy of Congress has since been to trench less on the military powers of the States, the militia of the United States, such as it is, has necessarily and always, when in actual service, been under the command of the President by constitutional right, and the Supreme Court have decided that it is for him alone to determine when it is fit to call them out.[1]

So, in regard to our standing military and naval establishment, the orders of the President are always absolute.

They may involve the pulling down or setting up the government of a State. Such was the effect of Presidential interposition in Dorr's Rebellion in Rhode Island, when the courts declared[2] that whichever government he recognized as the true and lawful one, they must respect.

They may bring a sudden stop to combinations of labor, which have put great railroads at their feet, and the commerce of the country in peril.

They may compromise our relations with foreign

---

[1] Martin *v.* Mott, 12 Wheaton's Reports, 19.
[2] Luther *v.* Borden, 7 Howard's Reports, 1.

powers, and even authorize an invasion of foreign territory or the blockade of ports[1] before Congress has declared the existence of war.

And when a state of war is fully recognized, what limits can be assigned of the executive power? As it was practically administered during the civil war, it extended, in States that were not the seat of active hostilities, to domiciliary visits; to arrests by military warrant; to refusals to obey writs of *habeas corpus* issued by the State courts; to trials by military courts, ending in decrees sometimes of exile, and sometimes of death. The courts and the bar, were at the time divided in opinion as to the question of right. The Chief-Justice of the United States denied that the President could suspend the privilege of the writ of *habeas corpus* where there had been no proclamation of martial law; but even he did not venture to enforce his decision by process of contempt. At this point Taney yielded before Lincoln, as Marshall had yielded before Jefferson as to the subpœna issued and disobeyed on the trial of Aaron Burr. Finally, after the close of the war, came the decision in Milligan's Case, annulling a sentence of death passed by a military commission, sitting in Indiana, for a political offence; but a decision rendered by a divided court, four of the nine judges, with the then Chief-Justice at their head, holding that, in time of insurrection or invasion, the President might rule by martial law, when public danger required it and there was no opportunity for Congress to act, in any part of the United States, though not the actual seat of war,

[1] The Prize Cases, 2 Black's Reports, 635.

if he found the ordinary law inadequate for public protection.[1]

It was Macaulay's criticism of the Constitution and government of the United States that we were "all sail and no rudder." He uttered it in the first half of the century, that half divided for us by so wide a chasm from that now closing, — the chasm of the Civil War.

No one who watched the progress of that great contest would have failed to see that there was rudder, no less than sail. There was a rudder, and there was but one man at the helm. Lincoln's course may be commended or condemned, but this, at least, all must agree, that his personality dominated the course of political events during those stirring years from 1861 to 1865.

It was far from being a consistent course. The Constitution, on his accession to the presidency, did not seem to him the same thing that it grew in his mind to be, as the long struggle wore on. He came to feel, as he wrote in 1864, "that measures, otherwise unconstitutional, might become lawful, by becoming indispensable to the preservation of the nation." This is a doctrine without limits, in the mouth of a military commander in time of war. It led him to the proclamation of emancipation, as imperial a decree as that by which the Czar of Russia, in the same year, abolished serfdom in his dominions. We need not stop to ask whether this proclamation was a legal act. It is one of the great facts of human history; its practical consequences were immeasura-

[1] *Ex parte* Milligan, 4 Wallace's Reports, 2, 142.

ble, and whatever else it accomplished, it demonstrated the absolute power of an American President, whether it be rightfully or wrongfully exercised.

The observation of Macaulay which has been quoted was written not long after the hard-fought struggle, with its varying fortunes, between Jackson and the Senate of the United States. As late as 1835 the Senate had successfully opposed his will in a matter which it was thought by many put the honor of the country at risk. Our relations with France had become strained by her long delay in paying an agreed debt. In President Jackson's annual message at the opening of the session in December, 1834, he recommended legislation to authorize reprisal by the capture of French vessels. France intimated that she was entitled to an apology for the tone of the communication. Jackson replied by threatening to recall our minister, and sent in a special message to Congress, in which preparation for war was suggested. Within a week the House of Representatives voted an appropriation of three millions, to be expended in whole or in part under the direction of the President of the United States for the public defence, should it, in his opinion, become necessary to do so, before their next winter's session. The Senate refused to concur. The general voice of the people blamed their caution, but Webster subsequently defended his vote against the measure by saying on the floor of the Senate that as for him he would agree to no such proposition were the guns of the enemy battering against the walls of the capitol, and that he had been amazed at the action of the house in "rushing with such heedless, headlong trust, such impetuosity of confidence, into the arms of executive power."

The growth of that power since then, and its growth since the Civil War as well, is illustrated by the very different reception given in 1898 to a similar suggestion, under quite similar circumstances, from President McKinley. Without a special message, as the result of a private interview at the executive mansion between him and a few of the leaders of the party in power, Congress unanimously put fifty millions into his hands, to be expended absolutely at his will for any purposes of national defence.

But it is not to times of war or of rumors of war that one should look for authoritative definitions of political powers. Those of every department of government are then commonly strained to the utmost, and all tend to support the military arm.

When Lincoln assumed to suspend the privilege of *habeas corpus*, Congress came to his aid by an Act[1] formally investing him with such a power, to be exercised anywhere and at any time at his discretion, and granting immunity for any acts in restraint of liberty done at his command. Similar action was taken in the Confederate Congress to strengthen the hands of President Davis, and his influence in shaping legislation was even more evident and effective, throughout the war, than that of President Lincoln at Washington.

Let us go back to times of peace and ask which President was the first to startle the country by the

[1] Of March 3, 1863.

exercise of powers not before generally thought to appertain to the Executive Department.

It was Jefferson, when in 1803 he bought the Louisiana territory from Napoleon, and by a stroke of his pen doubled the area of the United States. It inevitably moved the centre of political rule to the valley of the Mississippi. It destroyed the existing balance of power between the States. But it was fortunate that under our political system there was one man able thus to commit the country, without consulting it, to so great a departure from its earlier traditions.

A generation later, another executive act proved that the President was stronger than any combination capital could form, though supported by far-reaching political influences. The United States Bank was the greatest financial institution which the United States have ever seen. It had paid a million and a half to the government for its charter. It was made by Act of Congress the standing depository of the cash funds of the United States, unless at any time the Secretary of the Treasury should order their withdrawal. President Jackson believed that the affairs of the bank were being improperly conducted, and requested the Secretary of the Treasury to remove the deposits. The Secretary declined, stating that he saw no reason for it, and that the authority to decide had been lodged with him. His removal followed, and a successor was appointed who promptly complied with the President's wishes. The Senate denounced Jackson's action as unwarranted by the Constitution. He sent in a protest against this res-

AN AMERICAN INSTITUTION

olution, which they voted to be a breach of privilege. A commercial crisis followed, which shook the country to its foundation, and by one of the great parties of the day was attributed to Jackson's act. Whether the cause of it or not, the removal of the deposits was certainly the occasion, and it came by the absolute will of the President alone.

It was Jackson, also, who first showed the people how almost irresistible, in strong hands, and on great occasions, is the force of the executive veto. It is the common prerogative of royalty, but one to which modern royalty seldom dares to resort. Queen Victoria has, in law, the same absolute veto power as to every bill which Parliament presents to her for the royal assent which Queen Elizabeth or William the Conqueror had. But does she use it? No English sovereign since the Hanoverian dynasty came in has ever used it, and none ever will. It has fallen into desuetude because it is an absolute power, and because no men of Anglo-Saxon stock will ever again stoop to absolute power, exercised by hereditary right.

The disuse of the royal veto has brought on a silent but fundamental change in the whole system of British government. The ministry, unwilling to ask the sovereign to approve a bill that they do not, if such a measure is forced upon them, resign their offices or dissolve the Parliament. As the Crown cannot be held responsible to the people, the ministry must be, — a vicarious sacrifice at the altar of liberty.

In every form of government that stops short of despotism, the people must have some share or some semblance of a share in legislation, either by way of origination or approval.

In the palmiest days of monarchy in France the edicts of the King were submitted for registration to the parliaments of justice; and the convocation of the States General was always in reserve. Under the reign of the Cæsars the absolutism of the Emperor was rested on the assumption that the people had delegated to him their powers and the functions of their tribunes to intervene for them to defeat an unjust law.

But the American veto is supported by no legal fiction, and impeded by no fear of popular discontent. During his short term of office, and because of his short term of office, the President of the United States may set down his foot at any point and oppose his individual will to the judgment of the whole people, speaking by their representatives, and of all the States, speaking by their ambassadors in the Senate. If such a veto is sent in during the closing days of the session, as Congress is now constituted, with so great a number of members in each of the houses, and the opportunity for unlimited discussion in one, it is almost certain to be fatal to the bill; and under any circumstances it is fatal, if the President and Congress are in general political accord.

But if they are not, what then? He has a greater prerogative in reserve.

The executive power of the United States, and the whole of it, is vested in this one man. What are laws, if they are not executed? And who is to judge, except the President, or above the President, whether an Act of Congress which he is called upon to execute is or is not such an Act as Congress had power to pass?

We have, indeed, now passed from questions of expediency to questions of jurisdiction.

The President can veto a bill because he deems it inexpedient, or because he deems it unconstitutional. He can only decline to execute a statute which has become such without his approval, because he believes it to be no law at all. But the absolute power of decision, and of action or inaction, in either case is equally in him.

This was the position of Jefferson and of Jackson, but it required the Civil War to make it an unquestioned principle.

At its close society was confused and disorganized in every one of the States south of Kentucky. The *status* of almost half the population had been revolutionized. The natural political leaders had been set aside. A general readjustment of civil government to meet all these new social conditions was necessary. President Lincoln and after him President Johnson proposed to accomplish it by the exercise of the executive power. Temporary governments were set up under military authority. Executive orders were issued, authorizing popular elections, under certain conditions, to replace military by civil rule and home rule. Congress interposed to prevent it. The "Reconstruction laws" were enacted, and others, such as the Tenure of Office Act, intended to subordinate the President of the United States, as to military affairs, to the General then in command, and, as to civil administration, to the will of Congress. Of these Acts some were so incorporated into other legislation that they secured an approval under protest. Others were returned with the President's disapproval, strongly expressed. They were passed over the veto. They were treated with contempt. The Secretary of War was removed without the consent of the Senate and against its will. A great party, in full control of Congress, found itself hampered and thwarted at every step by one man, whom they had selected for a position of little authority, and the accident of death had elevated to the highest.

The President was impeached. His answer was, in substance, a justification of the acts complained of. He was accused, not only of disregarding the Tenure of Office Act, but of having stated in public addresses that the policy manifested in the Reconstruction laws led in the direction of disunion and the permanent disruption of the States; that they violated the fundamental principles of the government; and that they tended to consolidation and despotism. He avowed these opinions, and declared that they had been deliberately formed, and rightfully expressed. He was prosecuted and defended with the greatest ability. The trial was long. It was followed in every part of the country and of the civilized world with the closest attention. A judgment of acquittal came, and the one vote that saved him from conviction, I might almost say, re-made the Constitution of the United States. If such a President as Andrew Johnson, so defiant of opposition, so abusive to his opponents, so distrusted by the party that had elected him, on the one side, and by the party which had rejected him, on the other, could not be successfully impeached for following out, and to the end, in matters so all-important to the people and the States, his view of the Constitution against that of Congress, no President ever could be.

Up to that hour the great engine of impeachment and removal from office, left in the hands of the Congress and the Chief-Justice of the United States, had been looked to as a perpetual guaranty against the undue exercise of executive power. It had been thought by Madison and Pinckney to make the President too dependent on the favor of the legislature.[1] The test of use was applied, and it had fallen to pieces by its own weight. It had done no more than give the President a new forum and a wider audience for the proclamation of his right to administer and defend the Constitution as he might construe it, and to denounce before the people any legislation that he might deem to violate its principles.

There had been before, on one great occasion, a difference of opinion, strongly pronounced, as to his constitutional duty, between the President and the courts. Jackson declared, when he vetoed the recharter of the United States Bank, that he had sworn to support the Constitution as he, not others, understood it, and that the authority of the Supreme Court must not be permitted to control either Congress or the Executive when acting in their legislative capacities. It was left for another Tennessean, in another

[1] Elliott's Debates, v. 528.

generation, to vindicate the doctrine that the President was equally independent of the courts when acting in his executive capacity.

Can the President be prevented from executing an Act of Congress which the Supreme Court considers to be unconstitutional and void?

This was the great question which Mississippi brought to the bar of the Supreme Court of the United States in 1866.

The Reconstruction Acts purported to set aside the existing governments of certain States, — governments existing by the authority or sanction of the President as commander-in-chief of the military power of the United States. Mississippi was one of these. She asserted that these statutes were unconstitutional and void, and sought leave to file a bill for an injunction to prevent President Johnson from undertaking to enforce them.

No one would have been better pleased than he to see them fail. But he knew that it was his duty to defend the dignity of his great office. By his direction the Attorney-General opposed the motion of the State of Mississippi. It was denied, and the cause of Mississippi v. Johnson [1] established by judicial decision what had been only feebly and sporadically claimed by Johnson's predecessors, that the President was the absolute judge of his duty as to proceedings in the execution of a statute, subject only to the power of the courts to pass upon the legal effects of his action, should they afterwards become proper matters of judicial controversy.

[1] 4 Wallace's Reports, 475.

We have seen how far the military powers of the Executive may serve as a warrant to interfere with the administration of justice in State courts. In time of war and in the presence of war, it extends to their temporary abolition. When enemies' territory is occupied, or territory to which the rules of public law assign that name, though it be that of a State of the Union, the President can replace its courts by courts of his own, exercising both civil and criminal jurisdiction, and disposing of life, liberty, and property, not as instruments of the judicial authority of the United States, but as instruments of the executive authority.

Such was President Lincoln's Provisional Court, established by a mere military order in Louisiana in 1862. Four years later Congress ordered its records transferred to the Circuit Court for the Eastern District of the State, and made its judgments, in legal effect, the judgments of that court. The validity of this legislation was attacked, but it was finally supported by the Supreme Court of the United States,[1] and under this decision in the case of *The Grapeshot*, what were really decrees of the President, speaking by his military deputy, the judge of the Provisional Court, were made to stand for and virtually become, by legislative action, the judgments of a regularly constituted judicial tribunal, which could only have pronounced them by virtue of its judicial powers.

But how far, in time of absolute peace, can the President of the United States, in the exercise of his

[1] *The Grapeshot*, 9 Wallace's Reports, 129.

civil authority, interfere with the police of a State, and set aside its ordinary course of justice? Let Neagle's Case, which arose from threats of violence against Mr. Justice Field of the Supreme Court, give the answer. The President can surround civil officers of the United States, within a State, with armed guards, who can defend them, even to the death, without responsibility to the State whose peace may be disturbed. He may send such guards in the train of every judge upon the circuit, and however they may overstep the line of duty, the State cannot call them to account. There is, says the Supreme Court, a peace of the United States as well as of the State, which is broken by an attack upon such an officer, and although the peace of the State be also broken by the defence, this can be determined only by the courts of the United States.[1]

I have spoken of the President as the sole representative of the United States in our dealings with foreign nations, except, indeed, that the ordinary executive prerogative of declaring war has not been confided to him. If he cannot declare war, however, he can create one.

Take, for instance, his power to which I have already alluded, of receiving foreign ministers. To receive them as coming from what foreign sovereigns? From such, and such only, as he may choose to recognize as sovereign. From Hawaii, if he chooses to recognize the Hawaiian Republic. From Cuba, if he chooses to recognize the Cuban Republic. Such an

[1] Neagle's Case, 135 United States Reports, 1.

AN AMERICAN INSTITUTION 105

act of recognition in case of a political revolution that has obtained temporary success, may obviously constitute a *casus belli* in favor of the former government.

In all America that lies south of us we have long taken an especial interest. As to the foreign relations of our sister republics there, we may almost say that our will is law; and our will is uttered by our President.

Let one of these republics complain to him of encroachments threatened by a European power. It is Mexico struggling to free herself from an Austrian emperor sent and supported by Louis Napoleon. At a few words from our Department of State, in the name of President Johnson, the French troops are recalled, and Maximilian is led to execution. It is Venezuela, charging England with pushing too far the boundaries of British Guiana. A sudden message to Congress from President Cleveland asks for the appointment of a commission to aid him in determining which nation is in the right, and intimates that if Venezuela proves in the right she shall have right done. In an hour, by this executive act, we are brought face to face with a question of war with the leading power in Europe, and the danger of it passes away through a diplomatic correspondence, for the issue of which the President was again alone responsible.

The very ground of our interference in this quarrel of Venezuela — what was it but a doctrine proclaimed, and indeed invented, by a President of the United States? The Monroe Doctrine has laid down the law for our hemisphere, and it was the single act of the executive department.

Has any sovereign in Europe, of his own motion, ever done as much? There was some reason for the remark made at the time by the organ of the French ministry, that it had been "reserved for Mr. Monroe to show us a dictator armed with a right of superiority over the whole of the New World."[1]

The place of the President in our government was prepared for those who could be safely trusted with imperial power — for ideal heroes of the nation whom the leaders in each State, chosen by the people for that sole purpose, in the secret conclave of the electoral college, might agree on, — must agree on, — for in no nation at any time can there be more than one to whom all true men look as the foremost citizen.

The framers of the Constitution sat in convention under the Presidency of such a hero. It was for Washington that they prepared the place of President of the new republic. It was by such as Washington that they hoped the powers of this great office would be administered when he should fill it no longer.

Their forecast has been but half fulfilled. The electoral colleges have sunk to the condition of so many patent voting-machines. They are a survival of the unfittest. Human government, like natural government, is administered, in the long run, on the principle of natural selection; but we are more apt to

[1] This appeared in *L'Étoile*, the journal of the administration, as soon as news of the President's message reached Paris. See McMaster's "Origin, Meaning, and Application of the Monroe Doctrine"; Notes, p. 49.

change the substance than the form of political institutions. England has slipped into a republic without knowing it. They keep their Queen, indeed, and are proud of her reign of sixty years, but she is little more than a historical curiosity. Our Presidential electors were brought into being as the safest and surest way of declaring the will of the people. We have found a better way, in national conventions of great parties and the popular verdict upon their work, at the polls; but, by the force of the *vis inertiæ*, we still cling to the out-worn form of the electoral college. The tailors persist in sewing two buttons on the backs of our coats, because in the England of the Tudors, when all travelling was done on horseback, one had to button back the skirts of his riding coat, to keep them from flapping and fraying against the saddle-bags. The tailor is the despot of modern society, — he still insists on his two buttons, though we have forgotten their use; and so the electoral colleges seem destined to cling to the skirts of the Constitution, simply because nobody cares to take the trouble to have them cut off.

Their purpose was good, but it has become an impossible one. Only a great war can give us again a national hero, and even then the successful General can never be President unless he be formally adopted as the candidate of a great party.

The successors of Washington have been often weak men, — never, as yet, bad men; but it is hard to name more than three of them who can in any sense be termed the heroes of the nation. The great powers, however, are always there, if the great man is not; and every generation has made them powers greater still.

Time has also brought a greater permanence to them.

Thrones are allowed to descend by hereditary succession because it is believed that the son is most likely to follow the policy of the father, and to resemble him in character.

The election of our Vice-President is arranged with a similar view; but for a hundred years the vacancy that might occur by the event of his death was left by our laws to be filled by officers chosen by one or the other house of Congress. What might have been expected finally happened. A Vice-President became President, and the legislative officer next in succession was of a different political party. It was a time of deep party feeling, and there was serious danger that the President might be pushed from his place to make room for a representative of widely different views; coming into power, perhaps, by his own vote as a member of a Court of Impeachment. Twenty years later, when passion had had time to cool, a wiser law was enacted, under which the President, in such a case, names, in effect, his own successor, and so secures the continuance of the same policy until the people have had another opportunity to declare their will.

Aristotle said that the principle or spirit of two governments widely different in political form might be the same.

AN AMERICAN INSTITUTION

The principle of despotism may exist in any government. It may dominate in a democracy. It does when the popular majority legislates at will on matters of individual liberty or property. Despotism was never more terrible than in the hands of the people in the French Revolution.

We need not be surprised, therefore, that, beginning in 1787 by granting our President more extensive powers than the chief magistrate in any democratic confederation had ever received before in times of peace,[1] we have finally drifted into a kind of modified constitutional despotism. It was the logical outcome of our attempt to unite in one government the form of a confederation and the principle of a nation. If sovereign States were to be kept within the limits which the Constitution set, it must be by something in the nature of a sovereign power that was even greater than they. The people of the United States are greater than any or all of the United States, but they cannot meet together, and none to represent them can meet together, save in the extraordinary and yet unknown event of a second national constitutional convention. They must therefore speak by the chief magistrate of the republic; and so has come his transcendent power.

I have compared that power with the authority exercised in his dominions by the Czar of Russia. It has become a political aphorism that Russia is governed by despotism tempered by assassination. Enhance human power to a certain point, and it becomes to some men intolerable. As we look back

[1] 2 Woolsey's "Political Science," 258.

on the dagger of Booth, and the *sic semper tyrannis* with which he struck home his blow; at the shot of a disappointed office-seeker that cost the life of President Garfield, — we cannot but feel that there are fanatics in America also, who proceed by the methods of fanatics, and are actuated by the blind impulse of destruction in the presence of political absolutism.

But such men are few. There is despotism in American government; but all who look at it with open eyes and honest hearts know that it is despotism in reserve and despotism in division. Russia would centre absolute power once and forever in a single man. We part it for administrative purposes between three departments of government, and however great the share of the executive may be, it is still kept within limits, and held, at most, only for eight years. I say for eight, because American tradition has made a third term impossible.

Our ultimate despot is the people of the United States; but they are the knights in armor that from generation to generation may slumber in the enchanted chambers of the eternal hills. They lay down to rest when a declaration of their rights had been added to the Constitution of the United States by its first ten amendments in the third year of Washington's administration. They rose to action for a moment when, three years later, they found that their ministers of justice had so far misunderstood their meaning as to hold a sovereign State subject to the federal jurisdiction, at the suit of a private individual. Again, at the beginning of this century, they awoke, when party machinery had so far controlled personal patriotism that Aaron Burr had almost been seated in the place which they designed for Thomas Jefferson.

A longer period of inaction followed, till the time came to proclaim by law, what had been before only asserted by the sword, that slavery had become incompatible with free institutions. But the long war that made freedom national, had done much more. It had struck at States. It had conquered States. It had borne down with its strong hand barrier after barrier set by former generations to guard that vast and indefinable domain of rights "reserved to the States respectively, or to the people." It had brought into existence a new class of persons, a great class; utterly unfitted to their new position; surrounded by those who had been their masters, distant from those who had been their liberators.

Two great things remained to be accomplished. These millions of slaves, new-born into freedom, must be protected in it, or given some means of self-protection; and these new relations of the States to the United States, of the old States to the new nation, must be more definitely marked and secured.

Again the knights in armor stirred in the enchanted chamber. The Fourteenth Amendment succeeded the Thirteenth; the Fifteenth soon followed, and the chapter of the Civil War was closed.

But the freedom of the slave was the least of its political consequences. These three amendments of the Constitution readjusted and reset our whole system of fundamental law.

Down to 1868 each State had said for herself, My people shall be free from arbitrary arrests; their liberty and property shall be secure; their rights equal; the law impartially administered; the stranger within my gates protected from wrong as fully as my own sons. Now came back for a brief moment to the scene of action the people of the United States, to say, by the Fourteenth Amendment, that thenceforth every man should have their guaranty that the State would not recede from these obligations, but they should forever be the foundation-stones of American institutions.

We well know that this great change was not a welcome one to the whole people. Only absolute power, the absolute power of a three-fourths vote of the States under a written Constitution — the absolute power of a two-thirds vote of Congress, with the absolute right in each of its houses to determine as to the qualifications of its own members and the admission of members from any recalcitrant State, — with the right to pack the jury even, by admitting to statehood a row of mining camps on barren mountains, and giving to Nevada an equal vote with Virginia or Massachusetts, — this is what forced the Fourteenth, if not the Thirteenth, Amendment into our organic law.

But there it is. It was a slight matter that it hastened the day of negro suffrage, and paved the way for the Fifteenth Amendment, passed two years later. Whenever and wherever the American negro has education enough to enable him to cast an intelligent vote, he will cast that vote, and he ought to cast it. And whenever and wherever he has not such education, he ought not to vote, and, in the long run, he will not vote. Mississippi and South Carolina have put themselves upon solid ground in saying that education must be a condition of suffrage. It is no new doctrine. In the North there is more than one State in which such has been the law for nearly half a century.

The great change wrought by the Fourteenth Amendment has been to concede and perpetuate to the United States vast and far-reaching national powers; to unify and centralize their government, for good or ill.

It has been said that the ideals of the Teutonic race have been in perpetual vibration from one period to another, as the pendulum of time swung to and fro across the ages, between two social forces — Individualism and Collectivism; between the cry of each man for himself, *sauve qui peut*, and the broader note of each for all.

If absolute power has risen up in the United States, and for the United States, during this century, to a height our fathers never contemplated, it is because we have departed from our Anglo-Saxon inheritance of Individualism; because the people demand more of their government, and have given it more. When Coleridge declared that —

"We receive but what we give,
And in our life alone does nature live,"

he spoke what is, above all things, true of free institutions. For each of them, the individual citizen has parted with something. They are the great result of a common contribution; and whatever they give back we who receive have paid for, are paying for, whether we recognize it or not.

It was Collectivism that wrote the Fourteenth Amendment; Collectivism that ratified it; Collectivism that enforces it. It protects individual rights, as in no land were they ever, in any age, protected before. But this is only by the sacrifice of other rights of Individualism; only by extension of the sovereignty of the Union at the cost of the sovereignty of the State; only by giving to the courts new authority to control legislatures, and Congress new power to control the citizen; only by giving to the President new laws to execute, of such a kind as put him forward into fields before unoccupied.

Nor is it to be forgotten that when, by some such great act as this, the people have changed their government, it is for the executive power to proclaim the change, and so to give it its necessary consummation. It is for the Secretary of State, as the representative of the President, to notify the country of the adoption of every constitutional amendment.[1] Then, and not until then, does it become the supreme law of the land. His signature is wanting to make it such, and is sufficient to make it such.[2] Who but he is to decide whether the requisite number of States have given it their votes? Who but he is to say what are the States having the right to vote? Who but he is

[1] Act of 1818: Revised Statutes of the United States, § 205.
[2] See the remarks of the Supreme Court of the United States in Virginia v. West Virginia, 11 Wallace's Reports, 62.

to say whether a State which has once voted to ratify an amendment can reconsider its action?

All these questions were presented by the proceedings upon the Fourteenth and Fifteenth Amendments; and some of them were necessarily involved in determining as to the adoption of every preceding one.

The common practice has been for the Secretary of State to issue in each case a certificate stating that he has received due proof of ratification by a certain number of States, that these constituted three-fourths of the whole number, and that the amendment " has become valid to all intents and purposes, as part of the Constitution of the United States." He acts in this, of course, as an executive officer, responsible to the President for what he does and what he does not do. Until this certificate is issued (unless Congress is in session and intervenes), the Constitution remains as it was. The President may direct the Secretary to delay its issue. He may differ with him as to whether the necessary conditions of ratification have been fulfilled, and if so, he might remove him from office, and, as Jackson did in his contest with the Bank of the United States, when Duane was succeeded by Taney as Secretary of the Treasury, replace a refractory by a submissive agent.

Such is the great office around which modern republicanism has built up its government on American soil.

In the impeachment trial of Andrew Johnson, one of the managers of the prosecution described the

President as nothing but "the constable of Congress." Had that impeachment been successful, the contemptuous taunt might have seemed simple truth. It was not successful, because all honest men, not blinded by party passion, felt that the President held great constitutional functions, which made him, in his sphere, the spokesman of the republic.

The foe that threatens American institutions to-day is not absolutism, but anarchy; not the tyranny of a man, but a tyranny of the mob. To meet it we need the strong hand of power. If we were not a nation before the Civil War, we have been since. A nation must have a head. There is no ground to fear that the President of the United States, absolute as he is within his bounds of office, will ever act the part of Cæsar. The foundations of American liberty are laid too deep. The checks of the Constitution are ample for any strain, because they are backed by the sentiment of a free and intelligent people.

It might seem that there was grave danger of his acting rashly in great emergencies. Had he less power, there would be. But concentration of power brings concentration of responsibility. The most impetuous man is held back if a hasty word or act of his might put the peace or welfare of a nation in peril. It is his very absolutism that has made the President, in respect to all matters of foreign policy, — and there he is most powerful, — the great conservative force in our constitutional system.

CHAPTER V

THE EXEMPTION OF THE ACCUSED FROM EXAMINATION IN CRIMINAL PROCEEDINGS [1]

THE exemption of persons accused of crime from being compelled to testify against themselves is one of the institutions of English jurisprudence which we have fully adopted. It has been incorporated into the Constitutions of all but three [2] of our States, and was grafted into that of the United States at the instance of the first Congress, by the Fifth Amendment. This declares that no person shall be compelled in any criminal case to be a witness against himself, and the State Constitutions use language substantially similar.

The practical construction which these provisions have received from courts and legislatures has been such as generally to exclude any preliminary examination of a person charged with crime, by a magistrate acting for that purpose on behalf of the State. It is the purpose of this chapter to inquire whether that construction is the proper one.

And what, in the first place, was the reason for the original establishment of this rule of immunity? The

---

[1] In preparing this chapter free use has been made of a paper read by the author before the American Bar Association, in 1883.

[2] Georgia, Iowa, and New Jersey. Michigan did not introduce the provision until 1850, nor South Carolina until 1868.

slightest glance at English history leaves us in no doubt as to that.

Our fathers, in the era of our early constitution-making, were not acting the part of political theorists. They undertook to deal with practical questions in a practical way. It was their business to gather in the hard-won fruits of the Revolution. They had just struck off the hold of a government which had been always hard, and often hostile, — a government administered in the interest of the great and the rich; a government which was suspicious, jealous, overpowering, when it wished to overpower. Men were still living in whose boyhood torture, even, had been applied on British soil, to wring confessions from unwilling lips; and the common law gave no sufficient warrant against its future use, should public safety ever be deemed to demand it, by those in power.

If we turn to the leading writers on the English jurisprudence of their day, we find that Britton, indeed, had said[1] that felons must be brought into court without irons, "so that they may not be deprived of reason by pain, nor be constrained to answer by force, but of their own free will;" but Bracton puts this privilege as granted so that they might not appear compelled to offer to undergo the trial by ordeal.[2] Coke gravely tells us in his "Institutes"[3] that "there is no one opinion in our books or judiciall records (that we have seen and remember) for the maintenance of torture or torments," and that Magna

---
[1] Cap. v. 36.
[2] Bracton, lib. iii. 137, "Ne videat coact' ad aliquam purgationem suscipiendam."   [3] Vol. iii. p. 35.

Charta forbids it; yet a few years before (1619) he had signed, as privy councillor, a warrant to put one charged with treason to the rack;[1] and in his speech as Attorney-General, in 1600, in the prosecution of the earls of Essex and Southampton, he attributes to the queen "overmuch clemency to some" in the inquiry into the matter in hand, since, "out of her princely mercy, no man was racked, tortured, or pressed to speak anything farther than of their own accord and willing minds, for discharge of their consciences they uttered."[2] So in 1613, in the Countess of Shrewsbury's Case, Coke,[3] as chief-justice, mentioned it as a special privilege of the peerage in legal proceedings that, "for the honor and reverence which the law gives to nobility, their bodies are not subject to torture *in causa criminis læsæ majestatis.*"

It took, in truth, Cromwell and the Civil War to root out torture from the English courts; nor was it given up in Scotland until the succeeding century.

The whole criminal code of England was a bloody and heartless one when the Pilgrims sailed away for freer shores. Its severity, it is true, often prevented its execution. Juries stood ready to violate their oaths rather than send a man to the gallows for some trivial offence; and judges construed the strength out of many a Draconian statute. But there had been also a Chief-Justice Jeffreys, and indeed, wherever the interests of the party in power were involved in a criminal proceeding, the bench had proved but a feeble barrier against political passions and prejudices.

---

[1] Samuel Peacock: Ann. Reg. for 1790; Antiq. 96.
[2] 1 State Trials, 1336.   [3] 12 Rep. 96.

Under the guise of prosecuting crime, the ministers of justice had too often been seen to strike down the innocent and spare the guilty.

What might be the future of the new governments which a hundred years ago were being here called into life, to succeed to the rights forfeited by the British Crown, who could tell? They were to be clad with the same sovereign power. They might abuse it in the same way.

For this cause we find these solemn guaranties in our American Constitutions of the right of all accused of crime to have fair notice of the charge, defence by counsel, trial by jury, and exemption from being forced to testify against themselves.

That of defence by counsel is more nearly connected than one might think with that of immunity from enforced confession.

In Finch's "Discourse on Law," he speaks approvingly of the then English rule of refusing counsel when the prisoner denied the fact, and gives this as his reason: —

"For either his conscience, perhaps, will sting him to utter the truth, or otherwise, by his gesture, countenance, or simplicity of speech, it may bee discovered; which the artificial speech of his counsel learned, would hide and colour. Also himself can best answer to the fact." [1]

The power of a law can seldom be known or foretold when it is enacted. It will lie in the construction and operation to be given it by the courts and people.

[1] Edition of 1661, p. 386.

EXAMINATION IN CRIMINAL PROCEEDINGS 121

If it appeals to some popular prejudice; if it is rooted in some traditional principle of freedom, for which a former generation may have fought with their kings, and fought successfully; if it attracts human sympathy, or reassures human fears, it may rear up around itself a wall of protection and public reverence which will endure long after the reason of the enactment has ceased to exist.

A law may grow into an institution. It may be extended by analogy. It may be expounded and expanded by some course of judicial decision, far beyond the anticipations of its framers.

So did the little phrase, " impair the obligation of contracts " — like the genius of some Arabian tale — at the touch of the magic wand of Chief-Justice Marshall, rise and spread into the form of that invincible champion of chartered franchises, by which the whole theory of American corporations was to be revolutionized once and again. And so, by means perhaps less direct, but no less controlling, has a new meaning been read into many a provision of statute or constitution, by public opinion and the lapse of time, — a meaning by which the law, it may be, at last ceases to protect, and begins to oppress society.

Has not this been the history of the constitutional guaranty now under consideration?

The judges of England had given it as their opinion, in 1628, under the spur of the public sentiment that was then dictating the Petition of Right, that to compel a discovery by torture, from one accused of crime, was not allowable by the laws of the realm.

All precedent, however, was against them. The practice of the reigning sovereign continued to be against them as long as he had courts to control. The authorities which they could cite to sustain their opinion were uncertain. Britton, in the passage already quoted, was the strongest of all. Fortescue[1] had inveighed, with a manly outburst of feeling, against the barbarity and folly of the practice, but had not ventured to deny its legality. Jardine, in our own day, has not hesitated to defend it as an ancient flower of the prerogative. The maxim *Nemo tenetur accusare seipsum* first appears in English law books[2] at the era of the civil war, and certainly derives no authority from the language in which it is expressed. As Ortolan said of the theories of Roman law and legend evolved by the German historical school, it has the singular merit of having been wholly unknown to the Romans themselves. Hardly two authors quote it in the same words, and in one leading case,[3] it is cited twice in the same opinion, — once as *Nemo tenetur accusare seipsum*, and once as *Nemo tenetur prodere seipsum*.

Here, then, was a disputable doctrine of uncertain origin, — a doctrine that great men could assert in books, and deny in practice. It was a doctrine in advance of the utterance of the judges in Felton's Case. They only forbade torture. This went further, and forbade any form of compulsion. In the

---

[1] Cap. xxii., folio 24.
[2] Wingate's "Maxims," 1648.
[3] People *v.* McMahon, 15 New York Reports, 387, 390.

Countess of Shrewsbury's Case, already cited, while her rank and sex might save her from the rack, Coke and Bacon concurred in holding that a fine of £20,000 and imprisonment during the king's pleasure were but a just punishment for her refusal to criminate herself; and the poor lady, in fact, died in the Tower.

Our forefathers, then, approving to its full extent the principle formulated in Wingate's maxim, determined to give it a place in their Constitutions. They did so. But did they mean to do more, and in effect impede, if not prevent, disclosures of crime, not procured by force or threatened fine or imprisonment? Did they intend to forbid any preliminary examination of an accused person designed only to assist the proper authority in determining whether he should be prosecuted or discharged? For this is the result to which a hundred years of use has really brought us.

In few of our States[1] is the prisoner, on his arrest, even asked by the examining or committing magistrate if he desires to make a statement; and in almost every one of these the magistrate is enjoined to caution him that he need say nothing, and that whatever he does say may be used against him. Similar provisions were introduced into the English law by Sir John Jervis's Act[2] in 1848.

---

[1] Some sort of provision to this effect is made in Delaware, Louisiana, Mississippi, Missouri, New Hampshire, New Jersey, New York, North Carolina, Tennessee, and Texas, and in these States only.

[2] 11 & 12 Vict., cap. xlii.

Is it not plain that such an invitation to speak is rather a counsel to keep silent?

The object of criminal prosecutions is to detect the authors of crime, and to punish them. In the majority of cases the person arrested is the person guilty. In most countries the first step is to ask him to give an account of himself with reference to the crime in question; to say where he was and what he was doing at the time of its commission; to explain, if he can, the circumstances which fasten suspicion upon him. In most countries this inquiry is conducted by a magistrate or prosecuting officer, and instituted before the prisoner has consulted counsel, or had time to frame theories of defence. The result of the examination is put in writing by the same authority, and therefore preserved in an authentic form. If the accused be innocent, he will often be able to clear himself by a frank statement; if guilty, he will probably become involved in contradictions and absurdities.

Such was the practice in England until the Act of 1848. Her justices of the peace were originally more like our constables, — prosecuting, rather than judicial officers. From ancient times, and under the positive injunctions of an Act of 1554,[1] they had made it a principal part of their duty to examine the prisoner, and record whatever information he gave.[2] In the Countess of Shrewsbury's Case, we find Lord Bacon pressing her to a disclosure by this very consideration of ancient and reasonable practice.

[1] 2 & 3 P. & M., c. x.
[2] 1 Stephens' "History of the Criminal Law of England," 219, 221.

"No subject," he says, in his stately fashion,[1] "was ever brought in causes of estate to trial judicial, but first he passed examination; for examination is the entrance of justice in criminal causes: it is one of the eyes of the king's politic body: there are but two — information and examination: it may not be endured that one of the lights be put out by your example."

No prisoner, indeed, can hope to be exempted from examination simply because the law makes no provision for requiring it. Some such questioning, under any system of jurisprudence, he is certain to undergo. It may come from neighbors, from busybodies, from reporters, from constables, detectives, jailers. It will come from them if it does not come from authority of law. And the answers obtained, lying simply in human memory, will be easily twisted and perverted by the narrator, anxious, perhaps, to magnify the importance of the revelation his sagacity has secured, or perhaps to screen a friend or serve a grudge.

It is, in fact, the evils and inaccuracies of testimony founded on these extra-judicial confessions, which have led English and American courts to confine its introduction within such narrow bounds.

But for the very reason that those in authority have no right to require a disclosure, those without authority feel justified in seeking to worm it out by threats, by ill treatment, by fraud, by holding out false hopes,

[1] 2 State Trials, 770, 778.

by putting forward false pretences.[1] On information thus obtained rests a large part of the convictions for crime in any of our courts. The source of the information may not appear at the trial. Unguarded answers may have put the inquirer on the track of more certain evidences of guilt; and an explicit confession, however obtained, if once made, is likely to result in a plea of guilty.

In many cases, if not in most, the conviction of the prisoner, in this country as well as under the continental mode of procedure, results from words spoken by himself. But what European courts accomplish by direct means, we attain by indirection.

Unwilling to allow a magistrate to institute, as a matter of course, a formal examination, and place the result on record, we leave the same information to be fished for by the sheriff who makes the arrest, by the jailer, by a fellow-prisoner turned informer, or by the detective in disguise, and only require the witness who proves it to add, perhaps, perjury to fraud, in swearing that no undue means were used to elicit the confession.

The tendency of modern legislation has, for fifty years, been strongly in favor of admitting parties in interest as competent witnesses. The common law excluded them because it believed that they were

[1] In a recent case which has attracted wide attention, the mate of a ship was convicted of murder, largely upon the testimony of a police officer as to a reply he had made to a question of his, put to him after he had been stripped to the skin, and while being subjected to an inquisitorial examination in the police station, in that humiliating condition. The courts reversed the judgment for this cause. Bram *v.* United States, 168 United States Reports, 532.

likely to lie, and certain to be tempted to lie. But, for a generation past, England, and for the most part America, have received their testimony in civil actions for what it is worth, and have found the cause of justice advanced by it.

In criminal proceedings, the temptation to perjury, if the accused is allowed to testify for himself, is undoubtedly greater, — rising with the degree of the crime charged; and yet he is to-day a competent witness in most of our States, and has been since 1878 in all courts of the United States.

It is a general feature of these recent laws for admitting the accused to the witness-stand, that his failure to testify shall not create any presumption against him. I cannot but think that this proviso is only another proof that the spirit of the constitutional guaranty in his favor has been misconceived in its administration.

Were it not for that guaranty, who would say that if a man has the right to speak in his own behalf, to explain all the circumstances brought up against him, and declines to avail himself of it, it ought not to be deemed an indication that he cannot explain them? In the forum of common-sense it is such an indication. If our boy, our servant, our clerk, is charged with some fault, and denies it, we expect him to make a frank statement of what he did or knew. If he does not, we consider the charge half proved. Should we be more tender of the prisoner in the dock? If we have given him the new right to testify for himself, it does not follow that we should disturb the balance of justice by forbidding the jury to suspect him if he keeps silent.

Such has been the view of some,[1] but not of most courts, in administering justice in such cases, under statutes not containing a positive prohibition against comment on the position of the accused if he declines to testify. The general current of decision has been towards making his constitutional privilege as wide as the words will bear.

This course of construction has led to many rulings in favor of the defence which I cannot but think strained and unnecessary.

Thus, in a recent case in New York,[2] it was held that the person of a woman charged with killing her infant child, could not, without her own consent, be examined by physicians deputed by the coroner, to ascertain if she had recently been a mother. The same principle would seem to preclude searching the pockets of a suspected thief, or stripping a man arrested for murder, to see if his body shows marks of blood or violence.

In a later case in Georgia,[3] indeed, the court rejected evidence that the defendant's foot fitted exactly the tracks left on the ground by the perpetrator of a crime, because, to obtain the proof, his foot was placed by force in the necessary position.

A different and, as it seems to me, sounder conclusion has been reached in some other of our States, in admitting testimony of a similar character.[4]

[1] States v. Bartlett, 55 Maine Reports, 215–221.
[2] People v. McCoy, 45 Howard's Practice Reports, 216.
[3] Day v. State, 63 Georgia Reports, 667.
[4] State v. Graham, 74 North Carolina Reports, 646; State v. Ah Chuey, 14 Nevada Reports, 79; Walker v. State, 7 Texas Appeals Reports, 245. A more extended and thorough discussion of the

The leading authorities, however, are in accord in holding that the prisoner who accepts the benefits of a statute making him a competent witness, accepts them to the extent of becoming open to the same cross-examination to which any other witness may be subject, and in respect to whatever can legitimately throw light on the question of his guilt, whether or not it be connected immediately with his direct testimony.[1] When he voluntarily puts himself under oath, the logic of the law leads inevitably to this result; although where the statute simply allows him to make a statement, there are judges of eminence who have reached a different conclusion.

In fact, there are few parts of criminal jurisprudence in which American judges in expounding the law, and American legislators in framing the law, do not lean on the side of the defence.

Much is said with us as to the rights of criminals; so much that we almost forget that the State has rights against criminals and against those charged with crime, on the maintenance of which the public life depends, and that it is mainly for their maintenance that the State exists.

> "And sovereign Law — that State's collected will —
> O'er thrones and globes elate,
> Sits empress, crowning good, repressing ill."

A sharp lecture was read a few years ago to the American public by a well-known sociologist,[2] on

authorities will be found in the "Central Law Journal," vol. xv., pp. 2, 207.

[1] State *v.* Griswold, 67 Connecticut Reports, 290.
[2] Professor William Graham Sumner, LL.D., of Yale University.

"The Forgotten Man." He was the hard-working, law-abiding, unobtrusive man, whom legislators forgot, in their zeal to help the poor, reform the vicious, and grant relief to every interest that clamors and pushes for it.

The noblest feature of modern society is its attainments, not in science and art, but in humanity. We recognize the dignity and worth of man, as man, and recognize it even in the meanest and basest. There is but one temple on earth, says Novalis, and that is the body of man.

But there is a point at which humanity turns into sentimentalism. There is a point where selfishness — that is, putting forward self-protection as the first object — is becoming to a government.

The American system of criminal prosecutions is one which seldom convicts the innocent; but it is also one which often acquits the guilty. The proportion of acquittals to jury trials is probably three times as great as in England, and ten times as great as in Scotland or on the Continent. There are few civilized governments in which homicide is as frequent as in some of our western and southwestern States and Territories; there are none in which convictions for murder are so rare.

The defendant has, under all systems of criminal justice, a great advantage in the matter of pleading. The prosecutor must formulate his charges with precision and accuracy; but the plea of *Not guilty* leaves him utterly ignorant of the defence by which he is to be met. It may be an *alibi*, a justification, a claim of temporary insanity. Whatever it be, he learns it for the first time when the trial is begun, and must be ready to meet and disprove it on the instant, with no possibility of a postponement on the ground of surprise.

This embarrassment to the prosecution seems to be an inevitable one. Not so as to the embarrassments set up by our American administration of the rules of evidence; for it is these rules which have grown into an artificial net-work, through whose meshes a well-defended criminal can so often slip.

No fault is to be found with the fundamental principle that the State must satisfy the jury of the prisoner's guilt beyond a reasonable doubt. It speaks well for society when it can afford to say to a citizen who is pursued for a claim, however great, involving no moral wrong or civic degradation: You must pay it, if there is a bare preponderance of evidence against you; and yet say to the same man, if charged with crime: We will declare you innocent, unless we show that there is no hypothesis to be framed which is not inconsistent with your innocence. Only a free State can or will take this attitude. Perhaps no State which does not take it can be free.

But here is it not time to stop?

We have relieved the prisoner from the necessity, ordinarily imposed in civil cases, of pleading the nature of his defence. We have thrown upon the public a burden of proof heavier than it is thought just to impose on any private suitor. Why, at the same time, cut off the counter right which every private suitor has, of putting his adversary to his oath as to the merits of his defence?

The historical reason we have already considered. If government can ask a prisoner to testify, it can require it of him: if it can require it, it can force a compliance. All such force our Constitutions forbid; and far be it from any advocate of law reform to urge a recurrence to it; whether it be the Bavarian plan, now or lately in force, of giving only bread and water to an accused who refuses to make a statement, or the more downright English methods of rack and thumbscrew, fine and imprisonment, discarded two centuries ago. But between forbidding physical or moral compulsion, and inviting, or even urging a frank disclosure, the difference is wide. We have construed a prohibition to compel as a prohibition to request.

We assume a burden of proof unknown except where the English tongue is spoken; we demand a unanimity in the verdict equally unknown elsewhere; we often permit the jury — a thing unheard of in any other land — to go to their homes and mingle with the friends of the prisoner, while they are deliberating upon his guilt, — and yet we reject the aid of the simple expedient which would occur first of all to any child, of asking the accused what he has to say about the charge against him.

They are still jealous of their government in Great Britain. It is still a royal government, supported by an idle aristocracy; two of the estates of the realm ruling by no other right than that of birth. In prosecutions for political offences, the interests of these two estates are directly involved, and to one of them the bench itself, in its highest places, belongs.

EXAMINATION IN CRIMINAL PROCEEDINGS 133

It is not strange, therefore, that while not surrendering the procedure of preliminary examinations, close upon the arrest, they have been sedulous to require the magistrate to warn the prisoner that he need not answer, and that, if he does, his words may be used against him.

But with us, government has no other office or end than to order and protect the peace of society. The prisoner is tried before judges, and by prosecuting officers, who were, directly or indirectly, of his own choosing. The jury is made up of his neighbors. The law is one, directly or indirectly, again, of his own making. He had been, probably, educated at the expense of the State, for the very purpose of giving him the intelligence necessary to govern his conduct as becomes a good citizen. No private prosecutor, as in most countries, is pushing the case against him, for revenge or restitution. He has to contend only with the public, and the public have no interest except to discover the truth, whichever way it lies.

If, then, we would make the punishment of crime as certain here as it is in Europe — I might almost say, as it is in Mexico or China — is it not time to abandon our attempt to fight it without the use of the ordinary weapons that lie at hand; without asking the man who, of all the world, knows best what the facts are, to tell us about them; and without asking him in such a way as to facilitate, rather than to prevent, an honest statement? Let him be brought before the examining magistrate, as he is abroad, before he has time to fabricate an explanation; before he has seen counsel; when the proofs of guilt are fresh. Let him be asked if he desires to make any statement or explanation to be placed on record. And let all be done, not as a matter of favor from him, but of right to the State.

An innocent man, under such an examination, may become confused. He may answer confusedly or incorrectly. He may admit more than he intended, and more than is true. But he will certainly be less liable to do so than if questioned unofficially by a wheedling detective or incredulous policeman; and such questioning is as sure to come as it is to be but half remembered. A fair report, made at the time, in writing by an impartial magistrate, proves often the best evidence for the accused, and results in his immediate discharge.

Inviting a statement from the accused before the committing magistrate is, of course, a very different thing from allowing his examination by the court on his trial to the jury, or even by the magistrate himself, when sitting for the final hearing and disposition of the cause. Both form a part of the general Continental system, but it is the interrogation from the bench, when the issue of *Guilty* or *Not guilty* is before the jury for decision, which becomes often and justly a matter of reproach.

In France, for instance, the preliminary examination is conducted by the prosecuting officer, in order to determine whether there is or is not ground to prosecute; but when the accused is once informed against and put on trial, the judge is apt in practice to presume his guilt, and exercise all his ingenuity to twist some admission out of him, or perhaps to distort what is said, so that the jury may receive a false impression from it.

The embarrassment of the defendant when actually on trial, and confronting a charge of crime laid against him by the authority of the State, is naturally and necessarily greater than when, at an earlier stage of the proceedings, the State is simply inquiring whether it ought to be put to the expense of a prosecution. The very nearness of the final decision, by a verdict which may convict and may set free, must intensify the excitement of his feelings.

If the prosecutor is allowed to question him now, the interrogation is sure to be unfriendly: it may be, it is even likely to be, if conducted by the judge. Under such circumstances the contest between the questioner and the questioned is too unequal, and innocence may well seem guilt. Pomeroy, in his work on *Constitutional Law*,[1] has not hesitated to say that the rule " that no person shall be compelled to be a witness against himself can only be supported by that intense reverence for the past which is so difficult to be overcome," and that "there can be no doubt that the States will gradually abandon this provision and reject it from their Constitutions."

I doubt if the prediction comes true; I doubt if it would be well that it should. There may yet come a revolution in social forces which would make even the use of torture tolerated in courts, were there no

[1] p. 155.

fundamental law to forbid. The highest refinement in civilization has, in former ages, not been found incompatible with the highest refinement in cruelty; and the nature of man changes little, beneath the surface, from generation to generation. Lynch law, within our own borders and among our own people, has been no stranger to the arts of interrogation, aided even by torture, at the foot of the gallows.

Let us keep our constitutional guaranties as they are, but let us read them and apply them like reasonable men. It is enough to reject the use of force, without also refusing even to ask the defendant to speak for himself when first arrested, and so at a time when a frank statement may secure his immediate discharge.

These views are not presented without full consideration. They are the result of thirty years of practice at the bar, during which I have acted sometimes on behalf of the government in criminal prosecutions, and sometimes for the defence, and of five years upon the bench, during which I have had occasion to sit both for the trial of such causes with a jury on the circuit, and for their disposition on proceedings in error, as a member of an appellate court.

Nothing, of course, can now be done to remedy a practice so inveterate as that which has been the subject of this discussion, without the action of the legislature. What I would suggest is provision by statute that committing magistrates, upon whose warrant an arrest is made, should ask the defendant when first brought before them, whether he desires to make a statement, explaining clearly that he is under no obligation to do so. If he then makes one, whatever he says should be written down at length in his own words, and the whole read over to him for any corrections or additions which he may wish to have entered. He should then be asked if he is willing to sign it. If he declines to make any statement, or having made one, is unable or declines to sign, the fact should be recorded. In case of a foreigner unfamiliar with our language, the statement should be written down in his own, by an interpreter.

This is no new or untried method of procedure. It is our present method which is the innovation on the practice of all lands and all times.

I do not think I am mistaken in believing that the sober judgment of the country is tending to the belief that we have gone too far towards making the law serve as a shield of crime. There is a growing and just impatience of the delays and uncertainties of criminal procedure. The Supreme Court of the United States has reflected this sentiment in the course of its recent decisions in regard to the effect of the Fifth Amendment on the provision of the Inter-State Commerce Act. One statute after another was passed by Congress to enable the Inter-State Commerce Commission to compel witnesses before it to testify as to violations of the Act which it was created to enforce, and finally the court, limiting the scope of earlier decisions, held that a self-criminating answer could be compelled, under pain of imprisonment, provided the witness were assured against any prosecution for the offence.[1]

One of its leading members[2] not long since declared before the American Bar Association that justice would be promoted if, in cases of criminal conviction, no writ of error should ever be allowed. "In criminal cases," he said, "there should be no appeal. I say it with reluctance, but the truth is that you may trust a jury to do justice to the accused with more safety than you can an appellate court to secure protection to the public by the speedy punishment of a criminal. To guard against any possible wrong to an accused, a board of review and pardons might be created with power to set aside a conviction or reduce the punishment, if on the full record it appears, not that a technical error has been committed, but that the defendant is not guilty, or has been excessively punished."[3]

The denial of an appeal is in accordance with the English practice as respects their highest tribunal for the trial of criminal causes, but that court is presided over by members of the High Court of Justice, whose qualifications for correct decisions on points of law and evidence may well be superior to those of the ordinary trial judge in an American court.

I venture to think that we should begin at the other end of the case to seek our remedy, and look for it in giving the defendant an opportunity to clear

---

[1] Brown v. Walker, 161 United States Reports, 591.
[2] Mr. Justice Brewer.
[3] Reports of the American Bar Association, xviii. 448.

or convict himself by a preliminary statement to a proper magistrate on his first arrest.

It is no mean distinction to New Jersey that it is the only American State that has steadfastly adhered to this ancient plan.[1] It shows the same spirit of independent judgment and sound conservatism which, under the lead of Patterson, made her influence so great and so healthful in the Constitutional Convention of 1787. And more, perhaps, than anything else in her system of criminal administration, it has made "Jersey justice" proverbial along the Atlantic coast, to signify swift and certain retribution to wrongdoers, at the hands of the law.

America has tried many experiments in the art of government. She has tried none more hazardous than that which has been the subject of this chapter. There are parts of the United States where more criminals are yearly put to death by Lynch law, or by the hand of some private avenger of blood, than by judicial warrant. And is it not true that, in those communities, public sentiment justifies such deeds of violence because the courts afford too uncertain a remedy; not because they are corrupt, but because they are inefficient?

If we would make American justice as sure as American liberty; if we would banish pleas of temporary insanity from our court rooms, and mob violence from our frontiers, ought we not to begin by going back, — back to the ancient ways from

[1] General Statutes of New Jersey, i. 1119, sec. 2.

which a false humanitarianism may have led us off? Leaving our Constitutions as they are, let them, with such aid as appropriate legislation can afford, be interpreted in their true spirit, and the State, in its judicial contests with those whom it charges with crime, given once more an equal chance.

CHAPTER VI

FREEDOM OF INCORPORATION

THE Romans made the world over again, but among their many achievements none was more durable in its effects on the civilization of mankind than the invention of the corporation as an instrument of government and of trade.

The very word "civilization" describes the condition of the citizen of a municipal corporation, — a city or a city-State.

In the nature of things, of course, every sovereign and independent government claims the attributes of perpetuity and personality. What the Romans did was to establish in men's minds the conception of perpetual personalities of a lesser rank, subordinate to the State; each in its own small sphere subserving the interests of the State in the support of its political institutions, or the promotion of industry and commerce.

The city-State, as a public corporation, had always been known since the beginning of history. It was the first form of any real political organization. The group of neighboring villages, uniting around some common fortress of defence into a tribal settlement, grew to be a city, and the city came to be a State; governing dependent communities, in which perhaps other cities might be included. Such had been Nineveh, Babylon, Athens. What the Romans did, as far as municipal corporations are concerned, was to show how self-governing cities could belong to a city-State, subject to it as to national affairs, and practically independent of it as to local affairs.

They treated every such place as if it were a human being, possessing the right to life, liberty, and the pursuit of happiness in his own way, and yet owing allegiance to his sovereign and such public duties as allegiance implied. It was an application of the doctrines of private law, not to the relations of State and subject, but to the attributes of a new political subject which they had been the first to call into existence.

The private corporation of Roman law was even a more perfect form of an artificial political personality; composed of several human beings but occupying the place of one, with rights and duties of its own, distinct from theirs. It was formed on the model of the public corporation, but shaped with a freer hand.

The Roman mind was accustomed to deal both with men and with property collectively.[1] The family was the social and political unit. Succession to the property of the dead was by a universal title. Nothing seemed more natural than for men

[1] The effect of this national trait on Roman law is well stated in Cuq's *Institutions Juridiques des Romains*, 50. In Roman politics, it is manifested by the composition of each of their legislative assemblies. That of the centuries, as Niebuhr remarks (Hist. of Rome, i. 340), reflects the theory which regards the State as a joint-stock company.

to associate in some close and permanent way for the accomplishment of any large undertaking.

Guilds of workmen existed as early as the reign of Numa Pompilius, and the Twelve Tables confirmed and probably extended their rights.[1] Similar associations were soon formed by those who were not mere wage-earners, and had other ends in view than the protection of trade interests.

Such a body of individuals was at first regarded as a mere society (*societas*). It did not differ essentially from the Greek ἑταιρία. It was a fraternity, or, if for business purposes, a partnership. Later came the investiture of some of these associations with the attributes of personality and perpetuity. In the phrase of the lawyers, they received a *corpus;* the collective body being treated as something with a distinct life of its own.

The juristic person thus created served two important purposes. Holding the possessions of many natural persons, and acting with the united strength of all, it formed a counterpoise to the family, as a political factor in the State. It was also the natural opponent of that spirit of contempt for mercantile and mechanical pursuits which was universal among the upper classes of society among the ancients.

The Roman *familia*, in its original type, was the closest possible association of men; and one that had, in itself, much of the character of perpetuity. It massed property, acquired by the labors of many, in one hand, with a power of absolute disposal. It

[1] Niebuhr's Hist. of Rome, i. 432; Mommsen's Hist. of Rome, book ii., chap. 8.

put under the command of the head of the house, the *paterfamilias*, the services of his children and their children, who worked for his benefit on little better footing than his slaves, and with no greater reward, except that to be anticipated as heirs to the succession. In that capacity they were recognized as in some sort proprietors, even during his life;[1] and when that ended they were put so absolutely in his place that while they owned all his estate they also owed all his debts, as a personal obligation. The very name of such an inheritance, the "*universitas*," was one of those commonly used as descriptive of a corporation.

The political influence of such a family was necessarily great. Only another family of equal means could stand up against it, until the private corporation was invented. Then for the first time opposition could be made by capital and labor combined in another way, but with similar strength and power of resistance.

Then, also, for the first time, could mutual support give tradesmen and artisans, associated together, a position of consideration and of assured permanence. All merchandizing on a small scale was held to be a low and mean pursuit, but some favor was accorded to those engaged in commerce in a large way.[2] What trade there was of the latter character

---

[1] Dig. xxvii. 2, *de Liberis et posthumis Heredibus instituendis*, 11. "*In suis heredibus evidentius apparet continuationem dominii eo rem perducere, ut nulla videatur hereditas fuisse, quasi olim, hi domini essent, qui etiam vivo patre quodammodo domini existimantur.*"

[2] Cicero, *de Officiis*, i. 42.

in early Rome was conducted either by foreigners or by the heads of houses, acting through their slaves.[1] The commonalty had no share in it. Indeed, no Roman citizen, at this time, could follow trade as a profession without forfeiting his political rights.[2] It was a base thing to engage in any form of labor for which he was to be paid by another. Into this new form of commercial association, however, the poorer classes soon found their way; and from the confidence of numbers and the absence of any limit to the capital stock which might be contributed, the corporation gradually rose to a position of importance, if not of dignity. It could hold real as well as personal property, and by a title of perpetual succession.[3] Men of the highest rank found in them a convenient and profitable mode of investment. They often took shares in the name of some client or other dependent, and sometimes lent to a company in which they had no other interest. Plutarch tells us that Cato had, in the name of Quintus, one of his freedmen, two per cent of the capital of a trading concern, which was also a large borrower from him.[4] Senators were forbidden by law to engage in mer-

---

[1] Mommsen's Hist. of Rome, book iii., chap. 12; Institutes of Justinian, iv. 7, *Quod cum eo qui in aliena potestate est*, etc., 2. A *collegium mercatorum* was instituted about B. C. 495, in connection with the temple of Mercury, but probably only for purposes of religious worship. Livy, ii. 27.

[2] Niebuhr's Hist. of Rome, i. 447. Tradesmen in ancient Egypt were also excluded from participation in public affairs. Wilkinson's Ancient Egyptians, ii. 57 (chap. 7).

[3] *Corpus Inscriptionum Latinarum*, x. 444.

[4] Plutarch's Lives, Clough's translation, ii. 344.

cantile adventures; but who was to know if they were shareholders in this or that corporation (*collegium*) formed for gold-mining, or contracting for public works, or Egyptian trade?[1]

Under the influence of such causes, during the era of the republic, the formation of voluntary associations for purposes not in themselves of an unlawful character was at first unrestricted. Afterwards, when the lawyers and judges had clothed such bodies with the character of an immortal person, statutes were enacted which either specified the purposes for which they could be organized, or stated purposes for which they could not be organized. Whichever form was adopted, they apparently still left the privilege of incorporation open to all, provided the objects proposed were such as the law sanctioned.

Special legislation was foreign to the ideals of Roman jurisprudence. These demanded that all in like circumstances should be treated alike. The Twelve Tables made it, as regards public prosecutions, at least, a constitutional rule, by the declaration: PRIVILEGIA NE IRROGANTO.

All societies and corporations were, from the first, left free to regulate their internal management by such by-laws as they might agree on, provided only they were not contrary to any of the laws of the State.[2]

Towards the end of the republic, corporations had multiplied so greatly that the patricians became seriously alarmed. Political clubs, and ward organ-

[1] Mommsen's Hist. of Rome, book iii., chap. 12.
[2] Dig. xlvii. 22, *de Collegiis et Corporibus*, 4.

izations of the lower classes, were threatening to control all elections. Presidents (*Magistri*) of some of the moneyed companies were vying with senators in their style of living. The companies of craftsmen must have come in direct competition with the workshops forming part of the establishment of every great Roman *familia*, and conducted by the labor of slaves. Membership in these was not confined to those of the same trade. It seems most natural to suppose that the merchants and physicians who, as several inscriptions testify, were on their lists, had put money into the common stock as an investment, from which to receive dividends from the profits. Capital was thus combined with labor, to render competition formidable, and no limitation on the total amount of the assets or capital stock of a Roman corporation was then, or ever, imposed by law.

There had been also scandalous jobbery in letting State lands and State contracts to corporations in which public officials were shareholders.

These causes combined to raise a general cry of Down with corporations! and a statute was enacted in the year 64 B.C., which absolutely dissolved most of these organizations, leaving only a few, composed of those engaged in manual labor, such as the guilds of smiths and statuaries. It is probable also that this did not affect the peculiar form of quasi-corporations (*publica societas*), with a large money capital divided into shares (*partes, particulæ*) under which the public revenue was farmed and collected by publicans. Cicero styled this the "*ornamentum civitatis et firmamentum reipublicæ.*"

A reaction soon followed, and the Clodian law in B.C. 58 revived most of the charters which had been annulled, and gave authority for the foundation of new corporations for many purposes.

Under Julius Cæsar, a restrictive policy was again pursued, and it became the general law of the empire that no corporation could be formed except for certain specified purposes. These were few in number,[1] and even as to those it is not improbable that those desiring incorporation were obliged, in each case, to submit their scheme to the emperor for approval, and receive what was in effect a special charter.[2]

To usurp the franchise of being a corporation without due authorization was a high crime.[3] Notwithstanding this, however, the constant solicitude of the Romans to preserve rights of private ownership led to the rule that upon the dissolution by law of a corporation formed for illegal purposes, the capital stock, if any, was to be divided up among its members.[4]

A similar right to withdraw his share of the assets

---

[1] Dig. iii. 4, *Quod cujuscumque Universitatis Nomine*, etc., 1 ; Dig. xxxiv. 5, *de Rebus dubiis*, 21. They were undoubtedly more numerous than those specially mentioned by way of explanation in these texts. There was, for instance, a company of shipowners so highly favored that by a decree of Constantine if any member of it died intestate and without heirs, his property, instead of escheating to the State, should go "*ad corpus naviculariorum ex quo fatale sorte subtractus est.*" Code, vi. 62, *de Hereditatibus*, etc., 1.

[2] See this point discussed in Mommsen's *de Collegiis, etc.*, chap. iv., and his Hist. of Rome, book v., chap. 11.

[3] Dig. xlvii. 22 *de Collegiis*, etc., 2.

[4] *Ibid.* 3.

was conceded to one who had violated another of the imperial constitutions issued by Marcus Aurelius, by which it was provided that no one should at the same time be a member of more than one body having full corporate privileges.[1]

The reason for imposing this prohibition, if not its extent, must be considered doubtful. Mommsen argues that it has come down to us in the Digest out of its proper connection, and must have been intended solely for funeral aid societies; no man needing to provide twice for the cost of his burial. Heinneccius ventures the conjecture that, as many of these organizations met monthly for convivial purposes, the law was meant to prevent their members from getting drunk too often. It would seem more natural to attribute the enactment to either of three causes: (1) The corporations were so prosperous, that their members were becoming too rich. To restrain a man to investment in a single company tended to keep his accumulations within reasonable bounds. (2) The political influence of these organizations was a just cause of complaint. If the same man could belong to several, he might attach each to his interests, or, at least, imbue each with his own views on public affairs. It was in this way that Franklin's *Junto* at Philadelphia spread its influence over the whole city. Each member, or each who could, formed a new club on the same model, and without telling his new associates that he also belonged to the original organization, made it his business to put before them from time to time, as if they

[1] Dig. xlvii., 22 *de Collegiis*, etc., 1, § 2.

had occurred to himself alone, all the measures to which that might be committed, and engage them in their support.[1] Whether secretly or openly attempted, such an extension of one man's and one society's influence was something to be dreaded in a government resting on no more solid foundations than that of a Roman emperor. (3) Again, the shareholder in a Roman corporation was often, if not generally, an active participator in the business which it conducted, or the trade to which it appertained. The Egyptian rule,[2] that no artisan should follow more than one trade, because no man can do the best work in more than one, may have been in mind. "*Ne sutor supra crepidam.*" So far as the societies or corporations of artificers were concerned, membership was largely hereditary. The general rule was that every man must follow his father's rank and trade. "*Exemplo senatorii ordinis, patris originem municeps unusquisque sequatur.*"[3] He must also follow it in the same place; and if a college of workmen transferred the seat of their business to some new city, it was at the risk of being sent back, together with their children born there, to their original home.[4]

The general incorporation law which seems to have existed during the empire is known only by fragmentary references. The fullest of these contains no more than a single section, which relates to fun-

[1] 1 Franklin's Works, ed. 1834, pp. 40, 42.
[2] Wilkinson's Ancient Egyptians, ii. 57.
[3] Cod. Theodos. xii. 1, *de Decurionibus*, 101; Dictionnaire des Antiquités, *Collegium*, 1295.
[4] *Ibid.* xiv. 7, *de Collegiatis.*

eral-aid societies.[1] Other sections probably contained similar provisions as to corporations formed for other purposes. This seems to me fairly implied from a reference in the Digest to certain corporations "*quibus jus coeundi lege permissum est,*" among which are mentioned those of craftsmen, since they are engaged in work necessary for the public interest.[2] The authority of some such statute is often invoked by bodies of this kind in dedicatory inscriptions, in phrases of description, applied to themselves, as "*Ex S. C. P. R. quibus coire, conveniri, collegiumque habere liceat,*"[3] or, more briefly, "*quibus ex S. C. coire licet.*" Corporations of smiths, shipwrights, builders, musicians, castanet players, &c., &c., speak of themselves in this fashion.[4] It is not improbable that this statute, in its original form, was one of the many Julian laws. A *collegium sym-*

---

[1] This is found on a slab unearthed at Lanuvium, which probably was placed over the door of the hall where such a society was accustomed to meet. It is followed by a copy of their by-laws, prefaced by a warning to all those who propose to become members to read these first, and not to complain later that they did not understand what they were, or leave a controversy to their heirs. The by-laws, or "*lex collegi,*" are arranged in separate sections, and provide minutely for the rate of contribution, the kind of funeral to be furnished, and the conditions upon which it was to be obtained.

[2] Dig. l. 6, *de Jure Immunitatis,* 5, 12. Cf., however, Waltzing, *Étude Historique sur les Corporations Professionelles chez les Romains,* i. 118, 147.

[3] This is the phrase used in the Lanuvium inscription. That inscription is given at length in Giraud's *Novum Enchiridion Juris Romani,* 662, and at the end of Mommsen's *de Collegiis et Sodaliciis Romanorum.*

[4] See *Corpus Inscriptionum Latinarum,* x. 1642, 5198; Azuni's Maritime Law of Europe, i., chap. 4, *ad fin.*

phoniacorum is described in an inscription on an ancient columbarium found near Rome, as permitted to unite as such "*e lege Julia, ex auctoritate Augusti, ludorum causa.*"[1] The privilege of incorporation, however, so far as trades associations were concerned, was much extended at a later period, particularly under Alexander Severus in the third century.[2]

Private corporations in some form were found wherever there was a Roman city. Whatever their object might be, the members met together much more often than is common in similar organizations of the present day. The officers apparently did not engross the management of affairs like the modern board of directors.

The general meetings were often of a convivial character, even in the case of a burial club. In the corporations of fellow-craftsmen there was a strong sentiment of sodality. It was a common thing in the epitaph on a tradesman's tombstone to speak of him as "*pius in suos, pius in collegium.*"[3] An endowment was often held for the perpetual support of an annual banquet in honor of the founder.[4] In one instance five such feasts were provided for every year.[5] A common burial lot was often owned, — a practice still familiar in Europe.[6] So the gratitude of a corporation to some one who had been its friend or patron was often shown by its assuming the per-

---

[1] Giraud's *Enchiridion*, 662.
[2] Dictionnaire des Antiquités, *Collegium*, 1293.
[3] Duruy's Hist. of Rome, v. 398.
[4] *Corpus Inscriptionum Latinarum*, xii. 4393.
[5] *Ibid.* x. 444.   [6] *Ibid.* x. 5386.

petual care of his monument. A sarcophagus and family tomb in Ephesus was left by Apollonius, a comptroller of the provincial revenues, in charge of five designated colleges, one of which, at least, was composed of the freedmen and slaves of the emperor; and he expressly declared that it should not go to his heirs as part of his estate.[1]

The Roman corporation, under the empire, as it is painted to us in lapidary inscriptions, seems ordinarily to have been composed of men in quite moderate circumstances. The government looked upon them with distrust, on account of their political connections, and was slow to charter any for objects which did not fall within the terms of the general statute. Trajan was so far under the influence of this feeling that he refused to incorporate a fire company in Nicomedia, though it was especially requested by Pliny. Most of the corporations of which mention is made at this period have largely the character of fraternal associations of those pursuing the same calling, for mutual aid and assistance. The objects to be promoted are rather the good of the members individually than any common enterprise.

There existed the form of the modern corporation, but it was put to but few of the uses of which it was capable. The capital stock was never represented by certificates for transferable shares of the same par value. The paucity of such organizations for the prosecution of large business undertakings, and the slight importance, in respect to rights of prop-

[1] *Corpus Inscriptionum Latinarum*, iii. 6077.

erty, of those of the ordinary type, is well evidenced by the fact that corporation law, which is so large a head of modern jurisprudence, is not discussed, or so much as mentioned, in the Institutes of Justinian, the work prepared expressly for use as the first textbook to be put in the hands of the Roman law student.

The Digest gives it some attention, but slight as compared with that which it receives in any modern code. In its treatment of the subject, it classes with corporations partnerships of the nature of the English joint stock company, that is, those composed of a considerable number of persons, under an agreement that the death of any of them should not dissolve the organization, but his estate should succeed to his position in it. Under such a form (*societas publica*) the farmers of the revenue customarily associated.[1] They had a number of these societies conducting operations in the various provinces. Each had a *corpus* or was, in law, an artificial person, but all were united in a kind of "trust," with its headquarters at Rome, under the general management of a single man (*magister societatis*[2]).

This brief review of the development of private corporations among the people whose invention they were shows a fluctuating policy on the part of the government.[3]

[1] Dig. iii. 4, 1; Dig. xvii. 2, *pro Socio*, 5, 59.
[2] Heineccius' *Antiquitatum Romanorum Syntagma*, iii. 23-27, § 14.
[3] In the Theodosian Code, there are constitutions showing that the ancient guild corporations were decaying, and the emperors disposed

Springing originally from the free association of men engaged in the same pursuits; passing into the definite form of a distinct personality, with a certain resemblance to the *familia*, and like that with a religious cult of its own to bind it in one; feeling the strength of union, and commanding its influence; now favored and now repressed by law,— these Roman corporations changed as Rome changed, and there is little in common between those of the republic and those of the Byzantine empire.

If ancient history had been written as modern history is coming to be, we should have a clearer conception of their effect on the social and economical life of their times. We could well spare whole books of Livy and Tacitus, devoted to petty wars or dull oratory, for some such crisp chapter as Green or Taine in their place might have given us, on the work of associated capital and labor in Roman trade and manufactures. As it is, much must be assumed, on the *a priori* method, and there cannot but be disagreement between scholars in many of their ultimate conclusions. Waltzing, the latest and most industrious author who has dealt with the subject, is disposed to minimize the collective operations of corporations under the early empire, but gives them a new importance in its later ages. In these they became, as he paints them, the gigantic slaves of the State. Functions that they had at first assumed freely, as a matter of profit and contract, became a grievous burden from which they could

to prop them up. Lib. xiv. 2, *de Privilegiis Corporatorum Urbis Romæ*; 4, *de Suariis, Pecuariis, et Susceptoribus Vini, ceterisque Corporatis.*

not escape. They paid their taxes, so to speak, by doing service.

The individual did this also, at Rome, as later under feudalism. There was little money in circulation, and little use for it. The rich seldom bought, because they or their houses were the great producers. Like the New England farmer of colonial days, they raised on their own estates, for the most part, whatever they consumed. The poor seldom bought, because the government fed them, and amused them too.

But who was to bring their bread to Rome? The great corporations early assumed the task, and were well paid for it. The *navicularii*, whose grain ships were employed in this business, were men of means, and soon became men of position. Government contracts were as profitable then as now.[1] There was also a special encouragement to those who engaged in this business. It was deemed such a public service that they were exempted from rendering any others. This, however, did not apply to shareholders in such a transportation company who took no active part in its affairs, and invested less than half their fortune in the enterprise.[2]

Gradually this immunity seems to have been turned into an instrument of oppression. Members of a corporation in any line of business, the maintenance of which was necessary for the public interests, were compelled to remain in it; and their

---

[1] Waltzing, *Étude Historique sur les Corporations Professionelles chez les Romains*, ii. 45, 50.

[2] Dig. l. 6, *de Jure Immunitatis*, 5, 3 . . . 6.

property, outside of their shares in its capital stock, was, in some instances, at least, subjected to an implied hypothecation for its debts.[1] They were thus held irrevocably to the service in which they had once engaged. Their children were enrolled with them as members, and upon their death, of course, remained such.[2]

The State insisted that the public wants should be supplied by these public bodies. They must now bring the grain and bake the bread, not as a matter of mere adventure and contract, but of statutory duty. The individual life of the members in industrial corporations became largely merged in the corporate life. If one of them failed in business, his "college" must discharge his debts. If one of them committed a misdemeanor, his college might be obliged to pay a fine.[3]

Only a despotic government could thus crush into one a mass of citizens and hold them together by the strong hand. Private corporations in such a position were really nothing but forms of municipal government.

But as we look at the course of Rome towards her purely municipal corporations, composed of those living on the same territory, we find it consistent and liberal. They were treated, indeed, with greater favor under the empire than under the republic. Nor was this without strong reason. It was by

---

[1] Code Theodos., 14, 3, *de Pistoribus*, etc. ; 13, 5, *de Naviculariis*.
[2] Waltzing, ii. 360.
[3] Code Theodos., 16, 4, *de His qui super Religione contendunt*, 5.

their aid that, first, Italy was united, and then the world brought under the rule of Rome.

It was the settled policy of the republic to institute throughout its dominions the largest possible number of small, self-governing municipalities. This tended directly to dissolve any sentiment of attachment among their inhabitants to the pre-existing Italian confederacies. It made each city a centre, and the only centre to which its people could look, except to Rome itself. It set up local rivalries where there had been local union. Nothing could have tended more to bring Italy together. The expedient, as Mommsen says, was not generous, but it was effectual. And whether generous or not, it was popular. It sent men back to the beginnings of social order — to the home rule of the village community.

The emperors were wise enough to see that this same plan of maintaining and multiplying minor civic communities was the best way to reconcile the people to absolute power at the capital. The *municipium* and, to a large degree, the *colonia*, maintained the forms of republicanism at the important centres of population, and the inhabitants, choosing their own local magistracy, and so regulating for themselves the greater part of their political concerns, hardly felt the pressure of imperial power. Britain was divided into thirty-three townships or communes, each with considerable powers of home rule. Of Roman provincial cities there are some, such as Cologne, Rheims, and Lyons,[1] which have

---

[1] Lyons, in Roman days, was the seat of a number of private corporations. An old inscription in the collections of Gruter speaks of

survived in almost unbroken political continuity to the present day as witnesses to the sound principles of representative government upon which they were originally constituted.[1]

The dark ages found Europe under the influence of these political ideas; but what were now the dominant races, as they swept down from the North, looked upon each walled city only as another enemy to conquer and destroy. The ancient Germans con-

"*omnia corpora Lugduni licite coeuntia.*" The character of the modern city as a centre of socialism may find some explanation in this fact.

[1] The Roman *municipium* was almost autonomous. The ordinary *colonia* was subject to the laws of the mother country, which it was said to resemble in miniature. Aulus Gellius, in his *Noctes Atticæ*, lib. xvi. cap. xiii., explains this very clearly "*Municipes ergo sunt cives Romani ex municipiis, legibus suis et suo jure utentes, muneris tantum cum populo Romano honorarii participes, a quo munere capessendo appellati videntur, nullis aliis necessitatibus, neque ulla populi Romani lege adstricti. . . . Sed Coloniarum alia necessitudo est: non enim veniunt extrinsecus in civitatem, nec suis radicibus nituntur; sed ex civitate quasi propagatæ sunt; et jura institutaque omnia populi Romani, non sui arbitrii habent.*"

The *forum, conciliabulum, castrum*, and *castellum*, have sometimes been regarded as special forms of Roman municipal organization. The first two words, however, seem to be simply terms descriptive of the historical origin of towns which grew up around places once used as a forum or a place for consultation and debate. The magistrate who laid out a new road, e. g. the Appian way, often established upon it, also under his name, a market place and seat of justice, e. g. *Appii Forum*, and houses might afterwards cluster about it enough to constitute a village and perhaps to gain a new name. Municipal privileges might then be granted, and the inhabitants invested with Roman citizenship. See Sigonius *de antiquo jure Italiæ*, lib. ii. cap. xv.; lib. iii. cap. iii. On the other hand, *castrum* and *castellum*, like *oppidum* and *vicus*, denoted places having no peculiar municipal privileges, but viewed simply as aggregations of inhabited houses. *Ibid.* lib. ii. cap. i.

sidered it a badge of servitude to live in one. In their own villages the houses were scattered along at a considerable distance from each other. The feudal baron to whom a subjugated city was assigned built his castle out of the ruins of its defences, and laid down the law for the few inhabitants who might be suffered to remain there, at his will. With few exceptions, municipal privileges were for some centuries substantially destroyed, throughout all Europe. In the Codes of the barbarians we find no mention of them. The præfect, or mayor, is replaced by the feudal lord, the *comes civitatis*, or his recorder (*judex*),[1] and less attention is paid to the city than to the parish.

It is not till the beginning of the eleventh century that the benefits of incorporation seem to have been confirmed or extended to any organizations except those belonging to the Church.[2] Its abbeys and monasteries were supplemented by religious fraternities, some of which came finally to be anything but religious, and threw new discredit on the theory of corporate association for other than governmental objects. Such was that of the Knights Templar, founded by a few French crusaders at Jerusalem, by the name of the Poor Soldiers of the Temple of Solomon, and not taking the form of a corporation until long afterwards.

Brotherhoods for mutual protection and aid were

[1] Lex Wisigothorum, lib. ii. 31; Rotharis Leges, ccxlviii.
[2] The first city charter, that to Leon in Spain, was granted in 1020. Prescott's History of Ferdinand and Isabella, i., xlv.

common enough throughout the middle ages, but they had no special legal form or personality. By the side of these frith-guilds there grew up also the merchant guilds in the larger towns, and to them as well as to the craft guilds that sprang up among the wage-earners, charters were often granted. Some of these were probably constituted by a revival or continuation of a similar corporation, existing in the same place under the Roman laws.

Henry III. of France went farther, and, by general edicts in 1582 and 1587, following the policy of Alexander Severus, legalized and directed the association in every city, of those engaged in each of the leading arts or trades in a separate body, to which he gave a large regulative authority, both as to workmen and merchants. This system stood for two hundred years, but grew steadily more and more unpopular. In Paris it had thrown the entire trade of the city in the eighteenth century into the hands of six great corporations and forty-four lesser ones (*communautés*).

Wherever, in fact, throughout Europe, trades were incorporated, as the very object of incorporation was to give a special privilege, and to some extent rights of monopoly, and as it often deprived the ordinary courts of jurisdiction over the members of the new body,[1] neither the common people nor the higher orders viewed them with favor. Their essence was the promotion of self-interest by a policy of exclusion. Their practical effect was to raise up in each city an *imperium in imperio*. They filled its offices,

[1] The Case of Sutton's Hospital, 10 Coke's Reports, 30.

and obtained its sanction to whatever they thought most for their own benefit.[1] Either alone or in connection with the magistrates, they often succeeded in excluding the citizens at large from the right of suffrage.[2] The livery companies of London are a familiar example of this. It was so in Scotland until the era of the Reform Bill. The guild-hall, as to-day, in London, was the city-hall. Tending to oligarchy, unpopular in principle, bottomed on class distinction, they began to fade away as civil liberty entered upon its conquest of Europe. Their last vestiges were swept away in France by the French Revolution, and in England few have survived the Reform Bill and the Municipal Corporations Acts by which its principles were finally worked out into a uniform system.[3]

As the guilds declined, the great foreign trading companies arose.

Any such form of organization had been repressed by the development of the mediæval trade-city. Each of these, in truth, was one vast trading company. It had been an association of traders before it gained its municipal privileges, and it had procured these largely in order to protect its trade. The German conception of a municipal corporation still was that it only represented the joint rights and liabilities of all its inhabitants. The Roman notion of a collective body, with rights and liabili-

[1] Merlin's *Répertoire de Jurisprudence*, vi. 446 *et seq.*
[2] Motley's "Rise of the Dutch Republic," i. 36.
[3] An interesting example of the survival of their political power, though in a greatly reduced form, in Germany is furnished in the constitution of the legislature of the free city of Hamburg.

ties of its own, had not yet been adopted, or, indeed, generally understood.[1] It is, indeed, only of late years that Germany can be said to have fully and practically incorporated it into her jurisprudence. "To-day," wrote Mommsen, as late as 1843, "public corporations need most urgently the rights of a person, and loudly demand them; but our timid caution does not know how to interpret royal charters as common utility requires."[2]

The leagues by which neighboring cities in the middle ages bound themselves to each other from time to time, of which that of the Hanse towns was the most conspicuous, were not simply to strengthen their political power. They were in a certain sense great commercial partnerships. Their factories in foreign ports were like the department store of our own day. By the variety of their stock and its constant renewals they were able to command the market. By their political strength they could obtain concessions from the local sovereign which enabled them to dictate prices to his own subjects. The Hanseatic league, under the reigns of the Henrys, got possession of the best part of the carrying trade of England, and by their factory at Novgorod[3] monopolized the commerce of northern Europe.

[1] Sohm's "Institutes of Roman Law," § 20.
[2] Treatise *de Collegiis*, etc., 119.
[3] Under the fostering care of the league, Novgorod grew from a mean and inconsiderable town (into which it has since relapsed) to be a city of three or four hundred thousand people, holding the trade of Russia so firmly in its grip that it became a proverbial expression: *Quis contra deos et magnam Novogordiam?*

The decay of feudalism brought new strength to every throne, because it broadened its foundations. These were no longer an artificial framework of military construction, but reached down to solid ground, that is, the loyal consent of the common people. Cities became less necessary as a balance against the power of the nobles and the Church, and their privileges began to shrink and lessen. It became the aim of kings to make commerce a matter of national instead of municipal direction.

Pure business corporations, for foreign trade and adventure, were now first chartered. To the people at large they were generally odious, for they tended to repress business activity by the prohibition of competition.

They were of two descriptions, — the "regulated company" and the joint-stock company.

In those of the former kind, the original incorporators were required to admit associates who might desire to trade within the territory embraced in the charter, on payment of a certain fee. The amount of this was generally left to be fixed by the company: sometimes it was regulated by the State. Each member, whether one of the original set or a new-comer, traded separately for himself, on his own capital, and at his own risk. What he got by membership was the right to participate in the commerce within the jurisdiction of the company, and, in a general way, to enjoy its protection. There was no common capital or stock in trade, except the small amount derived from entrance fees.

The joint-stock company, on the other hand,

always had a common stock, and its trading was done on joint account under one management.¹

The first of the great trading companies was incorporated in Burgundy by the Duke of Brabant, in 1248, by the name of the Brotherhood of St. Thomas Becket of Canterbury. Its main trade was with England, and in the next century it transferred its seat to that kingdom, receiving a confirmation of its privileges from Edward III., and later from Henry VII., who changed its name to that of the Merchant Adventurers in London.² It was a "regulated company," and soon adopted a by-law forbidding any one to trade in the main ports in the Netherlands who had not first paid it an entrance fee of over sixty pounds. This charge was deemed oppressive, and the by-law was abrogated by a special Act of Parliament.³ A few years later a general law was enacted that no corporation should pass any by-law, without the consent of three of the great officers of State.⁴

By the close of the reign of Elizabeth corporate monopolies had swept five-sixths of the foreign trade of England into the port of London, and placed it there in the hands of two hundred men, shareholders in this or that company of merchants.⁵

As new markets were opened by discovery and colonization, new charters closed them against all

[1] Adam Smith's " Wealth of Nations," iii. book v., chap. 1. p. 108.
[2] Molloy, *de Jure Maritimo*, 453. Later it was known as the Hamburgh Company.
[3] 12 Henry VII., chap. 6.
[4] 19 Henry VII., chap. 7.
[5] Hume's Hist. of England, iii. 284.

but the favored few. The Russian Company, the Eastland Company, the African Company, the Levant Company,[1] and the East India Company were chartered under Queen Elizabeth, and the Hudson's Bay Company followed in 1670.[2]

All the patents under which the English colonies in America were settled, beginning with that to Sir Walter Raleigh in 1584, with which the history of North Carolina opens, partook largely of the same character. That of Virginia, granted in 1606, was nothing else, and particularly provides that a Council in England shall have the "superior Management and Direction" of both the proposed colonies, by a title paramount to that of the local council which each might set up within its own territory.[3] In other words, what the charter termed First Virginia, or the southern portion of the grant, and Second Virginia or the northern portion, were to be under the ultimate control of a board of directors sitting in London or Bristol.

The original Massachusetts patent was probably granted with no thought on the part of the Crown officers that the patentees would meet and hold their courts of election and management anywhere but on the soil of England. It was a bold stretch of authority on the part of Winthrop to transfer their

---

[1] This company acquired extensive interests in Turkey, to which country it accredited consuls of its own choosing. It surrendered its charter in 1825. Ann. Register for 1825; Hist. 113.

[2] The Russian Company, the Eastland Company, and the Turkey Company were all "regulated" companies. Smith's "Wealth of Nations," iii. 109.

[3] Poore's "Charters and Constitutions," ii. 1890.

seat of government to Massachusetts Bay, and no one appreciated this more fully than he. So far as concerns the Plymouth Colony, the commercial character of the enterprise is even more marked. Its promoters, so far as any pecuniary backing was concerned, were some seventy persons associated in a partnership styled the "Merchant Adventurers," with a capital of seven thousand pounds, acting first under a grant from the Virginia Company, and then under one from the patentees named in the charter of 1620 for Second Virginia, now, with its limits pushed two or three degrees further north, called New England.[1]

The grants which followed to the Duke of York and William Penn, and the Carolina charters, were still more proprietary in their nature.

Other European nations at this time reached out for the control of new markets by similar means. Henry Hudson, sailing in the service of the Dutch East India Company,[2] whose charter preceded that of the English East India Company by a few years, laid the foundations of the New Netherlands, and the port of New Amsterdam (now New York) was soon in the hands of another corporation, created to promote American trade, the "West India Company of the United Netherlands." In Sweden a company was incorporated for similar purposes in 1624, which

[1] Palfrey's "Hist. of New England," i. 187, 216, 221; Poore's "Charters and Constitutions," i. 992.

[2] This had a capital of $3,000,000, and the directors were chosen on a plan which gave the States-General, and also each of the main trading cities of the Netherlands a voice in the selection, Molloy, *de Jure Maritimo*, 454.

resulted finally in the first settlements on the Delaware. Two years later Richelieu, under Louis XIII., chartered the Company of New France, and gave it title to most of what is now the Dominion of Canada. Under the financial administration of Colbert were incorporated in 1664, the Company of the West Indies, that of the Senegal, and that of the East Indies, and in 1669 the Company of the North.[1] In 1695 the Scotch Parliament gave a perpetual charter to the Company of Scotland, trading to Africa and the Indies.

How the English companies were regarded at the time, and what their influence was in the development of the English law of corporations, may best be seen by quoting some observations made by Defoe, in his Essay on Projects, published in 1697.

"A while before this," he says, after describing the introduction of the London penny-post, "several people, under the patronage of some great persons, had engaged in planting of foreign colonies, as William Penn, the Lord Shaftesbury, Dr. Cox, and others, in Pennsylvania, Carolina, East and West Jersey, and the like places, which I do not call projects, because it was only prosecuting what had been formerly begun. But here begins the forming of public joint-stocks which, together with the East India, African, and Hudson Bay Companies, before established, begot a new trade, which we call by a new name, stock-jobbing, which was at first only the simple occasional transferring of interest and

[1] Voltaire's *Siècles de Louis XIV et de Louis XV*, iii. ch. 29.

shares from one to another as persons alienated their estates; but by the industry of the Exchange brokers, who got the business into their hands, it became a trade, and one, perhaps, managed with the greatest intrigue, artifice, and trick that ever anything that appeared with a face of honesty could be handled with; for while the brokers held the box, they made the whole Exchange the gamesters, and raised and lowered the prices of stocks as they pleased, and always had both buyers and sellers who stood ready innocently to commit their money to the mercy of their mercenary tongues. This upstart of a trade having tasted the sweetness of success which generally attends a novel proposal, introduces the illegitimate wandering object I speak of as a proper engine to find work for the brokers. Thus stockjobbing nursed projecting, and projecting in return has very diligently pimped for its foster-parent, till both are arrived to be public grievances, and indeed are now almost grown scandalous."[1]

The exclusive privileges held under the proprietary charters for the American colonies occasioned much dissatisfaction on the part of English merchants, who wished to trade with them. Petitions for their revocation, on payment of a proper compensation, were twice presented to Parliament, early in the eighteenth century, and made the subject of serious consideration. They were rejected, the last in 1715, but many years later some of these rights were extinguished by purchase, and the heirs of

[1] "The Earlier Life and Works of Daniel Defoe," Carisbrooke Library, iii. 42.

William Penn received on this account a perpetual pension from the British government.[1]

Monopolistic charters cannot be very numerous. The subjects of monopoly are soon exhausted. The trading charters, by the close of the seventeenth century, overlapped each other on every coast. As many banks were in existence at the great commercial centres as it was thought Europe could sustain, and each — the Bank of Venice, which had already flourished for five hundred years, and accumulated a capital of $16,000,000, that of St. George at Genoa, that of Hamburg, the Bank of England, the Bank of Scotland, the Austrian Bank at Vienna — had certain exclusive privileges from the State.[2] Capital was rapidly accumulating throughout Europe, and it became a subject of complaint that the natural channels of investment had been closed against its free circulation. Nowhere was this felt more than in England. The demand for corporate franchises was always in excess of the supply. A continually increasing number had money to invest, who, without desiring themselves to embark actively in business enterprises, wished to put it to productive use, and yet where, at any time, they could hope to turn it back into cash without much delay. The result was the formation of many voluntary associations of the nature of partnerships, between a considerable num-

[1] Rogers' "Economic Interpretation of History," 329.
[2] The Bank of Amsterdam was a mere form of municipal organization. The city was responsible for its deposits, and required all large payments to be made over its counters. It had no private capital or stockholders. 1 Douglass' "Summary, &c., of the Settlements in America," 106, *note.*

ber of individuals, with some distinguishing company name, such, for instance, as the "Amicable," or, as it was afterwards called, the "Hand in Hand" Insurance company, which finally obtained a charter in 1706.[1] Some of these were successful: many were not, and the dealings in their shares brought to a climax the condition of things so graphically described by Defoe in the passage above quoted. A strong push was made in Parliament for the establishment of a land bank in 1696, which should issue its notes in exchange for mortgages of real estate, but the ministry defeated the project by devising the scheme of issuing Exchequer bills, bearing a low rate of interest, and payable out of future revenue.

Defoe now proposed a remedy for the stagnation of capital by the establishment of fifteen local banks in the nature of "factories" or commission-houses, each of which should stand ready to make advances on staple or manufactured goods, and act as a warehouseman and factor for their sale. But how was their incorporation to be effected?

"Every principal town in England," he replies, "is a corporation upon which the fund may be settled, which will sufficiently answer the difficult and chargeable work of suing for a corporation by patent or Act of Parliament.

"A general subscription of stock being made, and by deeds of settlement placed in the mayor and

[1] Fire insurance was generally effected on the mutual plan; marine insurance by large syndicates of capitalists. The city water supply was furnished by companies formed under royal patents, the earliest of which dates from the sixteenth century. Ashton's "Social Life in the Reign of Queen Anne," 50, 53, 86.

aldermen of the city or corporation for the time being, in trust, to be declared by deeds of uses, some of the directors being always made members of the said corporation and joined in the trust, the bank hereby becomes the public stock of the town, something like what they call the rents of the town-house in France, and is managed in the name of the said corporation, to whom the directors are accountable, and they back again to the general court. For example: Suppose the gentlemen or tradesmen of the county of Norfolk, by a subscription of cash, design to establish a bank. The subscriptions being made, the stock is paid into the chamber of the city of Norwich, and managed by a court of directors, as all banks are, and chosen out of the subscribers, the mayor only of the city to be always one; to be managed in the name of the corporation of the city of Norwich, but for the uses in a deed of trust to be made by the subscribers and mayor and aldermen at large mentioned. I make no question but a bank thus settled would have as firm a foundation as any bank need to have, and every way answer the ends of a corporation."[1]

Here we have probably the first suggestion in England of anything of the nature of a general incorporation law for business purposes. One Act of Parliament, if Defoe's suggestion had been adopted, would have authorized the formation of fifteen different banks, in as many places, by such persons as might choose to subscribe the necessary capital.

[1] "The Earlier Life and Works of Daniel Defoe," Carisbrooke Library, iii. 55.

The State would favor no one, and name no one. It would simply allow money to talk.

The essential elements which go to make up a moneyed corporation are: a lawful object, a competent fund devoted to that object, suitable persons to direct its application, and an artificial personality through which they act.

A general incorporation law can secure all these with some degree of certainty, unless an exception is to be made with respect to the selection of suitable managers. Here it must rely on self-interest, but this rarely fails to answer the call. Those who contribute the capital are always anxious to protect it by placing it in the hands of competent directors, if their real object is to make money by the successful prosecution of the corporate business. It is only when their motive is to give the shares a fictitious value, and find their profit in selling out their holdings in the stock market, that their choice is apt to fall on men of a different class, rogues, or the dupes of rogues.

England was the first country, after the fall of the Roman republic, to venture on the experiment of authorizing the formation, by any who chose, of moneyed corporations; but she limited this to corporations of a single class. The dissolution of the monasteries and general confiscation of the Church lands under Henry VIII. had taken away from the poor the means on which they had relied for no small part of their shelter and support. Some of them became common beggars, and others common thieves. Acts of Parliament were soon passed to encourage the foundation of new charities of the nature of almshouses and workhouses; but they proved ineffectual. Men would not give largely for such purposes unless they were assured that whatever they established would remain in perpetuity. In 1597,[1] therefore, another statute was enacted, reciting the fact that the want of any grant of powers of incorporation had prevented the former legislation from having its anticipated effect, and providing that during the ensuing twenty years, any one, by a deed enrolled in the Court of Chancery, might found "one or more hospitals, *maisons de Dieu*, abiding-places, or houses of correction," and set over them such "head and members" as he might think proper, and that every such institution should be incorporated, and, being named by the founder, "should be a body politic and corporate, and should by that name of incorporation have full power, authority, and lawful capacity and ability to purchase, take, hold, receive, enjoy, and have, to them and to their successors forever, as well goods and chattels, as manors, lands, tenements, and hereditaments, being freehold, of any person or persons whatsoever, so that the same should not exceed the yearly value of £200 above all charges and reprises." The founder was also empowered to adopt a common seal for the corporation, and it was to have full capacity to sue or be sued in any courts. The only condition imposed was that the endowment must include a conveyance of the absolute title to real estate "of

[1] 39 Eliz., chap. v.

FREEDOM OF INCORPORATION 175

the clear yearly value of ten pounds." In the next reign this statute was made perpetual.

The scheme which it embodied amply provided for every one of the essential elements of a moneyed corporation. The class of objects was particularly specified. A competent fund was secured by the provision as to the *minimum* amount of the foundation. The appointment of suitable persons to apply it to the proper purposes was rendered reasonably certain by confiding it to the founder. An artificial person of the fullest description was created.

It seems strange that, with this simple and practical plan of corporate organization under a general law before them, the English people were content to go on from the sixteenth to the nineteenth century without giving it a more extensive application. But the English people grew gradually into power. English kings found in their prerogative of granting charters of incorporation a cheap and ready way of rewarding favorites, or adding to their own revenues. It was not until the accession of William and Mary, and the Resolution of the House of Commons, in 1693, that "it is the right of Englishmen to trade in the East Indies or any part of the world, unless prohibited by Act of Parliament," that such charters lost their main value. The Hudson's Bay Company had obtained the last great trading monopoly from Charles II., and soon grew to be almost as immense a power in northern America as was the East India Company in southern Asia. Such vast concerns, continually becoming more and more imperial in their character by the advances of their trading-posts to new frontiers, as well as by engaging in enterprises outside of their chartered purposes, and building up capitals without limit on watered stock,[1] brought the very name of corporation into disrepute. The unfortunate issue of most of the voluntary associations formed for business purposes, at the close of the seventeenth and beginning of the eighteenth century, was a further discouragement to any attempts to form permanent combinations of capitalists. Of the chartered companies also, several had proved unsuccessful. The African Company, chartered in 1588, passed through three successive reorganizations in the seventeenth century, under as many charters, each on the joint-stock plan. On the last occasion, the concern having failed with debts outstanding of £200,000, a majority of the stockholders organized a new African Company, under another charter from the crown, buying up the assets of the old one at their value, and using the money thus realized to pay a forty-per-cent dividend to the creditors. The result was to leave the African trade in the hands of the same persons who had previously

[1] The Hudson's Bay Company began business with a paid-in capital of £10,500. By a book-keeping entry this was trebled in 1690, and in 1720 it was trebled again, upon the payment of only ten per cent. During the Parliamentary investigation which terminated in the purchase by the government, in 1867, of its exclusive privileges in Canada, it appeared that its assets were of the value of over a million and a quarter pounds sterling, its ordinary annual net profits being £110,000. Winsor's Hist. of America, viii. 60. It also, early in the eighteenth century, embarked in the business of life insurance and granting endowment policies to apprentices; but the courts pronounced it an illegal usurpation. Child v. Hudson's Bay Company, 2 Peere Williams' Reports, 207 (1723).

controlled it, to be conducted in the same corporate name, and to wipe out sixty per cent of their obligations.[1] They had little better success, however, under their new name, and in 1750 their franchise was repealed on account of utter bankruptcy, and a "regulated" company formed, by Act of Parliament, to succeed them, which was expressly prohibited from trading in its corporate capacity.[2]

The Scotch company, chartered in 1695, to trade to Africa and the Indies, accomplished nothing but the foundation of a short-lived colony at Darien, and the stock soon fell to ten per cent of its par value. The shares were largely held by persons of political influence. Their support was needed to carry through the union between England and Scotland in 1707, and it was secured by the insertion of a clause in the Articles of Union providing that all the shareholders should be repaid the full amount of their investment from the English treasury. The opponents of the union were not slow to call this transaction "the selling of the country."[3]

In 1711 the South Sea Company began its singular career, which, so far as any foreign commerce was concerned, ended in 1748.[4] Its shares were so artfully manipulated, that, when in 1720 the capital was increased for the purpose of funding the national debt, by issuing its stock in exchange for government annuities, the final subscriptions were made

[1] Curson *v.* African Company, 1 Vernon's Reports, 121.
[2] Smith's "Wealth of Nations," iii. 115, 122.
[3] 1 Douglass' "Summary, &c., of the Settlements in America," 45, *note.*
[4] Smith's "Wealth of Nations," iii. 128.

at a premium of nine hundred per cent, and shares thus taken at £1000, of the par value of £100, were almost immediately sold at £1200, in the London market.[1] A few weeks later the price had fallen to £135, and Parliament was busy in confiscating the estates of the directors and passing a bill to suppress the "infamous practice of stock-jobbing." As the doings of the company were brought to light, it appeared that an over issue of stock, to the amount of half a million pounds, had been made, to aid in securing the passage of the Act authorizing the last increase of capital, ten thousand pounds of which had gone to one of the king's mistresses. The public creditors who had exchanged their annuities running for ninety-nine years, for stock in the company to the amount at par of no more than what would have been their receipts from the government for eight years and three months, were forced to be content with a dividend of 33⅓ per cent, thus saving less than three years' income out of ninety-nine.[2]

A general feeling of distrust now took possession of the public mind as to all forms of stock investment. The "Bubble Act" of 1720 was designed to prevent the formation of any companies for speculative purposes, and to a large extent it was for many years successful. Gradually, however, as a new generation came on the stage, the spirit of stock gambling revived. It became a practice in London, both of the three incorporated insurance companies and of the individuals who engaged themselves as

[1] Swift's Works, Nichols' ed., xix. 253, *note*.
[2] Mahon's " History of England," i., chap. xi.

underwriters, to offer to grant policies on lives to persons having no interest in the life insured. When George II. went to Bavaria in 1743, to take command of his army at the battle of Dettingen, policies were issued on his life, at a premium of twenty-five per cent. A few years later, the same speculators were writing policies on the life of the Pretender, and similar wagers were laid by their successors on the Exchange or at Lloyd's, on the lives of other public characters, until Parliament interfered by the passage of the "Gambling Act" of 1774.[1]

As early as the thirteenth century, there arose in France a practice of forming limited partnerships, one or more of the members of which conducted the active business and were alone responsible for the debts, the others simply contributing a certain capital and risking nothing but that. Colbert extended it, and made it the subject of careful regulation by law, in 1673. These "*sociétés en commandite*" offered an attractive mode of investment, and came into wide use in other parts of the Continent,[2] though never introduced into English law. While without the stability of a corporation, they had most of its other advantages, and in addition were always managed by those whose liability to creditors gave them the deepest personal interest in the success of the enterprise.

John Law, while the South Sea Company was still

---

[1] Smith's "Wealth of Nations," iii. 122.
[2] Their form has never been essentially varied. *Code de Commerce*, Art. 23; Law of July 24, 1867.

in possession of the public confidence in England, carried the notion of supporting public finance upon private trading adventure across the Channel, and found a favorable reception at the French court. In 1718 a charter was granted, at his instance, to the Company of the West, and it was endowed with the whole valley of the 'Mississippi, on condition of offering its stock of a hundred million livres, at par, to· the holders of the government paper currency, which was then at a discount of over sixty per cent. In a few months it absorbed all the old trading companies formed under Colbert (into one of which the Company of New France had been merged), and assumed the name of the Company of the Indies. A royal bank, at Paris, with five branches in other cities, was also organized in 1718, and consolidated with Law's Company two years later. The premium on the Company's shares rose even higher than that upon those of the South Sea Company at London, but it soon flooded the country with a new style of paper currency no better than that which it had absorbed. In May, 1720, a royal decree scaled these notes down to half their face, and a financial panic followed which shook the very foundations of society and put an end to any extension of corporate undertakings in France for the rest of the century,[1] although the Company of the Indies itself weathered the storm, by the aid of the government, and its shares were selling at more than ten times their par value in 1747.[2]

[1] Voltaire's *Siècles de Louis XIV et Louis XV*, iii. chap. 2.
[2] Douglass' "Summary, &c.," 80, *note*.

There grew up, however, something very like the corporation in the shape of a voluntary association, styled the *société anonyme*, or *société par actions*. It differed from other forms of partnership in not bearing the name of any of the partners, but a company name, indicative of the business which it was to pursue, and in that the interests of each member were represented in *"actions"* or shares, which were transferable. The management of its affairs was in the hands of one or more common agents, who were personally responsible for all the debts of the concern, although the rest of the shareholders were only liable to lose what capital they had put in.[1]

For France, and indeed for any nation following the principles of the civil law, some such modification of the partnership system was the most natural mode of advance towards the establishment of the corporation.

The theory of partnership in England and America is that it is a form of agency. The firm is the agent of each member, with power to bind him individually to the performance of its obligations, and, reciprocally, each partner is the agent of the firm to contract obligations in its behalf within the limits of the partnership business. On the other hand, the Roman law and the modern civil law recognize no solidarity between ordinary partners which would render any of them liable for the acts or contracts of another, who had not had special authority to bind the rest.[2]

[1] Merlin, *Questions de Droit*, xiv. 323.
[2] See Pothier, *Traité du Contrat de Société*, §§ 96, 103, 104.

The *société anonyme* of French law was originally a partnership conducted in the name of one of the members, otherwise styled a *compte en participation*. The others were strictly secret partners. To creditors of the firm they came into no relation and under no liability. To the active partner they owed an obligation to make the contribution which they had agreed to make to the capital of the concern, and, furthermore, if he were held personally liable to creditors to an amount which the capital would not enable him to satisfy, then to contribute to indemnify him for what he might pay in excess of the capital, so that each partner would sustain an equal loss.[1]

As thus used, the term was applied only to partnerships between a few persons not involving any large enterprise; those embracing more persons and formed for large undertakings being styled "*compagnies.*"[2] Later, by a gradual change of meaning, it came to be used only for such companies, with a share capital, and name descriptive of their object; and this is its signification in the Code of Commerce, framed by Napoleon in 1807.[3]

As there described (Art. 29 *et seq.*), it is identical with the private business corporation, except that it cannot be organized in perpetuity. A reasonable term of duration must be fixed in the articles of association.

By the code, as originally adopted, no such asso-

---

[1] Pothier, *Traité du Contrat de Société*, §§ 60–63.
[2] Pardessus, *Cours du Droit Commercial*, iv. 136.
[3] Rogron's *Code de Commerce Expliqué*, 15.

ciation could thereafter be formed without the consent of the government. That could only be had upon a petition from the promoters of the enterprise, stating all the particulars regarding it, and a report from the departmental prefect on their moral character and pecuniary responsibility. This was passed upon by the executive authority of the government as an administrative measure. Upon the approval and registration of the articles of association, the new company became an artificial person. The managing officers were not to be responsible for its debts.[1]

These provisions have been substantially retained ever since[2] in the statutes of France, except that, in 1867, the requirement of the authorization of the government before the formation of such an organization was repealed; and in place of this, regulations prescribed as to the *minimum* number of original incorporators, the accumulation of a reserve fund, shareholders' meetings, and other matters incidental to the proper constitution and management of such a body. This places France under what is equivalent to a general incorporation law, applicable to all kinds of business, save a few specially excepted.[3]

[1] Code of Commerce, Arts. 29, 32, 34; Mourlon's *Répétitions Écrites sur le Code Civil*, iii. § 859; Merlin's *Répertoire de Jurisprudence*, xxi. 277.

[2] By the law of May 23, 1863, authority was given to form a partnership of a similar character, without any petition for a license, by the name of *société à responsabilité limitée*. This was repealed in 1867.

[3] Law of July 24, 1867. Proprietors of land may also form quasi-corporations, for the construction of works of common benefit. Law of June 21, 1865.

Turning now to the United States, we find that in most of the American Colonies charters for private corporations were occasionally, and for public corporations often, granted by the Governor. Such were those of the city of New York, from the Dutch Governor, in 1657,[1] and the English Governor, in 1686 and 1730.

He was considered to speak for the crown or, as the case might be, for the proprietaries. Occasionally the grant came directly from the superior authority.[2] In Maryland, the city of Annapolis was chartered by Queen Anne in 1708, but in 1667 St. Mary's City was incorporated by a formal document running in the name of "Caecilius, absolute lord and proprietary of the provinces of Maryland and Avalon, Lord Baron of Baltimore," &c.[3] Several of our colleges — Princeton, the University of Pennsylvania, and Rutgers — had charters from the Governor. Harvard, Yale, and Brown were incorporated by the colonial legislatures, not without grave hesitation as to their powers in this respect.[4]

[1] A similar grant from Governor Kieft in 1644 to the settlers of Hempstead was upheld as a sufficient charter of incorporation by Chancellor Kent in the case of Denton v. Jackson, 2 Johnson's Chancery Reports, 320.

[2] Wilson's Works, ii. 561, Andrews' edition.

[3] 3 Bland's Chancery Reports, 416, note.

[4] The Massachusetts charter was adjudged, in 1684, by the High Court of Chancery in England to have been forfeited by several acts of usurpation, among which was this incorporation of Harvard College. In view of that decision, and at the suggestion of Judge Sewall, of Massachusetts, when Yale College sought a charter from Connecticut in 1701, the bill prepared was purposely shorn, as far as possible, of any expressions indicating that it was what it was meant to be. Papers of the New Haven Colony Historical Society, iii. 413.

The founders of William and Mary, Columbia, and Dartmouth, not caring to venture on so doubtful a title, secured their charters from the crown. Municipal quasi-corporations were freely created by the colonial assemblies from the first, and in 1639 Massachusetts also ventured to incorporate an artillery company, which still exists. Religious societies for the support of public worship were also often constituted corporations by special statutes.[1] Connecticut went much further in 1732, by granting a perpetual charter to a society for promoting and carrying on trade and commerce with any of "his Majesties Dominions, and for encouraging the Fishery, &c., as well for the common good as their own private interest."[2] The happy possessors of so generous a franchise, which the "&c." seemed to make capable of indefinite expansion, forthwith set up business as a land-bank. The subscribers to its stock paid for it in mortgages, on the credit of which the "New London Society United for Trade and Commerce, in Connecticut," as it styled itself, issued bills of credit, payable to bearer, in which it was recited that they "Shall be in Value Equal to Silver att Sixteen Shillings per Ounce, or to Bills of Publick Credit of this or the Neighboring Governments, and shall be accordingly accepted by the Treasurer of said Society, and in all Payments in said Society from time to time." Currency of this sort was set afloat in a few months, to the amount of several thousand pounds, and of course speedily gravitated

---

[1] See Revised Statutes of New York, iii. 298, sec. 12.
[2] Colonial Records of Connecticut, vii. 390.

below par, and, by Gresham's law, began to drive the bills of the Colony itself out of circulation. The charter was granted in May, and in the following February a special session of the Assembly was called to remedy the usurpation. It was promptly resolved that stock paid for by mortgages was not paid for at all; that the charter had been forfeited; and that it ought to be and was repealed.[1] Application having been made at the next session for a revival of the charter, with due limitations, the question of the power of incorporation which might belong to the Colony was brought up and argued at length by counsel, with the following result: —

"On consideration thereof, the following questions were put, and resolved as follows, (viz:)

"1st. Whether it be within the authority of this government, to make a company or society of merchants?

"*Resolved*, That although a corporation may make a fraternity for the management of trades, arts, mysteries, endowed with authority to regulate themselves in the management thereof: yet, (inasmuch as all companies of merchants are made at home by letters patents from the King, and we know not of one single instance of any government in the plantations doing such a thing,) that it is, at least, very doubtful, whether we have authority to make such a society; and hazardous, therefore, for this government to presume upon it.

"2ly. Whether it be for the peace and health of this government, to create such a society?

"*Resolved*, That such a society of merchants, whose undertakings are vastly beyond their own compass, and

[1] Colonial Records of Connecticut, vii. 421.

FREEDOM OF INCORPORATION 187

must depend on the government for their supplies of money, and must therefore depend on their influence on the government to obtain it, it is not for the peace and health of the government."[1]

Provision was then made for forcing the subscribers to the stock of the defunct company to contribute so much as might be necessary to redeem its bills, and they were allowed to substitute mortgages to the Colony for those given to the company, receiving in return Colony bills, with which to retire the company bills.[2]

In Massachusetts and New Hampshire similar companies were organized, at about the same time, by voluntary association, to put out paper money; and in 1739 two more were formed in Massachusetts for the same purpose, one among the merchants and tradesmen, and another among the farmers and mechanics, of whom eight hundred were enrolled among its members.[3] Governor Belcher opposed both schemes, and the result was an Act of Parliament, extending the "Bubble Act" of 1720 to the Colonies.[4] This prohibited, under heavy penalties, the association of more than six persons, with a joint stock, who had not been incorporated by law, and put an end, during the remainder of the colonial period, to all enterprises of the character described.[5] All subsequent organizations here on

[1] Colonial Records of Connecticut, vii. 449.
[2] *Ibid.* 450.
[3] Sumner's "History of American Currency," 28.
[4] Hildreth's "History of the United States," ii. 380.
[5] The Act was repealed in 1825.

a joint-stock plan sought a charter from Parliament or the Crown.[1]

During the course of the Revolution, in 1781, a government bank was chartered by the Congress of the Confederation. It was styled the Bank of North America, and its authorized capital put at $10,000,000, though but a small part of this sum was in fact subscribed. The right of Congress to do this was, to say the least, doubtful, and it was soon glad to accept a charter from Pennsylvania.

In the Convention that framed the present Constitution of the United States it was proposed to include in the enumeration of the subjects of legislative power, that of forming corporations. Madison and Pinckney both introduced resolutions to this effect,[2] but they were smothered in committee. Madison afterwards sought to secure such a provision at least for the formation of companies to construct roads and canals connecting different States, but his motion was defeated by a vote of eight States to three. Rufus King, in opposing any general grant of a power of incorporation, said that the States would be prejudiced and divided into parties by it, and that the public generally would be apprehensive of mercantile monopolies.[3] The Bank

[1] Such was the Ohio Company, incorporated in 1749. When the Susquehanna Company, of Connecticut, in 1753, proposed making an application for a charter, they obtained a recommendation from the Colonial Assembly. Colonial Records of Connecticut, x. 378. In Maryland, no private charter was ever granted prior to the Revolution. McKim *v.* Odom, 3 Bland's Chancery Reports, 418.
[2] Madison's "Journal of Debates," 549 (Scott's ed.).
[3] *Ibid.* 726.

of the United States, which the first Congress chartered for twenty years, under the lead of Hamilton, on the ground that other provisions of the Constitution implied that right, and the financial necessities of the country required its exercise, did not fail to justify Mr. King's anticipations. Its recharter afterwards became one of the leading political issues of the day, and the measure finally failed, because the people, as a whole, were afraid of it.

At the time of these discussions in the Constitutional Convention, an association of merchants for banking purposes had existed for several years in the city of New York. Alexander Hamilton had drawn their papers in 1784. It rested on nothing but a partnership agreement, and they were compelled to wait for some years before obtaining a charter from their State. Seven years more elapsed, and Aaron Burr was applied to by some capitalists who proposed to organize a second bank. He did not venture to ask openly for such a franchise, but had a petition presented to the Legislature for the incorporation of a company to supply the city with water. The capital was to be $2,000,000, and one section of the bill which he prepared provided that any surplus, not used in the construction of the water-works, "might be employed in any way not inconsistent with the laws and Constitution of the United States, or of the State of New York." A charter to the "Manhattan Company" was granted in this shape in 1799, and the Bank of the Manhattan Company was soon afterwards established, and still exists, though the city had to wait for other agencies, in later years, to supply it with water.[1]

It may be safely asserted that private business corporations were always viewed with disfavor by the mass of the community in every American colony; and also in the States which succeeded them, until the eighteenth century came to its close. The influence of English commercial corporations in engrossing American trade had rendered them justly obnoxious to the people, and there was similar cause of complaint against English manufacturing companies. The hatting industry offers a fair example. Beavers were originally so numerous here, that by 1731 ten thousand beaver hats were annually made in New York and New England, largely for export. The Company of Feltmakers of London thereupon petitioned Parliament to prohibit the future exportation of such hats. An Act to that effect was immediately passed, which also forbade any American hatter to employ more than two apprentices; and this remained the law until the Revolutionary War.[2]

The people of Great Britain, as a whole, shared the same sentiments.

In 1733 Lord Bathurst, who, though he had been an earnest antagonist of the South Sea Company, had had ample time since its collapse to revise any opinion he might have formed during the parliamentary struggle, wrote thus to Dean Swift, who

[1] Parton's "Life of Aaron Burr," 238.
[2] Documentary History of New York, i. 761, *note*.

FREEDOM OF INCORPORATION

had asked his good offices in regard to a matter affecting a certain corporation:—

"All corporations of men are perpetually doing injustice to individuals. I will attend it, but am as much prejudiced against them as it is possible, though I know nothing of the man, nor the matter in question. I have often reflected (from what cause it arises I know not) that though the majority of a society are honest men, and would act, separately, with some humanity, and according to the rules of morality, yet, conjunctively, they are hardhearted, determined villains." [1]

Hume, in his "History of England," published some twenty years later, in commenting on the times of Henry VII., observes that one check to industry then "was the erecting of corporations, an abuse which is not yet entirely corrected." [2] Adam Smith, in his "Wealth of Nations," which appeared in 1776, declares that without a monopoly no joint-stock company can long carry on any branch of foreign trade, as its directors cannot be relied on to give it that unremitting care and attention which individuals are willing to bestow on their own affairs. "The only trades," he adds, "which it seems possible for a joint-stock company to carry on successfully, without an exclusive privilege, are those of which all the operations are capable of being reduced to what is called a routine, or to such a uniformity of method as admits of little or no variation. Of this kind is, first, the banking trade; secondly, the

[1] Swift's Works, Nichols' ed., xii. 452.
[2] 2 Hume's Hist., chap. 26, p. 256.

trade of insurance from fire, and from sea risk and capture in time of war; thirdly, the trade of making and maintaining a navigable cut or canal; and, fourthly, the similar trade of bringing water for the supply of a great city. . . . To establish a joint-stock company, however, for any undertaking, merely because such a company might be capable of managing it successfully; or to exempt a particular set of dealers from some of the general laws which take place with regard to all their neighbors, merely because they might be capable of thriving, if they had such an exemption, would certainly not be reasonable. To render such an establishment perfectly reasonable, with the circumstance of being reducible to strict rule and method, two other circumstances ought to concur. First, it ought to appear with the clearest evidence that the undertaking is of greater and more general utility than the greater part of common trades; and, secondly, that it requires a greater capital than can easily be collected into a private copartnery. If a moderate capital were sufficient, the great utility of the undertaking would not be a sufficient reason for establishing a joint-stock company; because, in this case, the demand for what it was to produce would readily and easily be supplied by private adventurers. In the four trades above mentioned, both those circumstances concur."[1]

Similar opinions were generally held throughout Europe. The Abbé Morellet, one of the leading French encyclopedists, and a member of the Insti-

[1] Smith's " Wealth of Nations," iii. book v. chap. i. pp. 145, 146.

FREEDOM OF INCORPORATION 193

tute, had given strong expression to them, and fortified his positions by statistics of the fate of over fifty trading corporations, scattered over Europe, which, during the preceding hundred and fifty years, had been formed, only to bring ruin to stockholders and creditors.[1]

With the single exception furnished by the Act of Elizabeth to encourage charitable foundations, which has been described, no sovereign power in modern times had established anything in the nature of a general incorporation law. The privilege of combination into a political body clothed with the attitude of perpetuity, or at least of duration for a certain term, not subject to abridgment by the accidents of death, and whose obligations were distinct from those of its members, was universally deemed a matter of too grave importance to be left free to all. A special charter or license, from the crown or legislative assembly, or proprietary lord, was therefore held to be a necessary prerequisite to the existence of any such organization. An ancient custom, indeed, might found a prescriptive title; but only because long usage implied an original grant, although the record or other evidence of it might be lost.

The radical change of views, in the present century, which has brought such laws into existence in almost every civilized State, has been the result of

[1] The only great company of this kind which has been conspicuously successful in recent times, under a monopolistic charter, is the Netherlands Trading Company, chartered in 1824, with a capital of $15,000,000, and a monopoly of the trade with the Dutch East Indies.

new conditions of society. If these did not first appear on American soil, they were certainly viewed there with the least prejudice and appreciated with the least difficulty. Whatever action they called for had to encounter but slight opposition from traditions or received opinion, and almost none from vested interests.

We naturally expect the movements of a new social force to find expression in law first in new governments. We now look to Australia for experiments in legislation. A hundred years ago, the world looked to the United States.

The first general incorporation law of any kind which I have been able to discover was one enacted by New York, in 1784, to authorize the formation of ecclesiastical societies for the support of public worship in some particular church.[1] Pennsylvania, in 1791, adopted a similar measure, and extended the same privileges to associations for literary and charitable purposes. The articles of agreement by which the corporation was to be constituted were to be submitted to the Attorney-General for examination, and if he was of opinion that they conformed to the statute, he was to certify this to the Supreme Court. A like certificate of approval from the Court was also required, and if obtained, the record of the papers made the associates a corporation.[2] In 1796, another law of New York allowed any twenty persons who desired to establish a public library, and would

[1] The Revised Statutes of New York, iii. 292, give this as re-enacted and enlarged in 1813.
[2] Case of St. Mary's Church, 7 Sergeant & Rawle's Reports, 528.

contribute not less than forty pounds for that purpose, to become a corporation upon simply filing their agreement for record.[1] Vermont, the next year, declared the inhabitants of all towns, school districts, parishes, and religious societies formed for public worship, to be corporations, without any further act on their part.[2]

No harm having been found to result from legislation of this character, New York took the bolder step, in 1811, of allowing any persons to incorporate themselves, by filing the proper papers for record, who desired to contribute capital for carrying on the manufacture of woollen, cotton, or linen goods, glass, or a few other specified commodities, or engaging in ironmongery.[3] This policy was soon extended to other branches of industry from year to year, and was followed before 1850 by most of the other States. In an early Act of this description, passed by Vermont, it is worth remark that among the few occupations embraced within its terms was the construction of water-works,[4] not improbably in consequence of the opinion expressed in Smith's "Wealth of Nations," which has been already quoted.

The first extension of this principle to banking institutions was in Michigan, in 1837. The result was disastrous. Of forty banks organized under that statute, thirty-six failed within the next two

---

[1] New York Revised Statutes, iii. 288.
[2] Slade's "Compilation of the Laws of Vermont," 156, chap. 14.
[3] New York Revised Statutes, iii. 310.
[4] Revised Statutes of Vermont, ed. of 1840.

years. A similar lesson was taught by experience in other States.

Gradually it has come to be the general American policy not, as at first, to enumerate certain classes of objects for which the privilege of private incorporation is offered, but to throw it, with certain specified exceptions, open to those proposing to associate for any kind of business. Among these exceptions, banking, insurance, and all undertakings involving the exercise of the right of eminent domain are commonly included; but provision is then made for these by separate laws of a general character, in which special safeguards are set up for public protection.

There are also limitations which may be regarded as implied in the nature of things. Thus a power to incorporate for any lawful purpose ought not to be construed as including authority to pursue that purpose by extraordinary means, not open to the ordinary citizen, as an individual.

The ordinary objects of an association for the establishment of a college of learning, for instance, can be accomplished by the provision of proper instruction and suitable buildings and apparatus. It is not one of its necessary incidents that it should have power to grant degrees in arts or science, and thus confer upon their recipients a certain recognized *status* in the republic of letters. The academic degree did not come into existence until the thirteenth century. There had been great schools of learning in the ancient world, numbering thousands of students, and with professorships regulated and supported by law; but those who might successfully pursue their full courses of instruction received nothing but a simple certificate of that fact. The same thing was true of the colleges and universities that sprang up upon the revival of learning. The first collegiate degrees of the character with which we are now familiar were conferred by the University of Paris, by authority of a papal bull of Nicholas I. Their original purport and object was to grant the recipient the right to teach in any part of the world. The language of the modern diploma is the same. The University of Paris conferred the privilege by an authority then recognized as ecumenical. The modern college or university confers it by permission of a more limited authority, that of the particular State in which it is incorporated; but this permission must be distinctly expressed by the local sovereign. The University of Durham was incorporated by Act of Parliament, and opened for students in 1833, but it was not until 1837 that it obtained by royal charter the right to grant degrees. A general law authorizing the incorporation of literary institutions does not, therefore, authorize the incorporation of one with power to grant academic degrees.[1] The persons associating under such a law could not, as individuals, assume such a function, and their corporate character only enables them to do as a corporation what they could before have done without it, as private citizens.

It is to be regretted that in some of the States these principles have not always been enforced, and

[1] *Re* Medical College, 3 Wharton's Reports, 455.

that American diplomas from speculative colleges, formed under general laws, have been sometimes made the subject of bargain and sale, almost without disguise. Such degrees are simply counterfeits of the trade-mark of learning.

As a guard against such abuses of the law, it is provided in several States that those desiring to incorporate themselves for any purpose must submit their articles of association to some judicial authority for inspection and approval. Where the approval extends no farther than to the determination that the papers are properly drawn and the case one within the terms of the statute, this cannot be deemed a delegation of legislative power; but it may be otherwise where the approval is a matter of discretion, based on questions of policy or expediency.[1]

A provision of this character formed part of what is believed to be the first of the long line of American statutes throwing open incorporation for municipal purposes to all clusters of population on equal terms. This was the Pennsylvania law of 1834, giving to the courts of quarter sessions, with the concurrence of the grand jury of the county, power to incorporate any town or village into the form of a borough.[2]

The scheme of government and the extent as well as distribution of corporate powers are generally

[1] State v. Armstrong, 3 Sneed's Reports, 634; Mayor of Morristown v. Shelton, 1 Head's Reports, 24.

[2] The opinion of the grand jury is not considered as conclusive as to the expediency of incorporation. *In re* Incorporation of Village of Edgewood, 130 Pennsylvania State Reports, 348; 18 Atlantic Reporter, 641.

prescribed by the statute, and vary according to the number of the population to be affected. In two States, cities having over one hundred thousand inhabitants may, under certain restrictions, frame charters for themselves.[1]

Congress has imposed the policy, as respects both public and private corporations, of general incorporation laws on all the Territories.[2] It has also followed it itself in establishing our present system of national banks, and in giving a national character to associations of workingmen having branches in more than one of the States or Territories.[3] Its field of legislation is so limited that, except in the instances which have been mentioned, it has seldom had occasion to exercise the power of incorporation for business purposes, but when this has been done, it has taken the form of a special charter.

More than fifty years ago the principle of general legislation, in regard to corporate organization, began to pass into our system of constitutional law.

Not inappropriately, the first manifestation of this tendency was in a State whose institutions were founded on the civil law. Article 123 of the Constitution of Louisiana, which was adopted in 1845 to replace that framed in 1812, when the State was admitted to the Union, reads thus: —

[1] Beach on " Public Corporations," i. § 42.
[2] U. S. Revised Statutes, § 1889; U. S. Statutes at Large, vol. 24, p. 170.
[3] U. S. Statutes at Large, vol. 24, p. 86.

"Corporations shall not be created in this State by special laws, except for political or municipal purposes, but the legislature shall provide, by general laws, for the organization of all other corporations, except corporations with banking or discounting privileges, the creation of which is prohibited."[1]

Iowa went a step farther in her Constitution of 1846, and laid down the same rule for both public and private corporations.[2] The Constitutions of New York, in 1846, Wisconsin, in 1848, and Ohio and Indiana, in 1851, contained provisions on this subject more or less comprehensive, and special incorporation laws have since been prohibited in a large number of the other States.

The progress of British legislation in this direction may be said to date from the beginning of the "Victorian age."

A foundation had been laid, in 1825 and 1827, by Acts of Parliament conceding to workingmen the right of association in trades-unions, authorizing free banking on a basis of full partnership liability,[3] and repealing the Bubble Act of the preceding century.

The latter measures were due to the increasing pressure of capital seeking investment on the joint-stock principle,[4] and to the evils which had resulted from exclusive banking privileges, particularly in Ireland. During the period between 1783 and

[1] 1 Poole's "Charters and Constitutions," 721.
[2] *Ibid.* 546.　　　　　　[3] Act of 7 Geo. IV., chap. 46.
[4] In 1825, £18,000,000 was paid in by shareholders in various English companies. Annual Register for 1825, Public Doc. 42.

1825, when the Bank of Ireland enjoyed a complete monopoly, it opened no branches. The consequence was that private concerns received the country deposits, and speculated with them, involving losses in one year estimated at £20,000,000.[1] The Irish Parliament had endeavored to encourage legitimate enterprises on the principle of limited liability, in 1782, by adopting the device of the *société anonyme* in its original form; but it was not to be allowed to interfere with the Bank of Ireland. Any number of persons might enter into a partnership under the name of one of them "and company," for any kind of lawful business, except banking, to endure for not over fourteen years, and with a capital of not less than £50,000. The partner whose name was thus used was to have the sole conduct of the business and be liable for all the partnership debts. The others, who were styled "anonimous partners," risked only what capital they originally agreed to put in. The partnership articles were to be recorded in a public registry at Dublin; capital was represented by transferable shares; and the firm was not dissolved by the death of any of the members.[2] England did not care to follow this experiment in legislation, though it was preserved in force after the union by a special clause in the Joint Stock Companies Registration Act of 1844.

The causes leading to the adoption of that measure were briefly these. Many associations of individuals under a company name, which the ordinary people

[1] Daly's "Glimpses of Irish Industries," 66.
[2] Act of 21 and 22 Geo. III.; 12 Irish Statutes at Large, 347.

took to signify the possession of a charter, were trading under a fictitious credit thus acquired. Of the few full corporations which were in business under royal charters, the shareholders in some were liable individually to an amount proportioned to their stock, and those in others were under no liability except that of paying in the amount of their actual subscriptions.[1] Other companies which were merely great partnerships (including most of the larger and more solid concerns) had been successful in procuring a special Act of Parliament, based upon their organization agreement or "deed of settlement," which, without incorporating them, authorized suits to be brought by or against the company in the name of one of their number.[2] The Liverpool and London Life and Fire Insurance Company was one of these, and from time to time has secured successive special Acts of Parliament in aid of its growing business, each of which, however, contains a special proviso that it shall not be deemed an act of incorporation.[3] Important banking institutions existed by a similar tenure, and those whose seat of operation was more than sixty-five miles from London were issuing their notes for general circulation. Within that limit the Bank of England had obtained a monopoly. Two of the country banks, the Agricultural Bank of Ireland and the Northern and Central Bank in Manchester, were forced to go into liqui-

[1] Smith's "Mercantile Law," 41.
[2] *Ibid.*, chap. i. sec. 7.
[3] Liverpool Insurance Co. *v.* Massachusetts, 10 Wallace's Reports, 569.

FREEDOM OF INCORPORATION 203

dation at the outset of the commercial panic of 1836. Many others of the large companies formed on the joint-stock principle were shaken, and some fell. The British public then began to see that existing laws made no adequate provision for public information as to the financial condition of any of these associations. A demand that they should be invested with definite franchises which the State could control, and for the proper exercise of which they could be held fully responsible, became general in the community. It was a demand for the protection of creditors and investors against speculative and unsubstantial organizations, rather than one for more facilities for corporate organization.[1]

An Act passed in 1838 gave some slight relief,[2] but the first general incorporation law was not enacted until 1844. This (the Joint Stock Companies Registration Act) provides that no insurance company, and no partnership for any kind of business (except the construction of such works as would require a special grant of parliamentary authority), with a capital to be divided into transferable shares, or with more than twenty-five members, shall thereafter be formed until articles of association, duly executed, setting forth the proposed name, business, capital, stock subscriptions, term of duration, and other particulars which are specified, have been

[1] Bunyon on Life Assurance, 121.
[2] This (amending an Act of 4 & 5 William IV., chapter 69) left the members of joint-stock companies exempt from any individual liability, and made them quasi-corporations. Harrison *v.* Timmins, 4 Meeson & Welsby's Reports, 510.

put on record in a government registry office. It is then enacted that upon obtaining a certificate from the "Registrar of Joint Stock Companies" that a proper registration has been made, the shareholders and their successors "shall be and are hereby incorporated as from the date of such certificate by the name of the company as set forth in the deed of settlement, and for the purpose of carrying on the trade or business for which the company was formed, but only according to the provisions of this Act, and of such deed as aforesaid, and for the purpose of suing and being sued, and of taking and enjoying the property and effects of the said company; . . . and thereupon it shall be lawful for the said company" to do any act ordinarily incident to the business of a corporation, except that no lands could be acquired without the license of a committee of the Privy Council, except as a site for its place of business. Each shareholder, however, was made liable as fully as an ordinary partner to judgment creditors who could not collect their demand from the assets of the company. Ample provision was made for affording both shareholders and the public full information, from time to time, of the company's affairs.

This statute has not been construed by the English courts as giving the organizations which are effected under it the character of a full corporation; but it is difficult to see what of its essential qualities they lack. Subsequent Acts of Parliament have modified the system thus inaugurated, by allowing also the formation of limited liability companies, the members of which risk nothing but the contribution to the capital

FREEDOM OF INCORPORATION 205

which they originally agree to make in payment of their shares. Such a company must add the word "Limited" to its name. This provision dates from 1856; and in 1862 the legislation on the whole subject was revised in the "Companies Act" of that year, and the organization of unsubstantial enterprises rendered considerably more easy.

There had been a rush to take advantage of the Act of 1844, and a commercial panic followed in a year or two. Similar results followed the Act of 1862. The promoters of a new company, by gifts of shares, hired a few men of means and prominence to become directors; the arrangement being often made through some mutual acquaintance, who was also well paid for every name he brought in. Foreigners, whose own country offered no such opportunities, became promoters and purchasers. The stock of the "London Bank of Scotland, Limited," was divided into 10,000 shares, and a majority of them were held during one fortnight of its early history by six Greeks, all men of small means, who were brought into it because three leading merchants of their race were to be on the board of directors.[1]

Changes in detail have since been made in the English statutes, but in substance they remain the same.

A general banking law, with particular regulations for the conduct of that business and a prohibition against the issue of circulating notes, was passed in 1858.

The English have been unwilling to grant in terms

[1] Xenos' *Depredations*, 263, 316, 335.

the privilege of complete incorporation, as of right, to all who desire it, because in their law it has been regarded as essential incidents of a full corporation first, that its personality is wholly distinct from that of its members; second, that therefore they cannot, in fairness, be made liable for its obligations individually; and third, that it can exercise every power not prohibited by its charter. Coke had laid the foundations of this doctrine in discussing the attributes of an incorporated hospital, and it has been silently extended in course of time to corporations of every class,[1] notwithstanding the fact that a charitable institution is *sui generis*, and is, in effect, only the formal expression of an equitable trust.[2]

A striking instance of its practical effects may be found in the history of the British Linen Company. It was chartered in 1746 for the manufacture of linen, the stockholders to be under no individual liability for its debts. It soon added banking to its manufacturing business. The latter was afterwards abandoned, but the corporation still exists in active operation as a bank.

The American courts, untrammelled by English precedent, have proceeded on the theory that corporations have no powers which have not been granted

---

[1] Case of Sutton's Hospital, iv. Coke's Reports, 23, 30, b; Society of Practical Knowledge *v.* Abbott, 2 Beavan's Reports, 559; Pollock's Principles of Contract, 119, and note D, in appendix.

[2] Savigny would limit the use of the term "corporation" so as to make it exclude charitable foundations altogether. To English and American minds there is no difficulty in regarding a charitable corporation as a trustee of its funds for the benefit of the charitable objects prescribed.

to them either expressly or by reasonable implication; that it does not deprive them of their proper character to make it part of their original constitution that their creditors may resort, to any extent which the law may prescribe, to the members individually; and that in enforcing the duty of the corporation to the public, and sometimes in determining the absolute rights of its members, as such, between themselves, its artificial form can be disregarded, and it can be held bound by the acts of all its members.[1]

This difference between English and American law serves in great measure to account for the freer hand with which corporate franchises have been offered here to all who wish them, on equal terms.

Turning now to the modern development of corporations in Europe generally, we find that early in the century the *société anonyme* in its later form, as remoulded in the *Code Napoléon*, following the French arms, spread with the principles of that code over Southern Europe.

Belgium anticipated France by repealing the requirement of official authorization. This was effected there, with the aid of subsequent judicial interpretation, by the revolutionary decree of October 16, 1830, declaring that "impediments to the liberty of association are infractions of individual and political liberty."[2]

A year later Brazil adopted the same policy, and

[1] State *v.* Standard Oil Company, 49 Ohio State Reports, 137; 30 Northeastern Reporter, 279; Woodbridge *v.* Pratt & Whitney Co., 69 Conn. Reports, 304.

[2] Rogron, *Code de Commerce expliqué*, 15.

although its abuse by those engaging in the banking business caused a return to the old order of things a few years later, in 1882 absolute freedom of incorporation was again established, except for a few specified objects.[1]

Germany followed the example of France in 1870. It was to arm herself against her with her own weapons, for the struggle upon which they were about to enter. Capital was to be mobilized as well as troops. The law passed in June of that year by the North German Confederation, soon to become the new Empire, reproduced the main features of the French law of 1867, though the familiar designation, elsewhere generally adopted, of nameless society (*société anonyme*), was replaced by that of shares-society (*Aktiengesellschaft*). The speculative fever which accompanied and followed the war, found in this measure an effective support. Companies were organized on insufficient capital, a considerable portion of which were soon forced into liquidation.[2] This led, in 1884, to another law of the empire, adding new safeguards, particularly against the rapacity and frauds of promoters. The interests of minority stockholders were also given further protection, and regulations prescribed for partnerships *en commandite* (*Kommanditgesellschaften auf Aktien*), under which the partners' shares were made transferable. The benefits of free incorporation on favorable terms were extended to registered co-operative and mutual aid

---

[1] *Annuaire de Législation Étrangère*, for 1882, pp. 1080, 1082.
[2] *Annuaire de Législation Étrangère*, for 1885, p. 98 ; " Handwörterbuch der Staatswissenschaften," i. *Aktiengesellschaften*, iii.

societies (*Genossenschaften*), in 1889, and three years later to all who desired to engage in business of any kind, on a footing of limited liability. The shares-society was calculated, mainly, for large undertakings. Its stock was ordinarily distributed among numerous holders, and its business was often of a kind in which the general interest of the community might be concerned. The law had therefore required a certain publicity to be given to their affairs, which was needless and annoying in case of a small business in the hands of a few men. These could act more effectually if the corporate form were reduced as nearly as might be to the likeness of a partnership. The law of 1892 did this by allowing the formation of limited partnerships, with transferable shares (*Gesellschaften mit beschränkter Haftung*). They may have an ordinary firm name, made up of those of the individual members, or one descriptive of the business, but in either case the words above quoted to indicate limited liability must be added to it. Such a body is not formally declared to be an artificial person, but it has all the essential attributes of one. (Art. 13.) Each partner at the outset holds one share and one only. Its amount is that of his agreed contribution to the capital, so that the shares may differ widely in their par value. Subsequently they may be divided, but only by a general vote of all.

The result of the law of 1892 has been greatly to reduce the number of the shares-societies, capitalists preferring the new form of association because of the greater privacy with which its affairs can be conducted.[1]

[1] *Annuaire de Législation Étrangère*, 21st year, 154.

Hungary adopted the system of free incorporation for ordinary business purposes in 1875, Italy in 1882, and Spain in 1885. The Swiss Confederation incorporated it into their Code of Obligations (Art. 612, *et seq.*) in 1883, excluding from its benefits banks and insurance companies. It may indeed be said to be the general rule of Europe, Austria and Russia being the only considerable powers which have not given it their adhesion.[1]

Canada still holds to the principle of governmental authorization in each case, but by the " Companies Act" of 1886 allows the Governor in Council to grant charters, on written application, for any business purpose except those of railroads, banking, and insurance. Hawaii has a law quite similar.[2]

So far as concerns municipal corporations, the world at large has not been ready to follow the American lead.[3]

Perhaps no country is so situated politically that it could follow it with safety to its institutions. If there be one, it is Great Britain, but she is held back, both by what might be its effects upon her system of parliamentary representation, and by what they would

[1] *Annuaire de Législation Étrangère*, 14th year, 99.
[2] Civil Code of 1897, chap. 127.
[3] The Prussian laws for the government of country communities (the *Kreisordnung* of 1872, and *Landgemeineordnung* of 1891), to a certain extent look in the direction of free incorporation. They contemplate the formation, in certain cases, of new communities, or communal unions by grouping together several previously existing, by the action of the local and provincial authorities ; but this is only justified when the united communities were separately too weak to support the necessary public burdens.

FREEDOM OF INCORPORATION 211

be as to the inhabitants of the particular district respecting which incorporation might be obtained. While since 1835 she has had in operation a uniform scheme of municipal government, municipal incorporation is still by special charter in each case. The Reform bill of 1832 created a number of new boroughs for the purpose of parliamentary elections, without making them self-governing municipalities. Manchester did not secure a charter until 1838, though she then had a quarter of a million inhabitants. Newcastle until nearly the same time had no other than one early granted by the bishop of Durham. The Municipal Corporations (Consolidation) Act of 1882 went no further than to allow the inhabitants of any town or district to petition the queen for incorporation as a borough, and to authorize such a grant to be made upon a favorable report from a committee of the Privy Council. In 1888, however, the "Local Government Act" took a half way step towards the adoption of the American system of voluntary incorporation, by providing that cities and towns having not less than fifty thousand inhabitants shall *ipso facto* be distinct counties for administrative purposes, the duties properly pertaining to County Councils being performed, in every such case, by the municipal council.

Differences of legal theory as to the inherent attributes of a municipality have also had great weight.

In England the view taken by the courts as to the extent of corporate powers, which has already been noticed, extends to municipal corporations, and in the absence of prohibitions, they occupy much the position of a natural person as to the acquisition and disposition of property, and can do almost anything which is not a direct invasion of private right.[1] The same doctrine is practically applied to them in Europe generally, and we need not be surprised that, wherever it obtains, they are created only by special charter in each particular case, under the conviction that there is too much danger in their possibilities to make it safe to do otherwise.

The rule universally prevailing in the United States that a municipal corporation, in addition to the powers with which it is specially invested by the statute law, has by implication only such as are essential to the proper exercise of those, or necessary to attain the declared objects of incorporation, has led us naturally to a different result.

European history has also taught the lesson that municipal corporations are apt to come under the influence of particular classes of their inhabitants, organized for purposes of mutual aid and protection; and the extent of their powers under European law renders any perversion of them for class purposes doubly pernicious. We have seen how this was true of the mediæval trade guild. In recent times, trades-unions and socialistic organizations have made their power felt in a similar way, but not always with the same results. They naturally seek to promote their own views and objects by direct means, wherever the road is plain. Thus, for instance, in London, the trades-unions have made it a general feature of all city contracts for the erection of public buildings that

[1] Kyd on Corporations, i. 108, 182.

the contractor shall pay "the rates of wages mutually agreed upon by the Central Association of Master Builders of London, and the London Building Trade Federation." But instead of inclining steadily towards paternalism, it is often found that a city controlled by labor organizations is, in certain directions, held back from it. Appropriations for the relief of the poor, sick, or unemployed are discouraged, from the feeling that they should be left to insure themselves against want by membership in some appropriate mutual benefit society, under the principle that the sale of labor must be wholly controlled by organized labor. Such has been the recent municipal history of socialism in France and Belgium.[1]

Advancing standards of human comfort and a growing sentiment of municipal solidarity are, on the other hand, impelling cities everywhere to undertake new functions for the good of the citizen. They demand the right to pull down unsanitary tenement houses, and replace them by public ones; to establish savings banks, and pawn shops; to engage in great public works, even to the extent of reversing their natural geographical environment, as in the case of the Manchester ship canal; to erect cold storage warehouses for the convenience of importers;[2] to furnish power to manufacturers; to become manufacturers themselves.

The European city possesses far greater powers than the American, but it is also subject to a far

[1] Annals of the American Academy of Political and Social Science, viii. 208, 217.
[2] Manchester has done this also, on a large scale.

more stringent supervision by the State. The administrative side of government is, in theory at least, little regarded by us. As to municipal affairs, it is all important in the rest of the world. This, co-operating with economic conditions incident to the historical development of the nation, has led almost everywhere in Europe to the regulation of municipal government by general laws, reserving to the State large powers of intervention, to an extent hardly equalled yet in the United States. Under the municipal code of Austria, for instance, the government, in 1895, upon the election of a mayor of Vienna who was unsatisfactory to the emperor, dissolved the city council and assumed the administration of all the affairs of the municipality by an imperial commissioner.

The drift of workingmen's associations and trades-unions, both in Europe and in America, is towards the advocacy of larger home rule for the municipality, and less State interference with its concerns. The ordinary wage-earner comes closer to the city council than to the State legislature. Many of the "labor" leaders favor a transfer to the municipal corporations of a large share of the powers of government, even as to affairs of general concern to the nation.

The *commune* movement which succeeded the fall of Louis Napoleon, had for its avowed object the government of the French people through the local communes. The national government was to have as few powers as possible. France was to be a mere confederacy of 36,000 communes.

It is worth remark that in Milton's "Ready and

FREEDOM OF INCORPORATION

Easy Way to establish a Free Commonwealth," he sketched in outlines a similar plan for England. Every county, he says, should be made —

"a kind of subordinate commonalty or commonwealth, and one chief town or more, according as the shire is in circuit, made cities, if they be not so called already, where the nobility and chief gentry, from a proportionable compass of territory annexed to each city, may build houses or palaces befitting their quality, may bear part in the government, make their own judicial laws, or use these that are, and execute them by their own elected judicatures and judges without appeal, in all things of civil government between man and man; so they shall have justice in their own hands, law executed fully and finally in their own counties and precincts, long wished and spoken of, but never yet obtained; they shall have none then to blame but themselves, if it be not well administered, and fewer laws to expect or fear from the supreme authority; or, to those that shall be made of any great concernment to public liberty, they may, without much trouble in these commonalties, or in more general assemblies called to their cities from the whole territory on such occasion, declare and publish their assent or dissent by deputies, within a time limited, sent to the grand council; yet so as this their judgment declared, shall submit to the greater number of other counties or commonalties, and not avail them to any exemption of themselves, or refusal of agreement with the rest, as it may in any of the United Provinces, being sovereign within itself, ofttimes to the great disadvantage of that union. . . . Nothing can be more essential to the freedom of a people, than to have the administration of justice, and all public ornaments, in their own election and within their own bounds, without long travelling or depending upon remote places to obtain their right, or any civil accomplishment, so it be not supreme, but subordinate to the general power and union of the whole republic; in which happy firmness, as in the particular above mentioned, we shall also far exceed the United Provinces, by having, not as they, to the retarding and distracting ofttimes of their counsels or urgentest occasions, many sovereignties united in one commonwealth, but many commonwealths under one united and entrusted sovereignty."[1]

Since freedom of municipal incorporation exists only in the United States, and even there does not generally prevail, we should not expect and we do not find that it has been attended with any marked political or economical consequences. It naturally coalesces with our other institutions, and simply removes opportunities for favoritism and cheapens expenses of administration.

As to freedom of incorporation for private purposes, the case is different. This has secured a place among the institutions of the civilized world, and its effects are far-reaching and almost revolutionary.

How is it, we must first ask, that it has so suddenly attained this position? What are the causes that in half a century served to reverse a rule of legislation that had been everywhere accepted since the fall of the Roman empire?

First among these I should name the improvement in the arts, by which machinery has been so largely substituted for human hands. Household manufac-

[1] Milton's Prose Works, Boston ed. of 1826, ii. 329, 330.

tures have thus become unimportant. Individual skill and dexterity are little considered in such manual labor as is still required. All important products, except crops from land (and those also to a steadily increasing extent), come from a combination in a single workshop of laborers with capital in the form of costly mechanism moved by steam or electricity. It is also true that the largest workshops prove the most economical. Nor can the small producer contend with the large producer on equal terms in disposing of his goods. Steam and electric locomotion, aided by the telegraph and telephone, have annihilated the local market. Every manufacturer must compete with those of the whole country, or else combine with those of the whole country to an extent sufficient to prevent competition. Such combinations are merciless. Their aggregated resources allow them to establish prices below the cost of production long enough to ruin any small concerns that have not joined them.

Great undertakings are now almost the only successful undertakings: certainly the only ones which offer large profits to many people. Mere partnerships are no longer adequate to the necessities of the business world. They are not strong enough for the strain. In amount of capital, in term of duration, in unity of management even, they are no match for the corporation. Partners may differ, and the house divided against itself will fall. Stockholders in corporations may differ, but the iron rule of the majority guaranties consistent and harmonious action, when a board of management is once elected. This board, too, while more numerous than partners in an ordinary firm, unlike them acts as one man and by one man.

It was the contention of the old school of political economists, the school of which J. R. M'Culloch was one of the last leaders,[1] that directors of trading companies would not and could not give that personal attention to the business, which was necessary to ensure success, and so that trading partnerships, in which every member took an active part in the management, were a far safer mode of association. It is precisely because every partner in an ordinary mercantile firm is expected to take an active part in its affairs that the partnership is inferior in executive power to the corporation of equal capital. That principle of absolutism around which we have thrown so many checks in political governments, by the usages of modern business is recognized there as inevitable and controlling. Unity of policy, instant decision, immediate action, strict subordination, — without these the war of competition under present conditions cannot be waged with success. It must be regulated by military maxims, and with but one general in command.

Add to this the protection of limited liability which the corporation offers, and it is no wonder that nothing else will satisfy the modern capitalist. He is not ready to stake his whole fortune in the success of a particular enterprise. He prefers to scatter his investments, and risk by each only what he especially

[1] See his article on Companies in the "Encyclopedia Britannica," 8th edition.

devotes to it. He cannot give his personal attention to the management of each. He may not care to give it to that of any of them. The one man, then, who is to be directly in control of every large business is not often its owner. There are many owners; and not infrequently no one of them would be competent for such a position. By assuming the form of a corporation they can secure the services of one who is, without incurring the ordinary liability of an employer for the acts of his agent. The employer may lose his whole fortune by some injury which his agent carelessly inflicts upon another. The shareholder in an ordinary corporation cannot lose anything beyond his stock by such misconduct on the part of the president. He can also keep a certain watch upon him through his representatives, the board of directors. It is true that this is less real in practice than it seems in theory. Whatever powers may be placed in boards of directors, they cannot be always in session, and between their meetings some one will must be in control, and in emergencies in what is practically absolute control. But the next meeting of the directors or of the executive committee, and the report to be made to it, is always in prospect. A great capital is seldom sunk by any single act, or temporary course of policy. A vigilant stockholder, with a considerable interest, can always keep himself fairly well informed, if he asks questions enough of those who are acting for him, and looks with care at the books which he is entitled to inspect.

Whatever is the "law merchant" is not long in

becoming the law of the land. As soon as business men came to feel that their interests were safest in charge of a corporation, they began to demand that incorporation should be made as easy as the old forms of voluntary association. The rapidity of motion of modern trade is such that ordinary enterprises cannot safely be delayed by applications for special charters. They must be pressed forward with the despatch of the telegraph and the telephone. There must be the same liberty to form a corporation in a day that there is to form a partnership in a day, and the same freedom from outside interference in any of the initial steps.

The way to this was paved by what Lieber, writing in 1853, described as the "all-pervading associative spirit" so characteristic of English speaking peoples.[1] It long since ceased to be distinctively theirs. The same forces which led England to repeal her laws against combinations of workingmen in 1827, led France and Germany to repeal theirs, forty years later. The right of temporary association has gained in several countries of Europe, and even in one of the East,[2] a constitutional sanction.

The demand for this came mainly from the laboring classes, but the associative spirit had taken possession of the whole community. The legal expression of it was the result of the same social conditions already mentioned. The workmen found it necessary to unite in self-defence. They must accumulate a capital to support their claims to reasonable wages

[1] Lieber's "Civil Liberty," 129.
[2] Japan, Constitution of 1889, art. xxix.

FREEDOM OF INCORPORATION

and proper treatment. The employer did not oppose them in this. He could not with any degree of consistency, or any prospect of success. The modern trades-unions and fraternal societies are as much the fruit of steam and electricity as the factories where their members work.

Another cause, not less deep-seated, for offering corporate privileges to all who wish them, without discrimination, is the general acquiescence of our age in the doctrine that all men are born free and equal, and are entitled to a free and equal government, resting on their own consent. General laws further this equality, and special laws abridge it.

So far as concerns private corporations, there is also a certain sentimental reason for allowing them to be created at will. They serve to prolong, as it were, the life of the individual, by linking it with that which will not die.

The founder of an incorporated institution, whether it be a charity or a manufacturing company which bears his name, and every member of a scientific body or social club, has become a part of something that will live after him, and through which his memory may be perpetuated. Whatever he may contribute to the advancement of its interests will go into a common stock, in which those who are to take his place may share, and to which they may be expected to add. The union of those working for a common end is rendered doubly effective if, as one drops out, another enters in unbroken continuity of succession.

FREEDOM OF INCORPORATION

In former times, men were able to perpetuate their name by founding a family upon an entailed estate, and weaving it into the political constitution of their country, so that it partook of the same stability, and might endure as long. Now it is the society, the college, the church, the library, the factory, the business with which they have been connected, or in the usefulness of which they are confident, that they aid to a permanent establishment, and through whose continuance after they are gone they feel that they can best impress their ideas and their influence upon posterity. It is thus that we have found a way to prolong our passing lives, one might almost say forever. By such organizations, what is best of the activity and aspiration of one generation can be unceasingly transfused into the next, to gather new strength in the general upward progress of the race, and advance continually towards a fuller attainment of whatever objects they may be formed to promote.

As man learns better what is his relation to the world about him; as he understands more clearly how weak he is, standing alone; as he looks back to his origin and forward to his destiny, he feels more and more strongly the necessity of close human association for common ends.

The record written in the rocks and buried in caves, that modern science has brought to light, of the law of evolution, if one were to think only of the history of individuals, would make us tremble for the future of mankind. The lower animals, still true to the ancient rules of natural selection and the struggle for existence, are maintaining in their progeny the best characteristics of their kind. Man, who raises to maturity the puny and feeble of his offspring, only, perhaps, to perpetuate their weakness in another generation, seems to transgress in this the laws by which his physical being is regulated in the statutes of the universe. He prolongs and reproduces types of constitutions, which in the original order of nature would have been early borne down and swept away by something stronger. But that heaven-born mind that has made man the master of the earth has come to his support, and taught him the law of corporate vitality. The sickly child, who, in rougher ages, if not exposed to perish in infancy, would have fallen early in the struggle for existence, may now be tenderly reared to manhood. He will not stand alone and unaided in the community. He will be free to bind himself by a voluntary tie to stronger men and mingle his best qualities with theirs in indissoluble union, each giving something to gain more. The races of the civilized world number many of feebler form than their barbarian ancestors, or the savages of our own day; but by associations formed for perpetual succession to prosecute the same object steadily and always, as one man, they have in effect banished death and time from the domain of human achievement.

It is not easy to measure the weight of considerations like these in determining the course of human affairs. They are not the subject of statistics, and hardly of reasoning. But it is not always the motives that lie on the surface, or that are most commonly stated, which account for human conduct.

Sentiment has a large place in the development of institutions. Its place is all the larger because it is something indefinite and intangible, because it reaches out farther than thought can go, and belongs to that in our nature which in the life of earth is unknowable. It is this which makes it an enduring power, "for the things which are seen are temporal; but the things which are not seen are eternal."

Another ground of the demand for general incorporation laws which requires mention is the growing distrust of the people for their legislatures. Experience has shown that charters, from whatever authority they may proceed, go by favor, and quite too often to the least worthy. The modern tendency to overmuch legislation renders it difficult in the rush of business for committees to examine each measure that comes before them with the necessary care. There is ordinarily no opposition to an application for incorporation, and it is granted in the terms asked for, without the scrutiny which would attend an active opposition. Safeguards that are essential to the public interests are apt to be inserted in one charter and omitted from another almost by accident.

These considerations are of special weight in new countries, which are looking for a rapid growth in wealth and population; but the same causes are at work in all. The universal extension of popular representation in legislative bodies has brought the oldest governments face to face with the spirit of innovation and adventure, — the spirit of men who

FREEDOM OF INCORPORATION 225

have little to lose, and are risking the property and security of others rather than their own.

The immediate results of the adoption of general incorporation laws have been everywhere nearly the same. At first, it has led to many hasty and ill-considered ventures, which were a mere waste of the capital invested, and also brought some companies into existence which imposed upon the public by the issue of fictitious or unsound securities. A reaction in legislation has followed. New safeguards have been created against the abuse of corporate franchises. These have soon been found to bear too hardly on legitimate enterprises, and some relaxation has been granted. Each new law has thus been the occasion of others, but each has left the vital principle of free incorporation untouched. It is so in accord with the spirit of the age, that it must ultimately prevail in every country where any degree of individual liberty exists.

In attempting to estimate its general influence on modern society, it is not possible to discriminate closely between results due to the corporation on its original footing and those following from its creation under general laws.

This, however, is certain, that those laws have been everywhere followed by an immediate and large increase in the number of business companies and the amount of capital invested in active enterprises. Between the adoption of the Companies Act of 1862 and 1890, there were organized in Great Britain nearly thirty-five thousand corporations, with

226 FREEDOM OF INCORPORATION

limited liability, of which those surviving in the latter year had a total capitalization of over £220,000,000.[1] In Prussia more were created in 1871, the year following the first general incorporation law, than in the whole of the first half of the century, and in 1872 the number was more than doubled.[2] Before the close of the year (1892) in which Germany enacted her limited liability quasi-corporation Act, sixty such companies had been formed there, with an aggregate capital of over $7,000,000, and nearly fifty more were added during the next three months.[3] The French law of 1867, during its first full year of operation, produced nearly two hundred *sociétés anonymes*, and in 1881, when the movement reached high water mark, 976 of them were organized, besides fifty co-operative associations and 143 partnerships *en commandite* with transferable shares.[4] In the United States the movement has been much more rapid. In the larger States more corporations are formed under the general laws every year than existed in the whole world at the close of the eighteenth century. Connecticut has a larger number than the Russian empire.[5]

[1] Brockhaus' Konversations-Lexicon, *Gesellschaft mit beschränker Haftung*.
[2] Handwörterbuch der Staatswissenschaften, *Aktiengesellschaften*, 126, 127.
[3] Brockhaus' Konversations-Lexicon, *Gesellschaft mit beschränker Haftung*.
[4] Handwörterbuch der Staatswissenschaften, *Aktiengesellschaften*, 159.
[5] Russia entered the nineteenth century with but one trading corporation. In 1881 she had 833. There were over 1500 formed under the general law of Connecticut during the first 33 years after its

English capital is largely represented both in German and American corporations. On the other hand, American capital seeking investment in maritime commerce is often put into shares in an English limited liability company. Many a steamer thus plies under the British flag, and was built in a British shipyard, which is substantially owned by citizens of the United States, who find that they can in this way get the most for their money.

In countries where general incorporation laws are not fortified by constitutional provisions, special charters are occasionally granted, but seldom except for undertakings of an international character.

What, now, have these myriads of new-born corporations, coming into existence at the mere will of their promoters, accomplished of good or evil?

To those who have put money in them, they have often brought severe loss. Such was notably the effect of the Italian general incorporation laws in stimulating the attempt to rebuild Rome in a day, which resulted not only in new splendors, but new ruins. The same thing may be noted of the German law, under the influence of which Berlin became the subject of a disastrous " boom." But the failure of a joint stock company is not as unmixed an evil to the community as that of a private individual with an equal capital. He may be ruined for life, and for him there is no financial resurrection. Even

enactment. Special Laws of Conn., iv. 957. This number has since probably been more than doubled.

a discharge in bankruptcy will not restore his original credit. The company, on the other hand, can be easily re-organized under a new name, and the new possessors of its plant will take it at a low capitalization upon which they may be able to work it at a profit. Nor need the losses of the former owners be crushing to any of them. It will involve only what they invested in this particular concern, and men seldom risk their all in the stock of any single corporation.

To such failures and re-organizations, Thorold Rogers attributes in part that general depression of prices throughout the world which has marked the closing quarter of the nineteenth century.[1]

In the trade of our times goods are sold in large quantities and at small profits. The cost of production is largely determined by the cost of the plant. The re-organized corporation which rises out of the wreck of an unfortunate predecessor, representing generally its bonds instead of its stock, has acquired its plant so cheaply that it can afford to sell low, and yet pay dividends. This gives it the command of the market. It undersells other manufacturers. They fail, and from the new ruins emerge new corporations, to repeat the process, and work their plants, acquired at foreclosure prices, on a basis of diminished capitalization. The public thus gain what the original stockholders lost.

A much more obvious and certain cause for the universal fall in values, or rise in what measures values, is to be found in the inexorable law of supply

[1] The Economic Interpretation of History, 311.

and demand. The more easily corporations are formed, the more easily capital is massed at its best for productive work. It is the corporation which owns the machinery and directs the power which are so multiplying the force of human hands, that with their aid ten men now turn out more manufactured goods in a day than ten thousand once could in a year. Asia and Africa must be civilized and educated to demand the comforts of European and American life, before the market will be wide enough to satisfy the natural demands of corporate enterprise under modern conditions.

And what is the influence of the corporation on the men whom it employs? It is a hard master. It can always take the tone of a trustee. It represents others. Its only money is their money. It has no right to give away; none to retain the sick and feeble in its employment at their old wages, unless it can be made to appear that this is, on the whole, for the pecuniary advantage of the concern.

Against the incorporated employer has therefore risen up the incorporated employees. One of the great forces of modern society and modern politics is " organized labor." It has been a natural product of the factory system. That brings large bodies of workmen together under one roof, and subjects them to one rule. It tends also to centre manufacturing of a particular kind in a particular place or district. The boot and shoe business of the United States, for instance, radiates from eastern Massachusetts; Lyons is the great seat of silk manufacture, and Manchester of that of cotton goods. Laborers in the same trade, whether in the same factory, or in neighboring and competing ones, have naturally supplemented their association by day, by association in their evenings or Sundays for the promotion of their common interests. These re-unions began to take the form of regular and permanent organizations in this country early in the nineteenth century. Charters of incorporation were soon granted to such bodies, and they have since shared with all others the privileges of our general incorporation laws. In 1886, the national government took action in the same direction in favor of those labor organizations which branch out in several States. By an Act of Congress of that year,[1] "any association of working people having two or more branches in the States or Territories of the United States for the purpose of aiding its members to become more skillful and efficient workers, the promotion of their general intelligence, the elevation of their character, the regulation of their wages and their hours and conditions of labor, the protection of their individual rights in the prosecution of their trade or trades, the raising of funds for the benefit of sick, disabled, or unemployed members, or the families of deceased members, or for such other object or objects for which working people may lawfully combine, having in view their mutual protection or benefit," is termed a "National Trade Union," and on filing articles of incorporation in the office of the Recorder of the District of Columbia, shall "become a corporation under the technical name by which said National

[1] 24 U. S. Statutes at Large, 86.

Trade Union desires to be known to the trade;" with power "to establish branches and sub-unions in any Territory of the United States."

In England, trades-unions have been legal organizations since 1825; in Italy since 1865; in Prussia since 1866. France adopted the same policy during the Revolution of 1848, and again after the fall of the second empire. It may be said to be the rule of the world that labor is now free to combine for its own protection, and of most countries that it can obtain, if desired, the favor of incorporation on easy terms. The result has been a multitude of incorporated benefit and insurance societies among workingmen, handling considerable funds, accumulated in a common treasury from small dues or assessments contributed by many. In Great Britain four per cent of the entire population belong to some form of labor organization, and in 1883, the aggregate capital of those which give financial aid to their members or their families exceeded two million dollars.

A man who has such means of protection, on which he has the right of a proprietor to rely, against loss of work or of capacity to work, is less likely to lay up any separate capital of his own. He saves enough to pay his weekly dues or occasional death assessments to his society, and spends the rest of his wages, from day to day. If he falls sick, or meets with any accident, — if he joins in a strike or suffers by a lock-out, the society treasury will supply his needs; when he dies, it will pay a considerable sum to his family. What need, then, to scrimp and save? *Dum vivimus vivamus.*

FREEDOM OF INCORPORATION

The social consequences of this condition of things are most marked in the United States. Here, with high wages, cheap food, and low rents, the workman has always had the best chance to raise himself into the position of a capitalist, and formerly often accomplished it. He might do it still, with equal or greater ease, but the motive has been so largely withdrawn, that in cities or manufacturing villages he commonly dies poor, trusting to his benefit society to provide for his family. Ordinarily his trust is not misplaced, but there are not seldom cases, where it is found, when the time for heavy payments comes, that corporate mis-management and reckless investments have led these organizations into insolvency. Failures of this kind again react upon the members, and incline the less serious minded of them still more to the philosophy of Epicureanism. Why save at all for future needs, if their own mates, even, cannot be trusted to keep what is entrusted to their care?

No student of American life has failed to note with regret the rapid decrease, during the latter part of the nineteenth century, of the number of freeholders among our factory operatives. I believe the main cause has been their growing dependence on associated capital, administered by the various forms of mutual aid societies and fraternal or co-operative corporations. "Organized labor" is unfavorable to individuality. It merges the man in a class of men. He is no longer working out his own destiny: others, to whom he gives but slight assistance, are working it out for him, and seeing that it rises no higher than theirs.

FREEDOM OF INCORPORATION 233

To one form of association among workingmen the principle of freedom of incorporation has proved unfriendly. It is that of the voluntary co-operative society. This may have some degree of success, in the absence of competition by corporations in the same business; but only then. If it becomes incorporated in self-defence, it is no better off, unless either the necessary capital is very small, as in the cooper's trade, or it is contributed in unequal shares, and the majority in interest control the management. France, in 1848, tried the experiment of lending such concerns, formed for productive industry, the necessary funds for starting in business. Half a million dollars was advanced to fifty-six of them from the treasury of the republic, but in four years thirty had gone into insolvency, and nearly half of the public money was irretrievably sunk.[1] Co-operative trading societies have also in most cases fallen before the competing corporation; though in England they were of lasting benefit to all the larger towns in forcing the system of selling for cash on the retail stores.

In the matter of political influence, incorporated workingmen's associations have also achieved less than was anticipated. Jealousies between different organizations and among the leaders in each, as well as the strong hold of the great parties of the country upon their members, have stood in the way of united action, except under unusual circumstances and on rare occasions.

[1] Villetard's "History of the International," Day's Transl., 24.

Passing now to the more general question of the reflex influence of the modern corporation upon the economic conditions and administrative policy of the State whose laws gave it its being, we cannot fail to see that it has been an important one, and particularly as to methods of raising revenue.

Rome was a great military power because of its political constitution. It was a collection of great families, each with its throng of poor dependents; each with its single head. Rome knew on whom to call for supplies and troops. The modern State, following on lines that are almost parallel, has found an easy way to raise its taxes; or at least to add to them. Each of its business corporations stands much in the position of the Roman patrician house. Its concentrated capital cannot be concealed. Its political relations to the State, as the holder of a public franchise, place it under a perpetual obligation, for practically, under modern law, the franchise may be withdrawn by the power that granted it, at will. The consequence is that in this country, at least in most of our larger and richer States, the corporation has become the great tax-payer, or to state it perhaps more accurately, the great tax-gatherer.

De Tocqueville, in the first half of this century, noted this as a peculiar feature of the American system of municipal administration. In France, he said, the nation assisted the commune in collecting its revenues: here the town served the same office for the State, the local authorities including in their own tax levy whatever sum the law required the rate-payers of the municipality to contribute to the general government, and as to that taking substantially the position of farmers of the revenue.

During the last half of the century, the immense increase in number and importance of private corporations has worked a great change in this respect. The State has turned to them for the discharge of the function which it before committed to the municipalities. It has thrown upon them, without any intermediate agency, the great weight of State taxation. Its revenue is now largely derived from impositions on railroads, savings banks, insurance companies, and other corporations of lesser magnitude. They of course collect it from the public, with whom they deal, or the capitalists for whom they act, by adding it to the charges for service which they would otherwise make, or deducting it from the interest or dividends which they would otherwise pay.

This policy is economical in one point of view and wasteful in another. It greatly reduces the expenses of public administration. There are fewer tax assessors and tax collectors. There are fewer and richer paymasters, and not one of them can hide himself or his property from the public eye. On the other hand, the revenue is so easily obtained, and those from whom it is really exacted are so far unconscious of their loss, that there is less opposition to free appropriations for unnecessary objects. When the county or town added a certain percentage to the local tax as the contribution of its inhabitants to the expenses of the State, every one of these felt the increase of burden, and looked to his representative in the legislature to see that at least it grew no greater, from year to year. The corporation tax, also, falls more upon the city than the country. It is of little concern to the small farmer who seldom travels by rail, who has no money in the savings bank, no insurance upon his life, and probably none upon his house. Our State legislatures are generally controlled by the agricultural interest, and burdens that do not affect that unfavorably are easily assumed.[1]

No single State can pass a law which will not disturb the equilibrium of its old laws in some unanticipated direction. The civilized world during the nineteenth century has given its sanction to the general incorporation law, and we see its effect on other laws and other interests as yet but " through a glass, darkly." Already the new creatures which it has called forth control its commerce; they conduct its manufactures; exploit its mines; own its timber lands. They name the prices for its agricultural products. We look to them for protection against the casualties of fire, of accidental injury, of death itself. They have charge of our religious worship; of the higher education of our children; of the regulation, largely, of the social duties of those who are fellow-workers in the same calling, both to each other and to the general community.

This vast, impersonal force has grown up so slowly from its Roman foundation, to a work of which the Romans never dreamt, that we find it hard to see how

[1] The new policy was fully adopted by Connecticut, in 1890, when the State tax, which had been annually laid for over 250 years, was abandoned. The expenses of the State in 1889 were about a million and a half. In 1896, they were nearly two millions and a quarter.

far it has stepped outside of its former self. It is harder to forecast its future progress. Is this child of the State, made in its image, sharing its powers and immunities, to grow until it becomes re-united to it, re-absorbed into its being, and the State itself assumes these functions at the cost of all the people, and for the profit of all its people? Or will individualism re-assert itself, and these monster corporations fall to pieces by their own weight to make room, under governments which have no end but to promote the good of their citizens, and already protect property and personal security as never before in human history, for the great man to re-appear in a new race of merchant princes, and railroad kings beholden to no stockholders for their palace cars?

Of these two possibilities the latter is far the more remote. The Barings, early in the century, were heroic adventurers for fortune, but towards its close were glad to seek safety under the mantle of the "Baring Brothers & Co. (Limited)." The "young Napoleon of finance," whose successes dazzled Wall Street not many years ago, soon ended his career in the penitentiary. The Rothschilds are a survival of other days. The Goulds and Vanderbilts have worked through corporations.

The tendencies of our age towards Collectivism for capital demand it both for the accumulation of funds and the aggregation of owners. It is demanded, if for nothing else, because the millionnaire in active business has become an object of general criticism. The corporation doubles its capital, and no one complains. The new stock is widely distributed, and no one man is conspicuous for his ownership. Not so when the millionnaire is known to have laid by another million by some successful enterprise or speculation. He has taken from many. It may be that he has also given to many, but this is forgotten. By a large part of the community he is looked on as a sort of enemy to the human race, who has run up the black flag. His plan may be economical. He has no dividends to pay to others. There is little chance for waste, if he is active and vigilant. But his very activity and vigilance are counted against him by half the world.

Karl Marx, in his *Das Kapital*, says that the natural and inevitable end of modern society is expropriation of the many by a few usurpers, but that this simply makes it easy and certain that a new order of things will follow, beginning with the expropriation of these few usurpers by the many, whom they have been plundering.

If the great operations of modern business were conducted by single capitalists, in their own name and on their own account, there would be much more in this prophecy of socialism. That they are conducted by the corporation and the trust — that is by many for many — takes half the sting out of his saying, half the foundation away from his philosophy.

CHAPTER VII

AMERICAN JURISPRUDENCE [1]

THE truest gauge of a nation's civilization is its system of jurisprudence. It is a thing naturally of slow growth and of upward growth. If it ceases to rise and spread, we have a certain sign that the vital forces of the people are exhausted, for the people are the real sources of what is enduring and uplifting in legal institutions.

The United States and the States of which they are composed are building up on American soil a distinctively American jurisprudence. The great stretch of territory to the north of us is a dependence of a distant government, and looks for leadership there. Our sister republics to the southward have been content, for the most part, to follow the lines of the Roman law. But to us, the spirit of independence that came so early to give life and character to forms of government and judicial establishments, brought with it a transforming power. Latin civilization had lent color to the far south and southwest. The Dutch had brought something of it, and more of their own rugged republicanism, to New York. The Puritans

[1] In preparing this chapter free use has been made of an address by the author, delivered before the Ohio State Bar Association at Put-in-Bay, July 14, 1892.

had learned in Holland much that they afterwards put into the institutions of New England. But it is not what we owe to Spain, or France, or Holland, that has made American so different from English jurisprudence. The nation that has governed itself for more than a century, that has within it States that have governed themselves for more than two centuries, cannot but have a law and life peculiar to itself, the fruit of the ground on which they grew.

It has been said that there is a Great Britain and a Greater Britain. But no one land can now be called our mother country. Once Boston and Philadelphia might well give that name to England, and New Orleans and St. Louis to France; but now, when, if we count by nationalities, there are few cities in Germany containing more of German birth than does New York or Cincinnati, and few in Norway with a Norse population like that of some of our Northwestern towns; when the best half of Ireland is in America; when the face and tongue of the Italian and the Hungarian have become familiar on our streets, — we may say, with Cicero, that we have ourselves commenced our line of ancestry.

There is to rise here, Herbert Spencer has told us, from the mixture of allied varieties of the Aryan race, a finer type of man than has hitherto existed, — a type more plastic, more capable of the modifications needed for the completer social life that is to come. For this new race we are to prepare the way; and we and those who went before us have prepared it by the foundation of a broader and humaner jurisprudence.

Into the law of nations we of America have introduced the principle of voluntary expatriation. It is, indeed, the condition of our existence. The doctrine of perpetual allegiance was undisputed in the Old World. Its application to Americans by the British Crown was one of the grievances recited in the Declaration of Independence; but we ourselves asserted its obligation long after independence had been achieved.

Jeremiah Mason once said that the development of an American jurisprudence could only be looked for from the courts of the national government. Upon this question, however, it was a court of a State, that of Pennsylvania,[1] which, following the language of her Constitution, framed by Franklin, first declared expatriation an original and indefeasible right of man; and this at a time when those of the United States adhered to the rules of the common law.[2] Thus it was left to Congress to affirm by statute the American principle, as soon as the nation felt strong enough to assert it against the world,[3] and treaties which have been made, in pursuance of this declaration, have now obtained its recognition in almost every country that can call itself civilized.

This new rule of American jurisprudence is the work of the bar, rather than the courts. Its earliest supporters were Adams and Jefferson, and to our Attorney-Generals, and the great lawyers who, from time to time, have had the direction of the Department of State, we owe especially its international authority.

---

[1] Murray v. McCarthy, 2 Munford's Reports, 393.
[2] Williams' Case, Wharton's State Trials, 652.
[3] U. S. Revised Statutes, § 1999; Act of 1868.

For ourselves, also, we have changed the law of nations as to treaty obligations, in its fundamental conception. Treaties are not for us mere contracts, with no higher sanction than the military power of the other government. The Constitution of the United States has raised them to the position of the supreme law of the land, as binding as an Act of Congress in every American court.

Passing from the relations of States to States, to those of the State to its own citizens, we find a distinctively American system of criminal procedure.

We have viewed the punishment of crime from a new standpoint, that of the reformer. Nine-tenths of those who, in England a hundred years ago, would have been hanged, have been here, instead, condemned to labor for a term of years in what we have named, with kindly hope, a penitentiary. Pennsylvania was the first of civilized communities to inaugurate this change, under her Constitution of 1776.[1] The release of one convicted of crime on probation, under a suspension of sentence, also, and reformatories for young offenders, are distinctively American innovations.[2]

It is difficult for men of our day to believe how much of "man's inhumanity to man" was shown in the criminal law of England, when the institutions of this country first took shape. The common law was rigorous enough, but in the days of the Stuarts and the Georges the number of capital offences was in-

[1] 2 Poore's "Charters and Constitutions," 1547.
[2] See Chapter IX.

AMERICAN JURISPRUDENCE

creased by nearly two hundred. It was not until the beginning of this century that hanging ceased to be the punishment of a pickpocket.

To arrest a man on a charge of crime was almost equivalent to a conviction, for he could produce no witnesses in his own behalf, nor have counsel to plead his cause. It makes one's blood boil in his veins to read one of the shorthand reports of the State trials of the seventeenth century: such, for instance, as that of Stephen College, at Oxford. If a conviction did not lead to the gibbet, the criminal was either transported or turned loose on the community after some mark of bodily degradation, perhaps with his ears cropped, or a hand struck off, to fix the memory of his shame upon him as long as life should last. Degrees of punishment for the greater crimes were marked simply by the degrees of barbarity with which the wretch was executed. Hanging was, indeed, a mild penalty, when compared with burning, quartering, and disembowelling.

Not until the great popular movement which found voice in the Reform Bill, and has made England more of a democracy than the United States, were these cruelties swept away from English law.

But in guarding against their presence here, American jurisprudence may have gone too far. To forbid the examination of the accused by torture, or under any form of compulsion, was right; but was it necessary to forbid the committing magistrate to ask him anything, except whether he admits or denies the charge? I believe we have put the State at a disadvantage in preventing it from calling upon the prisoner to give an account of the transaction out of which the charge arose — to tell his own story in his own way, knowing that whatever he says may be used against him on the trial.[1] And is there a reason which is really good for giving the convict an appeal to our highest courts on the most trivial points of law, when the rights of the public are generally determined finally by the trial judge? It is this over-kindness to the individual, to the prejudice of the State, which renders possible, and, as many say, defensible, such things as the killing of the Italians at New Orleans, and the lynch-law executions that, in some of our States, outnumber, every year, those had pursuant to the sentence of the courts.

In one respect, our criminal law is perhaps less favorable to the accused than was that of England. We adopted early the Continental method of prosecutions by public officers, instead of leaving them to be brought or dropped according to the dictates of personal feeling, or the desire for pecuniary reparation.

The strength and value of government by party have led us to place party conventions under the protection of the criminal laws. Fraud in balloting at a nominating caucus is punished in the same way as frauds at public elections. A new order of rights is recognized: those which flow from the duty of political organization; for it is the duty of every citizen to use his elective franchise in the most effective way.

[1] See Chapter V.

That way, the law feels, is through party combinations, and therefore our jurisprudence is enlarged to embrace their recognition and protection.

The law of libel, in any government, is one of the surest tests by which to estimate its hold upon the people. The United States were the first to renounce, for their rulers, the protection of this law. When the decemvirs were framing the Twelve Tables of Rome, few as were the subjects they thought it important to cover in their code, they were careful to make libel against the State a capital offence; for they were the State, and they were turning a republic into a despotism. When the people of England were beginning to demand a greater share in her government, it was the law of libel to which the Crown resorted for its surest weapon of defence, and it was the pride of the English bar that, in criminal cases, they nullified it by the aid of the jury. With us, to the United States the law of libel is unknown, because they have no common law, and because the only statute ever passed by Congress to replace it, on this subject, was swept away in the first change of administration, and, indeed, in no small part was the cause of that change of administration; while in our States we have almost everywhere come to the position that, both in civil and criminal cases, truth is a justification, unless actual malice is proved.

We have ventured farther than any nation ever dared to go before in forbidding all *ex post facto* laws; and this and other guaranties of individual right we have woven into our written constitutions, so as to make them the supreme law, as unalterable as the frame of government itself.

In the same irrevocable way we have severed the relations of Church and State.

The famous definition of jurisprudence given by the Roman law, that it is *divinarum atque humanarum rerum notitia, justi atque injusti scientia*, has been sharply attacked by modern critics, as confusing notions of law and religion. But in what nation, before our own, were law and religion ever separated in their relations to the State? From the first beginnings of patriarchal society the world has looked at them as coming from a common source, upheld by a common sanction, and forming parts of the same administration of government. The authority of each was deemed necessary to support the other.

First of nations, the United States, without the least reflection on religion of any form, severed the Church from the State, and freed the current of its jurisprudence from all ecclesiastical control.

Nor has this mutual independence been found incompatible with restraining power in the civil courts where private rights were affected by unjust acts of those in ecclesiastical authority. In the organization of the great mother church of Christendom, the bishop has the power to remove any priest in his diocese from his parish, at his discretion. An American bishop exercised this power, for what seemed to him sufficient cause, but without notice or hearing. The priest applied to the courts for redress, and it was held, in granting it, that though it might be according to the laws of that church to deprive a man of his livelihood, on a charge of failure in duty, unheard, it was not in accordance with the laws of the land.[1]

The jurisprudence of most countries has been based on the conception of the rights of the State as against individuals. American jurisprudence rests equally on the rights of the citizen against the State. We believe that the State owes an active duty to its people, and that its welfare is only important as reflecting theirs.

I have spoken of our public prosecutors for wrongs to individuals. Their appointment is but one illustration of a principle of American government which demands that all business, in the well doing of which the public have an interest, shall be done by or under the inspection of a public officer, and so that the public may have full knowledge of it. This has brought a new security to landed interests. It makes it possible for any man of ordinary education to trace a land title, because the material is at his command, systematically arranged, in a public record office, not stored in some muniment chest in an old tower, nor even buried in the files of a notary, whose position is but half official.

Our rules of civil procedure are our own. A few States may still adhere in name to the cumbrous methods of English origin, but in most we have, and

[1] O'Hara v. Slack, 90 Pennsylvania State Reports, 477.

in all soon shall have, the simple rules of what, for want of a better name, we call Code Pleading. Originating in New York, not fifty years ago, it has, in the lifetime of its distinguished author, David Dudley Field, not only overspread a large part of our own country, but supplanted the forms of the common law in the very land of their birth.

Our attachment to the principle of personal liberty has modified the law of civil process. Insolvent debtors had been treated in most countries as a kind of criminals. America began to open their prison doors, at the era of the Revolution.[1] It has led to the extension of liberty of contract. It encouraged us to initiate a new policy which the world has copied, that of giving free liberty of incorporation to all who wish it, on equal terms, under general laws.[2]

The law of evidence has been changed in a vital point. In no country before our own has every man been admitted as a witness in court. There have been distinctions of class, exclusions from interest, exclusions for infamy.

American jurisprudence is unwilling to condemn the lowest or worst of men unheard; it is unwilling to believe that pecuniary interest necessarily leads men to forswear themselves, or to assume that every party to a suit would naturally perjure himself to get a verdict. The Roman law and the rules of English Chancery allowed you to force an oath upon your

---

[1] See the Constitution of Pennsylvania of 1776, art. 1, sec. 28; 2 Poore's "Charters and Constitutions," p. 1546.

[2] See Chapter VI.

adversary, but only at the cost of making him, so to speak, your own witness. We have done more wisely, I think, in admitting testimony from all, on equal terms, leaving it for the triers to give it, in each case, such weight as it may deserve. The first statute of this kind in America was enacted in Connecticut, in 1848. Its author[1] soon afterwards went abroad in the diplomatic service, and, when in England, brought it to the attention of some men of influence, through whose efforts an Act of Parliament, of a similar nature (14 & 15 Vict., ch. 99) was passed in 1851.

We have given a new character to trial by jury.

The right of the jury to judge of the law we have extended to all criminal cases, and the Continental plan of giving them partial control over the sentence, in case of conviction, has been extensively followed.

The authority of the court has also been weakened in civil cases, by securing greater privileges to the bar in shaping the terms of the charge. The dangers of these changes in the jury system were forcibly portrayed in a paper read before the American Bar Association, by Mr. Justice Brown of the Supreme Court of the United States, in 1889.[2] This mode of trial, as it existed at common law, was well adapted to secure the rights of the masses against the classes. But it was a system of exact balances. It demanded a free and fearless judge as well as a free and fearless jury. The jury may drag the car of justice, but the

[1] The late Charles J. McCurdy, LL.D., afterwards an Associate Judge of the Supreme Court of Errors of Connecticut.
[2] Reports of the American Bar Association, xii. 265.

judge must drive, or they will drag it to destruction. The inroads of the bar upon his prerogatives seem to me a mark of what I venture to term, on the whole, the degrading effects of the American plan of an elective judiciary. It indicates a distrust of the independence or the intelligence of the court. It foreshadows the gradual extinction of the jury trial in civil causes; because that can never be permanently satisfactory unless a large discretion, not to say despotism, is left in the hands of the thirteenth man.

We have given, I cannot but think, an undue prominence to judicial precedents as a natural source or enunciation of the law. The multiplication of distinct sovereignties in the same land, each fully officered, and each publishing in official form the opinions of its courts of last resort, bewilders the American lawyer in his search for authority. The guiding principles of our law are few and plain. Their application to the matter he may have in hand it is his business to make, and if he spent more time in doing it himself, and less in endeavoring to find how other men had done it in other cases, he would, I believe, be better prepared to inform the court and serve his client.

There have been lawyers bold enough to attack bad precedents in our highest courts and to destroy them. A conspicuous instance of coming to a right decision by overturning a wrong one is furnished by the history of the Supreme Court of the United States. In 1825, a libel in admiralty for seamen's wages, earned upon a steamer on the Missouri River, was dismissed

AMERICAN JURISPRUDENCE 251

for want of jurisdiction, and, on appeal, Mr. Justice Story delivered the unanimous opinion of the court, that admiralty furnished no remedies for services that were not rendered on tide-water.

There was no better authority for this than that such had been the rule of the English Admiralty. But a quarter of a century later the same court speaking through a greater though less learned judge, and with but one dissenting voice, reversed their position, and declared that America could not adopt the English definition, by which, in the terse phrase of the Chief Justice, "the description of a public navigable river was substituted in the place of the thing intended to be described." This last decision in the case of *The Genesee Chief* illustrates the manner in which the development of our law has been affected as time has gone on by changes in our commercial conditions, and perhaps in our national mode of thought. During the last half century there has been a gradual but marked substitution of practical for theoretical canons of decision. This freer spirit of selection and adaptation has done much to differentiate our law of private corporations from that of England, and to make the English reports of continually decreasing value as authorities here. The practical necessities of the case have driven American courts to extend to private business corporations the general Chancery doctrine applicable to charitable corporations, that the managing officers or directors occupy the position of trustees. The English courts admit the trust relation as regards the shareholders, but deny it as respects the creditors of the company.[1] And as to the latter, we ourselves have begun to doubt whether our decisions have not gone too far, and to draw the line between transactions attacked by creditors who were such before the thing was done, and those impeached only by parties to whom the corporation became afterwards indebted, as well as to limit the "trust-fund doctrine" to concerns already in the hands of a court of equity or insolvency for winding up.[2]

We have also from the first sought for the powers of a corporation in its charter, and denied it any which were not in that either given or implied. The English courts have held to the assumption that a corporation has all the powers which it has not been forbidden to exercise. The difference is wide, and has done much to lead England to that distrust and jealousy of corporations which has marked her legislation upon that subject from early days.

The case of *The Genesee Chief*[3] to which allusion has been made, is one of the eight or ten decisions that stand out as the great landmarks of American jurisprudence. I should put first in time that of *Marbury v. Madison*,[4] in which Marshall asserted the right of the courts to declare any statute void which was in conflict with the Constitution. The second place I would assign to *Fletcher v. Peck*,[5] where a private individual was protected against the revocation of a public grant.

[1] Poole's Case, Law Reports, 3 Chancery Division, 322.
[2] Hollins *v.* Brierfield Coal & Iron Co., 150 United States Reports, 371.
[3] 12 Howard's Reports, 455.   [4] 1 Cranch's Reports, 137.
[5] 6 Cranch's Reports, 87.

Then comes *Dartmouth College* v. *Woodward*,[1] in which Marshall read into the words of the Constitution a meaning which he admitted might never have been thought of by the men who framed or the people who ratified it. It made the subjection of the sovereign State to the performance of its obligations, at the command of the civil court, a rule of our jurisprudence. It brought a new theory of corporate rights into existence. If they rested on a public contract, that contract the public must perform.

To *Milligan's Case*[2] we turn when we seek the limitations of individual liberty in time of war; to *Cummings* v. *Missouri*[3] for its safeguards against *ex post facto* legislation. The *Slaughter House Cases*[4] brought sharply out the distinctions between the citizen of a State and the citizen of the United States. In *Loan Association* v. *Topeka*,[5] those limitations on the legislative power, which are inherent in the nature of a free government, are stated with telling force, in their bearing on questions of a public use.

There are other decisions of the Supreme Court of the United States which are as often referred to as these, because they settle hard-fought controversies over the meaning of our Constitution in its political aspects. Those that have been mentioned are of especial note in their bearing on the relation of the law to the individual.

That a woman is an individual, even if she be a wife, and does not forfeit her personal identity by

[1] 4 Wheaton's Reports, 518.
[2] 4 Wallace's Reports, 2-124. [3] *Ibid.*, 277.
[4] 16 Wallace's Reports, 78. [5] 20 Wallace's Reports, 655.

marriage, is another of the positions of American law.

Our treatment of the property relations of husband and wife, as it is now fixed by the statutes of most of our States, is almost as far from the Roman or Continental as from the English rule. Its principle is not community but independence.

This separation of property rights is but one of the inroads made by American law on what had been regarded throughout Christendom as the natural characteristics of the marriage relation.

The Church of Rome had declared marriage to be a sacrament, and indissoluble except by its authority. The Protestants of the Reformation denied this, and, under the Puritans, civil marriages and civil divorces were early American institutions. With the gradual extension of the causes of divorce, and the gradual abbreviation of the trial of a divorce case in our courts, all are now familiar. There have been countries before in which divorce was as free in law, but none where it has been so free in fact. For five hundred years the Roman husband could put away his wife at will, and for five hundred years only one availed himself of his right, and he was, like Napoleon, unwillingly driven to it by the demands of the State.

It seems to me that the number of causes of divorce recognized in American law might well be substantially reduced. Indeed, a movement in this direction has been made, which within the past twenty years has had considerable success. There is a National Divorce Reform League, which has been active and successful, and only three States[1] now retain the "omnibus" clause in their divorce statutes, which permits divorces for any cause satisfactory to the court.

But the evils of our divorce system lie quite as much in our method of procedure. A recent report on this subject by the Commissioner of Labor of the United States showed that a fifth of all American divorces are granted to parties who were married in some other jurisdiction. It is well known how short a residence on the part of the petitioner is generally made sufficient, and on how slight a notice to a non-resident respondent, the court proceeds. Such a notice is always dictated in the first instance by the petitioner's attorney, and his discretion in the matter is seldom revised, if he keeps within the letter of the law, however improbable it may be that the other party has in fact any knowledge of the proceeding.

So far as divorces obtained on default, upon newspaper publication, against non-residents, are concerned, the general rule of jurisprudence, here and everywhere, is that they are totally void, unless the petitioner was domiciled within the jurisdiction of the court, or the marriage was celebrated there. Just such American divorces have been disregarded in England and in Canada, and a second marriage by the divorced party treated as bigamy.[2] The American Bar Association, ten years ago, drafted a statute to remedy this evil, by making domicile, instead of

[1] Washington, Kentucky, and Rhode Island.
[2] Briggs v. Briggs, English Law Reports, 5 Probate and Divorce, 163.

residence, the test of jurisdiction, which has been adopted in two States.[1]

I have sought to state only such of the leading features of American jurisprudence as are not found in other systems or not found under similar conditions. One may be added of minor importance, but interesting, as the natural and spontaneous growth of the soil. It is the new rule of partnership law by which the death of a partner in a mine does not dissolve the partnership. The rough and dangerous life of the mining camp demanded the innovation and obtained it, at the hand of the courts, without aid from statute.

The drift of American jurisprudence, particularly in the Pacific States and the New West, is towards the expression of the law in an orderly and official form; in other words, towards codification. It has approached the question from the practical side, and in a practical way. The early colonies soon put their scanty statutes into print, arranged in some convenient way for ready reference, the various heads often following each other in alphabetical order, as in our digests of reports. New York led the way towards a more systematic and comprehensive treatment of the subject, by her Revised Statutes of 1827, — a revision which, though in many points revolutionary, was so well considered and well done that it has held the ground for over half a century, while in most of our States revision succeeds revision every ten or fifteen years.

[1] Minnesota and New Hampshire.

But there is nothing distinctively American in codification. It is simply un-English. It is the natural aim and end of every system of jurisprudence,—of jurisprudence itself, apart from any particular system of it. Jurisprudence is the science of law, and the orderly statement of its rules can be called by no better name than Code.

I have used the term "American jurisprudence" as meaning the scientific conception of that system of law judicially administered within the United States,— not alone the science of American law, or the science of law as applied to America. It is the judicial administration of law which, with us especially, gives it a character and vitality of its own.

It was a true and profound remark of De Tocqueville, that the extension of judicial power in the political world ought to be in the exact ratio of the extension of elective offices; for if these two institutions do not go hand in hand, the State must fall into anarchy or into subjection.

Our county courts, our justices of the peace, with combined administrative and judicial functions, our judge-made law, our Constitutions, as interpreted and expanded from the bench into something far wiser and better than their builders knew, these, quite as much as our printed statute-books, are the sources and safeguards of our rights and liberties.

There are few countries where the removal of public officials is as difficult, often as impossible, as with us. There is no country where the power of the courts to direct their action and to punish their misconduct is as great.

Nor is it the executive office only which is thus amenable to judicial control. The subjection of the legislature to written rules, enforceable by the courts, is a feature peculiar to American jurisprudence.

The honor of framing the first written constitution of government which deserves that name, belongs, I believe, to the early settlers on the banks of the Connecticut; but it was not till another century that we find the judiciary recognized as the guardians of Constitutions, and, as such, the superiors of the legislature.

It is a power that could only be intrusted to a trained bench of trained lawyers, and which could only be exercised in a land where government is settled on deep foundations and protected by the free force of public opinion. It has given birth to what is really a new science of political law, for constitutional law, as we use that term, is wholly an American creation. This function assigned by us to the judiciary has found no place in the institutions of our sister American republics. Colombia has made it the subject of a singular compromise in her Constitution of 1886.[1] No bill can become a law without the approval of the President of the republic, unless passed over his veto by a two-thirds vote. If his disapproval should be based on the belief that it is unconstitutional, the Supreme Court are to decide within six days whether his opinion is well founded. If they agree with him, the bill fails; if they hold it constitutional, it becomes

[1] Supplement to Annals of the Am. Academy of Political and Social Science, 1893, pp. 38, 56.

the law. The judges are thus brought, in a most objectionable manner, into direct and public collisions either with the executive or the legislature. Such a device only belongs to a country whose history is that of revolutions.

The occasional and peaceful exercise of the active sovereignty of the people in direct legislation, through special delegates meeting for a special purpose, is an American idea, — American, that is, as applied to governments embracing an extensive territory and founded on representative institutions. The city-State could furnish no precedent for us, and we were equally remote from that state of society which Tacitus describes as existing in his day among our Teutonic ancestors: "*De minoribus principes consultant: de majoribus omnes.*"

We call upon the people to act only on matters of fundamental law. In our constitutional conventions they resume, at long intervals, for a few weeks' time, their delegated powers, and re-found the State.

Conventions of the people, national assemblies, are common enough in history, but their work has been, or come to be, that of revolution. Our sister republic, France, has not ventured to follow us in trusting the people with this great power, and in waiting for them to act, whatever the emergency may be. Her plan is that if each house of the legislature deems a revision of the Constitution necessary, they may meet at once in joint assembly and effect it by a bare majority.

A direct reference to the people, at the polls, of proposed changes of a constitutional character is also one of our American institutions. The Colony of Connecticut introduced it during the seventeenth century, and it was incorporated in the Constitution of the State, in 1818.[1] It has become familiar in European practice, under the Swiss system of the *referendum*, but perverted to the questionable use of submitting mere questions of administrative policy to popular decision.

This system of American jurisprudence whose lines I have tried to trace, is the living voice of the American bar, — of the American bar of many generations. The spoken word, uttered by a Thomas Lechford, or James Otis, or Patrick Henry, or John Marshall, in other days, may be forgotten. But, if it stirred men's hearts; if it sank into men's minds; if it carried conviction; if it was the foundation of verdicts and judgments, customs and statutes, the circle of its influence is widening still.

There are those who tell us that all that is said on earth, when it dies to the human ear, floats on, upon the wings of air, to remain forever a witness for or against us, in the life beyond. It may be so; but whether physical force be or be not eternal and inextinguishable, it is so that the influence of human thought in the development of institutions will last as long as the history of civilization.

The science of American jurisprudence is just

[1] Papers of the New Haven Colony Historical Society, v. 182.

beginning to crystallize into form. The new race, whose character it speaks, is still but half developed.

The bar in this is their mouth-piece. The practising lawyer finds his days passing all too swiftly in the common routine of the office and the court-room; and as he is advising his clients, or advocating their causes, hardly feels that he is doing anything which can outlive the occasion that calls it forth. But the consultation, the argument, the opinion, by which the conduct of men, the disposition of controversies or their prevention, is determined, have an influence wider than we think.

These are the materials from which is being built up, by slow and imperceptible accretion, a new jurisprudence. The philosophy of the law must be founded on the practice of the law.

Others in after years may be the ones to trace out the succession and growth of general ideas, to formulate propositions, to array conclusions in scientific arrangement; but, after all, what they give is only form. The substance of our jurisprudence must be the work of the plain, average American lawyer. It is a monument like the great pyramid, to perpetuate, not the names of those who made it, but, what is better, their work; and, better still, it is not to perpetuate all their work, but only what was best in it.

It has been finely said by one of the first of living American jurists [1] that, "The glory of lawyers, like

---

[1] Judge Oliver Wendell Holmes.

that of men of science, is more corporate than individual. Our labor is an endless organic process. The organism whose being is recorded and protected by the law is the undying body of society."

This work in America began with the first beginnings of its history, and will continue till that history ends. It has had at all times the stamp of individuality. It has called no man master. It has never copied where it served its purpose better to originate. It struck out primogeniture because it believed an equal distribution of property the best foundation of republican government. It forced every deed on record, without respect to feelings of family pride. It brought justice within the reach of every man by a system of county courts and magistracies, under which the judge comes to meet the parties, instead of forcing them to travel to the seat of government.

It is now perplexing the national judiciary, as they are called on to declare the limits of public management of private property. Must a man, whose business has been established under one law, submit, uncompensated, to its destruction by another? Can a State demand of its railroads that they shall reduce their fares or freight-charges so low as to preclude a dividend upon their stock? Can it require them to build new stations, or reconstruct their roadbed, with no regard to their financial ability? Is the police power of a State susceptible of legal definition — that is, of legal restraint? Such questions are now occupying and often dividing the Supreme Court of the United States. They are peculiar to our system of government. They illustrate its merits and its defects. They are but the latest instances of a long series of great judicial problems which have arisen under our institutions, and which could have arisen nowhere else.

For the first of them we may look back to the very beginning of our colonial records. Nor need we be surprised that American jurisprudence should have taken, so early, a trend and aspect of its own. The general circulation of ideas, the general diffusion of knowledge, that was rendered possible by the invention of printing, was not rendered practicable until books became so plenty as to be cheap, and instead of being published in Latin, were given to the common people in their own language. This time came to England about three hundred years ago. The Elizabethan age was a creative age in literature and philosophy, and the English, who planted our first colonies, came here under the influence of its inspiration. Their business was to found governments; their literature was statute law; their gathering-place, if not the church, was the court-room or the town-meeting. Such men, thrown upon their own resources, under new conditions of society, could not fail to make a better law for themselves than they could find anywhere, whether in use or in history.

The political and commercial differences between the English colonies and England, which showed themselves as soon as property began to accumulate here, and which culminated in our independence, kept alive this spirit of free inquiry into the reason and causes of things.

The repellent influences of the Revolution taught us to look more to the Continent for our examples. Montesquieu's *Esprit des Lois*, published about the middle of the last century, had a profound effect throughout America. The same may be said of Beccaria's work on Crimes and Punishments, which appeared twenty years later. Then came the French alliance, and the French ideas that Jefferson and Franklin brought home from a long residence abroad. And from those days to these, not only have Americans been familiar with what comparative legislation has to teach, but they themselves have been growing more and more into a new, composite nationality, the roots of which strike back into every land whose institutions are in sympathy with the spirit of modern civilization.

Our system of jurisprudence has been built up during an era of ever-increasing power and prosperity — the glad youth of a new race. It has served us well thus far. Will it be found equally adapted to those other days that are sure to come, when a denser population will crowd the land; when immigration is discouraged or repelled; when there are no more virgin forests or virgin fields; when, perhaps, added duties of the general government give it a still greater weight, relatively to the States?

So far as we can forecast this future, it may, I believe, be our hope and our confidence that the forces of universal education, and of universal suffrage, bringing individual responsibility, will keep it in healthy and symmetric growth.

The American race has built up an American jurisprudence. It knows its value. It will modify it, as new conditions arise, but it will never surrender its essential characteristics, its spirit of self-reliance, its principle of equal, even-handed justice to all.

CHAPTER VIII

THE DECADENCE OF THE LEGAL FICTION[1]

NO student of political science or legal history is ignorant of the large part which fictions of law have assumed in the development of both. The steps of human progress are slow and uneven, and those who direct it have often found that the shortest way is not the straightest. The legal fiction is the invention of a rude people struggling towards the light. It comes from rulers who find the existing law not sufficiently pliant to serve their purposes. They may be kings, or priests, or judges. They may be the power behind the throne, the altar, or the bench: commonly they are; and it is to lawyers acting, not as the court, but as the advisers or officers of the court, that most legal fictions now in use owe their beginning.

Law and society are the two forces that produce government, and they seldom pull together. One or the other is in the advance. One or the other must always be in the advance, dragging the other after it, as best it may, save under those governments which are at the dead level of low-tide or of high-tide. In the masterly chapter of his "Ancient Law," in which Sir Henry Maine touches this general question, he

[1] In discussing this topic use has been made of an address delivered by the author before the Tennessee State Bar Association, on Lookout Mountain, in 1884.

THE LEGAL FICTION 267

tells us that the gap between them, in the past history of progressive nations, has always been filled by the agency of three things: Legal Fictions, Equity, and Legislation, succeeding each other in that order, the roughest first. Not, of course, that development by legal fictions stops when equitable principles are first adopted, or that equity cannot be embodied in statute form. All these devices may be resorted to at the same period, and in disposing of the same case; but the origin of each is at a different epoch.

In all English-speaking peoples of our day it is society which is ever in the lead; law which is ever holding back — as the conservative force, as the representative of the past. Our race in the past found legal fictions so useful in the development of its system of public administration that it multiplied them, more rapidly than any other people. Of late it has shed them more rapidly than any people.

That the king can do no wrong was one of them. Put in the form of an axiom, it long had the force of one, and became almost an article of faith for half of England. It did not survive the Stuarts as a national belief, but as the expression of a sound maxim of national policy, it did, and, as such, is still the foundation of her system of government by a responsible ministry.

A legal fiction may take the shape of a judicial presumption, which it is not permissible to controvert. Title by prescription or adverse possession was originally rested on the assumption that there must have been a grant, the evidence of which had been lost, of what had been long and peaceably enjoyed. There are few titles that could be traced far back without reliance on this means of support. Every one knows that, in fact, there was often no grant, but a mere usurpation, — that too often "property is robbery." In many cases it would be possible to prove this with absolute certainty; but no such proof is allowed. It was excluded, in early times, by force of the fiction of a lost grant, because that was the easiest mode of satisfying the popular conscience. In our day, it is excluded because all men have come to agree that it is a necessary rule of public policy that long continued and undisturbed possession should be defended at all costs.

Legal procedure in the English courts was long disgraced by fictions of mere convenience, sanctioned by courts that were anxious to extend their jurisdiction by indirect or covert means. Many of these were copied in America. Writs, judgments, and indictments were alike full of them. One could not sue for the value of an article which had been lent and carelessly destroyed, without setting up that it had been lost and casually found by the defendant, and that he had afterwards converted it to his own use. An action to compel the payment of a disputed claim could only be maintained upon the statement that there had been a promise to pay the money, although in fact it was not pretended that such a promise was ever made.

Most of these legal fictions have gradually faded out of existence during the last half century. They have perished by a biologic law, as applicable to legal conceptions as to physical beings. They were incapable of adjustment to their environment in modern society.

Maine has said that " no institution of the primitive world is likely to have been preserved to our day, unless it has acquired an elasticity foreign to its original nature, through some vivifying legal fiction."[1] If this be so, it is also true that no such institution can flourish in a civilized community of our day, unless it can throw off its form of fiction, and found itself on solid reasons and sober truth. The " common recovery" by which a fictitious suit was so long allowed to change the course of succession to landed property, was a convenient means of accomplishing a desirable end, but its basis of false assumptions made it intolerable to modern England, and it gave place sixty years ago, by Act of Parliament, to the " disentailing deed."[2] Where a statute can thus perpetuate a policy which is found in accordance with the social ideas of an age later than that which gave it origin, a legal fiction dies like the phœnix, to live again in higher form. But that which does not merit the sanction of legislation seldom ought to be retained by the sufferance of courts.

A few such still linger as a reproach to American law. One may serve to illustrate the rest, and it is one to which I particularly desire to direct attention in the hope that this may assist in forwarding its ultimate disappearance. It has served its day, and is embedded in our jurisprudence only as the fossil shell of a distant age.

---

[1] Ancient Law, chap. viii. p. 256.
[2] By a statute of 3 & 4 William IV.

I refer to insanity as a legal fiction. It bridged the way for us, as it did for the Romans, from rude conditions of society to better ones; but the bridge is passed and nothing is to be risked by burning it behind us.

The significance of human acts is their intent. A man really does only what he means to do. It is all he can do, and all he can be held, in the forum of conscience, responsible for doing. The only absolute proof of an absence of intent is by showing an incapacity of forming it. The sane man may at times intentionally do very unreasonable and very wrong things. The insane man never can; because to him there is no reason and no wrong.

What wonder, then, that under a criminal code of great severity, yet acknowledging to the fullest extent that *actus non facit reum, nisi mens sit rea*, the English bar should have early resorted to the plea of insanity, when there was little to sustain it but the sympathy of the jury and the eloquence of the advocate? What wonder that the coroner's inquests of a land where suicide doomed a man's family to beggary, and his corpse to outrage, should seize upon the same device to protect his grave, transparent as the veil might be? What wonder that the will that stripped wife and children of their just expectations was by the same makeshift set aside in favor of the distribution made by law?

It is no wonder that these precedents are stamped deep upon the pages of English law. It was the natural and happy expedient by which outgrown statutes, that Parliament refused to alter, were forbidden by English judges and English lawyers to oppress the innocent.

But it was still, at best, a pious fraud. It would have been unworthy of a people who controlled their own legislation. It was the protest of the community against statutes that they could not alter and would not obey. We have no such excuse for perpetuating the era of legal fiction. Our legislatures are the quick reflex of public sentiment, too ready to stamp with their approval anything that their leaders can suggest.

Has not the time fully come when the American lawyer should be relieved from ever claiming insanity when he knows that it does not exist?

Take, first, the case of a hard will, which thrusts aside children in favor of strangers, or enriches one at the expense of others more deserving but less importunate.

It is no new case. Every will disturbs what the law deems the natural course of descent, and many wills, from earliest times, among all nations, have disturbed it unreasonably. What remedy did Rome, the great mother of most modern law, have to suggest? A formal suit, called the complaint of an undutiful will, which was known in practice at least as early as the best days of the republic.[1] In this action, the contestant did not claim that what was propounded as a will was no will, but that it was an unreasonable will.

Rome, too, was originally forced in framing her

[1] Heineccius, *Antiq. Rom.*, lib. ii. tit. 17, § 5.

writ to resort to the legal fiction that the remedy rested on the ground that the testator's mind could not have been well-balanced; but this pretence was soon virtually abandoned.

"The action concerning undutiful wills," says Marcian,[1] "sets up a colorable ground, as if the testator was not of sound mind enough to make a will. And this is said, not as though he were truly a madman or demented, for his will he has indeed made well enough as a will, but not in accordance with the duty of natural affection; for if he were truly a madman or demented, there is no will."

To say that a will was undutiful was to say that some one had been improperly disinherited or passed over, which, said Marcellus, often happens when parents act under some false prejudice against their children. You might claim that a will was void, or that it had been revoked, or that it was undutiful, but you could not make all these claims at the same time. Each must be heard and decided by itself.[2] The legatee who attacked the will as undutiful, and lost his case, lost his legacy too, unless he abandoned the attack as soon as the defence appeared to be well founded.[3]

Nor did Roman law stop here. The legacies which could be charged on the executor and residuary legatee, who was generally the next heir, were restricted in amount by a succession of statutes, and finally limited, in the time of the early empire, so as never to exceed three-quarters of the net estate.[4]

[1] Digest, v. 2, *de inofficioso Testamento*, 2.
[2] Dig. v. 2, 12.   [3] Dig. v. 2, 14.   [4] Dig. v. 2, 9.

Similar provisions are to be found in most countries of modern Europe,—in most civilized countries of the modern world. They were brought into English law by the Normans, and remained there until the days of Henry VIII.

"Let the goods of gavelkynd persons," says the old Custumal of Kent, also, "be parted into three parts, after the funerals and debts paid, if there be lawful issue in life; so that the dead have one part and his lawful sons and daughters another part, and the wife the third part; and if there be no lawful issue in life, let the dead have one-half and the wife alive the other half."[1]

No doubt these limitations on the power of bequest originated in nations where the family, rather than the individual, was the unit of society. But be the political theory of government what it may, we never can eradicate family affection and family duty from their dominant position among the controlling forces of civilization. They must be recognized, and they must be protected. The father who causelessly disinherits a dutiful child commits a wrong which, in some way, governments must redress. The Parliament of England, in the Statute of Wills, might sweep the old way out of the common law, and provide no other; but this simply left it for the people and the lawyers of England to devise some new mode of protection. They devised the fiction of insanity, and for three hundred years they and we have gone on, solemnly setting aside wills of unreasonable men on the pretence that they were insane men.

[1] Crabbe, Hist. Eng. Law, 93.

May it not be wiser to-day to acknowledge that in this matter, as in some others, Henry VIII. was wrong and the world right? Some of our States have already moved in this direction. In many, of late years, we find statutes limiting bequests to public charities; in a few, statutes guaranteeing a certain portion of the estate to the children, if any there be. There will be more such laws as time goes on; and as their legitimate result, there will be less of legal fiction in our probate courts.

Next come a class of cases where the compassion of a coroner's jury has been accustomed to hide itself behind the verdict of temporary insanity.

In ancient times we all know that suicide was looked on with no unkindly eye. No man, they said, could rightly complain that his life was miserable, since he had it in his own power at any time to open the door and step out of it. That is no prison which one can leave at will. The Greek and Roman moralists did not, indeed, consider it often a right act. It was desertion of the post of duty to which the gods have assigned us. It was withdrawing from your country the services she had a right to demand. It was cowardly not to be able to stand up under suffering, however heavy the load.

The State went so far as to punish the act of suicide by a criminal with confiscation and with infamy, but it was because otherwise he would escape unpunished for his original offence.[1] The man who killed himself from weariness of life, or mortification at being insolvent, or impatience of disease, stood uncondemned.

---

[1] Dig. xlix. 14, *de Jure Fisci*, 45, 2.

THE LEGAL FICTION

No Roman law-giver, no Roman philosopher, ever dreamed that suicide was a natural mark of insanity. They knew, and we know, that it is too often the fruit of long and cool deliberation. It occurs oftenest in highly civilized communities. It is not a thing that always and instinctively shocks the moral sense. On the contrary, apart from considerations founded on religion, the question, Is life worth living? is one which many a man may hesitate to answer, and as to which the man who thinks most deeply and most clearly might hesitate longest. It is, no doubt, an awful thing to enter unbidden into the presence of the Almighty. There is an audacity in it to which few are equal. There is a recklessness in it of which few will be guilty. But that the fatal act may come from an unclouded mind and a steady hand who can doubt? Many is the man to-day who would willingly let go of life if it could be relinquished painlessly to himself and honorably to those left behind him, and if he had no hope, no fear of a life beyond. It would substitute certainty for uncertainty; rest for toil, anxiety, apprehension: it would, that is, if he were unaffected by the teaching of revelation, or the instincts of natural religion. The law is unaffected by them, and it is a legal question only that is now under consideration.

It was Saint Louis, of France, who first introduced the practice of confiscating the estate of every suicide, which, long since discarded in the country of its origin, remains still a disgrace to the statute-books of England. It was one of the first acts of Tennessee, in her original Constitution, to forbid such inhumanity to the innocent; nor is it now recognized in any American State. This penalty of beggary to the deserted family, coupled, until the present century, with the refusal of decent burial to the corpse, was the sufficient cause for the adoption in English practice of the legal fiction of temporary insanity.

The censures of the church, too, involving, when Europe was under Roman Catholic auspices, the denial of its rites at the grave, or its masses for the departed soul, tended strongly in the same direction. So did, and so does, the natural horror and disapprobation with which suicide is regarded by the majority of the community.

This last reason for calling it by another name is the only one that remains with us,—the only one, I say, for it includes the censures of religion, though not of popes and councils. "Though there are many crimes," says Madame de Staël, "of a deeper dye than suicide, there is no other by which men appear so formally to renounce the protection of God."

I would not relieve the memory of the suicide from the reproach of a breach of religious duty, and of social obligation. I would give the real, and not the conventional reason for his act. Poverty, hopeless disease, shame, loss of friends, loss of reputation, mere weariness of an empty life; when these exist, why shut your eyes to them and frame a fiction to occupy their place? In very charity to the dead man's kin, let the truth be told, rather than throw on them a still darker shadow.

THE LEGAL FICTION

The true duty of the coroner in such a case is to see to it that the verdict is true. Let public sentiment require him to instruct the jury that the law at least does not presume insanity from the fact of suicide, and that they should not find that to be the cause of death, unless satisfied by the surrounding circumstances that it really was.

But the worst form in which this fiction still survives is that in which it serves the living as a defence in criminal prosecutions. Its legitimate use for this purpose is of common occurrence. Its illegitimate use, I believe, is still commoner.

A class of crimes exists in which we always expect it; in which it is seldom well founded; in which it is generally successful. They are crimes in the eye of the law, and not in the eye of the community; crimes of blood and crimes of deep provocation. Human honor is held cheaper in law than it is in life. It is held cheaper in modern law than it was in ancient law. It is held cheaper in English law than it is in Continental law. Honor and infamy, — honor as the great prize of life, infamy as its heaviest burden, — these were great agencies of the legislator of the days before the Christian era.

The doctrine that no words can justify a blow, that the mortal stroke that punishes an insult is murder, but that violence to property will warrant violence to defend it, would have seemed somewhat incongruous to a Roman. These are the maxims of a pacific people, — of a nation at which Napoleon sneered as a nation of shop-keepers, though he found, at last, that when roused they could fight, and could conquer. They are maxims also which, however just in theory, do not regulate the actual conduct in life of Englishmen or Americans. They rest upon the plane of religion, rather than of ordinary human intercourse. Society may some day reach their level, but it has not yet.

In the practice of courts, they are softened by the sympathy of juries, or the good sense of the bench.

In cases of simple assault, this protection has been found enough. Where the punishment of fine or imprisonment is in the discretion of the judge, he will not fail to make due allowance for the man who has been provoked to right his own wrongs in a rough way. Even revenge, says Lord Bacon, is but a wild sort of justice.

But in capital cases, we are brought to face a question quite different. Here is no room for the infliction of a nominal punishment. The verdict binds the court to an invariable sentence. It is a simple question between guilt and innocence; between the last penalty the law can exact, and an absolute acquittal. It is this narrow alternative from which the common law allows no escape, which has driven the English and American jury to lay hold so often of the pretence of emotional insanity.

A hundred and sixty different capital offences blackened the criminal code of England, so late as when Blackstone wrote. The ground was strewn with dead after the assizes, as it is behind an invading army. Parliament refused to mitigate the laws. Lawyers and juries were found ready to nullify or

THE LEGAL FICTION

evade them. So will it always be when laws cease to represent justice. The people are stronger than any statute. They may be long misrepresented by their legislators, but they will not be long thwarted by them. The fiction of insanity as a defence in homicide had a natural origin in English law. It was the protest of the community against rules of decision which failed to recognize some of the finer feelings of our nature.

Our very forms of legal procedure were at once the occasion and the opportunity of this practice. We are unlike almost every other people in tying our juries down to single issues. To this result we directed our art of pleading in civil and criminal cases alike. The great thing was to give the jury but one point to settle,— one question to answer. It is now agreed that this system was a failure in civil cases. It became, ages ago, one of simplicity and certainty in theory only. Successive relaxations in practice by slow growth choked the clear spirit of the ancient science of pleading till it became a corpse, and have driven us to a system radically different.

But in our criminal procedure we still cling to the forms of the days of Alfred. *Guilty* or *Not Guilty* — this single issue, single in terms, but all embracing in scope — is still all that England and America put to their juries in the most important causes with which the law has to deal.

The Roman panel, before which the State brought its prosecutions, had a third answer open to it, — *Non liquet*, I am not certain. The Scotch jury too can say, *Not proven*. The Continental jury can do more. They can, and must, if they find the prisoner guilty, return written answers to a series of questions, proposed by the prosecution or the defence, and sanctioned by the court.[1] These questions relate to facts evidencing the degree of criminality involved in the commission of the offence. They may tend to aggravate it; they may tend to extenuate it. In either case, they are to be passed upon separately and on due consideration.

By the present laws of France,[2] if circumstances of mitigation are found in a capital case, the court may reduce the penalty from death to a limited term of imprisonment. In the Austrian Code of 1852, we find among the extenuating facts which may reduce the punishment, the case when the prisoner was urged on to the act complained of by violent mental excitement, growing out of the ordinary feelings of man. Temptation, opportunity, provocation, contrition, all these things, that, to the common judgment of men, give color to an act, and make one pity or condemn, these penal codes bring directly before the trier, to aid in ascertaining as to the prisoner's guilt and its degree. In a word, all the matters of palliation which, under the prevailing American practice, have been brought before the court, only after verdict, to mitigate the sentence, and shown by statements of counsel, letters of friends, or at most by affidavit, other nations allow to be proved on the trial, and placed on record as a permanent characterization of the offence, — as a necessary part of determining what that offence is and is not.

[1] See the French *Code d'Instruction Criminelle*, Art. 336 *et seq.*
[2] Law of May 13, 1863.

Under such a system, I need not say that they are ignorant of the plea of temporary insanity. They have no need to bring in fictions when they boldly accept the fact. The irresistible impulse that leads an outraged husband to clear his house of the seducer by his instant death, they calmly pronounce to be no crime at all.[1] The transport of passion under which a son may shoot down his father's murderer, though met years after the deed on some distant shore, they declare to be a legal matter of excuse.

Who is there that has not watched the progress of some such case on trial in an American court as it is photographed by the daily press? A man perhaps has avenged his daughter's or his sister's wrongs. He has followed the wretch who destroyed his happiness, and shot him down as he would a wolf. The sympathies of the community, of the audience, of the court, are with the prisoner. He has offended against the law; but is it a just law? It imposes on him the same penalty which it metes out to the lowest and basest criminal that defiles the dock. It refuses to hear the story of the injuries that drove him to revenge; or if it hears them at all, treats them as proof of malice and premeditation. The jury must find him simply *Guilty* or *Not Guilty*. The judge is the mere spokesman of the statute law. Some punishment the prisoner deserves, but he must receive the most severe, or none. He receives none.

[1] "Code Pénal" of France, Art. 324. By English law it is manslaughter; but men were once branded on the hand for it, by burning. T. Raymond's Reports, 212.

The tears of his family, the eloquence of counsel, the atmosphere of excitement and pity that pervades the court-room and the county, supply the want of proof, and the man who was sane the moment before the fatal deed, and sane the moment after it, is found *Not Guilty*, on the ground of temporary insanity. Twelve men have violated their juror's oaths; but they have done it to save a life which the law would have unjustly forfeited.

Which is better, to break a law which is unjust, or to make a law which shall be capable of being respected? We, of the American people, have it in our power to do either. Law is what we please. The general adoption of the humane principles of foreign codes, as to motives for homicide, would go far to drive the fictitious defence of temporary insanity out of our court-rooms. Are they not more in accordance with the instincts of the human heart than those which we have inherited from our common law? Are they not, on the whole, safer for society?

It was the great thought of Stoic philosophy that all things were ruled by law, — by one law, everywhere one and the same. Physical science in our day has come forward with new and commanding proofs of its universality. Let it be the language of heaven, or let it be the mere expression of material or mortal forces, it is in either case the highest, the ultimate conception of the human mind. To apply this law to the affairs of men is justice, and those to whom it is committed to administer this sacred trust should be free to do so in that spirit of sincerity and truth which its nature calls for.

The cycles and epicycles of Ptolemy might serve to indicate the laws of planetary space, till the eye of Copernicus pierced to the very heavens and saw the truth. Five thousand years of human knowledge were against it, but, once proved, Science, and Theology, as well, bowed to the discovery, and the earth shrank away into a corner of the great universe, of which her inhabitants had so long thought her the centre and moving cause. A surface reading of holy writ had made the Christian church believe that our earth, again, was but the six days' work of its great Maker. Geology read another story in the silent rocks, — dead witnesses of other times, — and a thousand centuries were added to the pages of history. The imperfections of human laws have at least been as great as the imperfections of human conceptions of cosmogony and of nature. It is the part of the modern legislator to be as loyal to truth as is the astronomer or the geologist. If any rule of right or practice, of those used in our courts of justice, comes to be recognized as false, there is but one way open, to strike it out, cost what it may of old traditions unseated and old ways abandoned.

For other times, for the rough days of Saxon kings and Norman conquerors, of Common Law struggling to keep out Canon Law, of peasant juries and royal judges, these legal fictions that linger still, may have been necessary. But they were ever necessary evils. One language alone befits the court of justice — the language of truth. If the surrounding society be such that the truth cannot be comprehended or acted on, then indeed it may be permissible and wise to veil and disguise it. But such a policy can be only a temporizing one. If there is real life in that community, if its people have the capability of better things, if its rulers are leaders, the hour will soon come when justice need no longer wear a mask.

Has not this hour come to the American lawmaker, as regards, at least, this pitiful fiction which we have had under particular consideration? Shall we go on for another century acquitting the husband who kills the betrayer of his household, on the false plea of temporary insanity, instead of the outspoken verdict of justifiable homicide? Shall we go on for another century listening to the same empty lie from every coroner's inquest that sits on the body of a suicide? Shall we go on for another century setting aside hard wills on the plea of testamentary incapacity, instead of protecting heirs by law, against a father's mere caprice or injustice?

We cannot say that our people are too ignorant to be trusted with the truth for their own good. It is the people who are laughing at their courts and lawyers for an ignorant and slavish adherence to precedents of former and ruder generations. America, that has taught all other lands the duty and the blessings of popular education, need not distrust the juries whom she has trained up in her own free schools. If there be an American citizen whom any State could ever put in her jury-box, too blind to see through these legal fictions of ancient time, that State has a worse enemy to contend with than legal fictions;

she must be the victim of legal facts, — of bad laws of administrative justice.

It is with a just pride that we look back on a thousand years of Anglo-Saxon life — its sturdy growth, its glorious expansion, its rugged self-reliance. Old England is dear to us still as our fatherland : —

> "A land of just and old renown,
> A land of settled government,
> Where freedom broadens slowly down,
> From precedent to precedent."

But precedents may mislead. They do if they run counter to the general sentiment of an educated community in a Christian land. In matters political our race has never allowed legal fictions to stand long in its way. The oldest of all, that "the king can do no wrong," was invoked in vain by Charles I., as he stood before his judges at Westminster; and by George III., when he undertook to tax the American Colonies.

But in questions of mere judicial practice, we have been ever slow to depart from the ancient ways.

No fault need be found with this spirit of conservatism. It has given us, and guaranteed us, the freedom we enjoy. No new-made law can have half the hold upon the community, can exercise half the power over men, which belongs of right to settled rule and ancient precedent. We have grown up with and into this notion of fictitious insanity. It is part of our criminal jurisprudence, and probate law, as well settled and familiar as any other. It ought not to be uprooted without strong cause. But is it not true that strong cause exists? All these fictions were once useful; we can see where. They are now outgrown; we can see how. Often they stand in the way of a manly declaration of the truth, in matters of judicial procedure, and they alone stand in the way of it.

The term legal fiction has been sometimes defined, and was by D'Aguesseau, so as to exclude whatever it is impossible should be true. The ordinary use of the term is more extensive. It embraces what is obviously untrue, as in the maxim that the king never dies, or that a will speaks from the death of the testator. Thus employed, it is a convenient figure of speech, — a bit of picture writing. It is no more than a correct statement in proverbial form of a legal fact.

Such fictions may well continue a part of any system of jurisprudence. It is those which assert what might be true, but is known not to be, that are falling into desuetude, and deserve to fall.

Conservatism is the peculiar characteristic of the Anglo-Saxon race in everything that belongs to law in government. But there may be a conservatism of forces, without a conservatism of forms. We are the heirs of strong natural traits, tendencies, aspirations. We prize the results they have attained for English law and English liberty. We prize more the high aim, the free spirit, the loyal soul, of which these results have been, after all, but an imperfect expression.

That people best honors its great progenitors that stands above them, on a higher plane of life and thought and law, gained by following out their principles of action in a better way; by standing on their foundation; not to stand still, but to step higher.

The statute law of an historic race, which has once attained any considerable civilization, should be a pyramid. The base will be broad,— too broad for anything except a base. It will be built of the customs of many ages crystallized into positive law, lying confusedly together, except as at the points of greatest advancement they may face the structure with what rises to the dignity of institutions. Each higher course will be a smaller square, because from each will be rejected that which has been found unnecessary.

The best statutes, says Mr. Buckle, are those that repeal some former statute. And why? Because under and around every system of legislation, like the free air of the desert that embraces the pyramids themselves, is the great sustaining presence of that unwritten law which every people makes for itself, and changes for itself, as time goes on. To this law they are remitted by the repeal of statutes, and it is a law seldom other than equal and just.

What says this unwritten law, as to the succession to the estates of the dead? That its natural course is descent to the next of kin. What says the statute law? That this course may be varied at the pleasure of the dead, if they leave a paper which we call their will. Repeal this statute and you remit the succession to the rightful heirs. Repeal it, in part, as by providing that they cannot, without just cause, be wholly disinherited, and you remit them, for that part, to the protection of the customary law. Is it said that this would be to establish a restriction upon the power of bequest, left untrammelled by the wisdom of former generations? Who have the opportunity to know best the wants of the present age, they or we?

In Bacon's *Novum Organum* are some words in regard to the wisdom of our ancestors which are as true for our time as they were for his. Reverence for antiquity, he says, is often founded on a mere misapplication of terms. The old world was not antiquity. That was a younger world than ours. In its relation to our times, it was old. In its relation to all times, it was young. As we look for better judgment in the man of experience than in the youth, so far more is to be expected from our age than from former ones, for it has had greater opportunities of knowledge.[1]

[1] Lib. i. lxxxiv. 37: "*De antiquitate autem opinio, quam homines de ipsa fovent, negligens omnino est, et vix verbo ipsi congrua. Mundi enim senium et grandævitas pro antiquitate vere habenda sunt; quæ temporibus nostris tribui debent, non juniori ætati mundi, qualis apud antiquos fuit. Illa enim ætas, respectu nostri, antiqua et major; respectu mundi ipsius, nova et minor fuit. Atque revera quemadmodum majorem rerum humanarum notitiam, et maturius judicium, ab homine sene expectamus, quam a juvene, propter experientiam, et rerum, quas vidit, et audivit, et cogitavit, varietatem et copiam; eodem modo et a nostra ætate (si vires suas nosset, et experiri et intendere vellet) majora multo quam, a priscis temporibus, expectari par est; utpote ætate mundi grandiore, et infinitis experimentis et observationibus aucta et cumulata.*"

The nineteenth century closes as an age of light, of truth, of sincere investigation, of candid judgment. It is intolerant of shams. It needs none. Least of all does it want them in its courts of justice. Surely, before that high presence, where we poor mortals invoke the aid of the God above us to keep our testimony pure, our judgments right, we may say with George Herbert —

"Dare to be true: nothing can need a lie."

CHAPTER IX

THE RECOGNITION OF HABITUAL CRIMINALS AS A CLASS TO BE TREATED BY ITSELF[1]

THE last quarter of the nineteenth century has witnessed the development of a new science, — that of Criminal Anthropology. It deals especially with the relation of crime to the criminal, and seeks to discover what were the causes which have made him what he is, and what regard society should pay to those causes in determining what to do with him. Since the publication of Professor Lombroso's *L'uomo delinquente*, in 1876, a considerable literature regarding this subject has come into existence, and one to which there have been contributions in many languages. The fundamental proposition which he has brought forward is that he who commits a crime commits it in consequence of a peculiar constitution of mind and body, acted upon by his physical and social surroundings. This seems almost a commonplace, but there are many anthropologists who contend that the environment is the sole responsible cause, and others by whom peculiarities of bodily conformation, race instinct, or climatic conditions are denied to have any determining influence at all.

[1] In discussing this topic use has been made of a paper read by the author before the American Social Science Association, in 1886.

Fortunately for Lombroso, his views were soon reinforced by proofs of a convincing character. In 1881, Alphonse Bertillon made public his new method of personal identification.

There are practically no changes of dimension in the bones or ears of the human body after it once attains its full stature. In no two skeletons do the bones have precisely the same relative dimensions to each other. These relative variations are particularly noticeable in the length and width of the skull, the length of the middle and little fingers, foot and forearm, and the stretch of the arms as compared with the height.

Bertillon asserted that if these and certain other dimensions were accurately taken in the case of any individual, and supplemented by photographs, a scientific analysis and description of the features of the face and an anatomical localization of all permanent scars, marks, or bodily deformities, he could be identified with certainty after any lapse of years or change of circumstances. While serviceable for many purposes, it is obvious that the principal utility of this method of "anthropometric identification," as it is termed, must be in its application to those arrested on a criminal charge. The system was put into use at Paris by the prefecture of police, in 1882, and soon spread over France, Belgium, Switzerland, and Russia. More recently it has been introduced into the English prisons.

At the Columbian Exposition at Chicago in 1893, the French exhibits, by which it was illustrated, went far towards convincing the American public that

Criminal Anthropology had fairly gained the rank of a science.

It was the least of the lessons taught by an examination of the photographs and files of measurements and descriptions, that escaping criminals, if they had been once convicted in any court or country could be infallibly identified, if arrested in another. They established the existence of a class of men, of peculiar physical characteristics, and facial expression, the members of which seemed formed to gravitate towards crime. In the contour of the skull and the great reach of the outstretched arms as compared with the height, many of them bore a striking resemblance to the ape or "simian" family, out of which it may be that man originally emerged. In most there was a want of symmetry and due proportion as to the features of the face, as well as the larger members of the body. Those in whom these abnormal characteristics were most marked generally had the worst record.[1] They were the old offenders or "recidivists." They constituted a class within a class, — that of the habitual criminals. If one coming into the world fashioned in such a shape, unless he be reared and educated with exceptional care and success, be placed in circumstances of want, an opportunity to satisfy it at the expense of another, will not go unimproved.

The philosophy of Lombroso, and the invention

---

[1] A French physician, as early as 1841, had called attention to many of these facts, as disclosed by a study of the convicts in the galleys at Toulon. Lauvergne, on *Les Forçats*, considérés sous le Rapport physiologique, moral, et intellectuel, pp. 43, 199, 279.

of Bertillon, came in good time to serve the interests of American society. Crime with us has become of late years to assume a new aspect. Our population has begun in more than one State to press upon the limits of subsistence. It is less easy than it once was for every man to find work at wages which satisfy his wants. It is more easy than it once was to gain a living by burglary and theft, roguery and fraud. It is more easy for the successful sharper, robber, or counterfeiter to find a way to spend his ill-gotten gains without attracting any more attention than he desires to their possession. Such men have come to have a social circle of their own; a certain pride in their profession; a following of respectful admirers; a Police Gazette literature to proclaim their exploits and perpetuate their kind.

We have been slow to recognize the existence of this class among us, and we have been slower in applying the remedy. But as no considerable city is now without them, and no village bank or store is secure against its forays, it is full time for every State to do what but a few thus far have done, and settle on some general plan of dealing with criminals of this description.

They are mainly the offspring of city life; their crimes are directed against property; their line of action is craft rather than violence, — violence only when craft fails.

Cities are transforming American society. They crowd the good and the bad of vast districts into a single centre, where, if the good become better, the bad become worse. We are repeating the history of ancient times and of the dark ages, though from a different cause. Not now for safety, but for pleasure and for gain, our people are deserting the country hill-sides for the manufacturing village or the more distant city. Political influence, industrial enterprise, capital accumulated elsewhere, go with them. If you would find the daring, venturesome, restless, ambitious spirits, such as were first in earlier days in pushing on the frontiers of civilization, you look for them on pavements rather than on farms. They go where there is not honest work enough for all, and so some take to what is dishonest. They take to it with the energy and skill that belong to the American character, with the intensity of purpose that marks the struggle of city life. It is thus that crime, if it fastens on some man who is ready to receive it, becomes a profession; that children are bred to it; that it has its own language, — its own tools.

In every country where modern institutions prevail, the same movement is to be seen. The great cities of England and Germany have been becoming greater during the last thirty years, with almost, if not quite, the rapidity of Chicago and New York.

And with what weapons has American society been opposing these new criminal classes? With none but those forged in the early days of English history, — in the days of another type of civilization. She has, to meet the Springfield rifle and the Gatling gun, nothing still but the old pike and shield of the middle ages. She has even less. The humanity of our times has given the man accused of crime rights of defence undreamt of by the common law, and has thrown aside half its punishments.

The laws of England regulating criminal proceedings, which we have inherited, were good for the times and the men whose work they were. In a land of headstrong kings and feudal lords, the common people had scant justice at the best. They needed all the guarantees of personal liberty which they could get. There was often little guilt in acts for which capital punishment was imposed by Act of Parliament. Crime was not without its romantic side. There might be a certain dash of chivalry in the freebooter of the Border, or a Robin Hood of the Great Forest. We shall find none in the city burglar of the nineteenth or the twentieth century.

The professional criminal of modern times is a product of a highly civilized society. He is armed with its arts. He must be met with the best means it has at its command. He hides himself in the crowds of great cities from the neighborhood watch which follows every individual in a thinly settled community,—which kept England safe in the days when every Hundred was responsible for its own good order. Society, then, must set a watch over him of some new kind; if there is likely to be none without law, there must be one by law. The habitual criminal is a perpetual well-spring of crime. The stream must be checked at its source, if it is to be checked at all.

It may be necessary to treat him in a manner incompatible with the traditions of our race. We may be forced to trench upon his personal independence. The time may come, even, for us to make suspicion evidence, and assume guilt where we cannot prove it. If so, the price is a great one, but the peace of society is worth it.

It is a rule of biology, to which I had occasion to refer in a previous chapter, that, in the natural order of the universe, a being disappears who cannot live in unison with his surroundings. The habitual criminal is such a being. He is habitually inclined to do and apt to do that which is forbidden by the general voice and sentiment of the political community in which he resides. He does not belong where he is found.

A sharp and efficient remedy was applied in ruder times. His first crime was apt to be his last. Before he had had time to harden into a criminal by trade, he was summarily put out of harm's way forever, by private vengeance or public execution; or disabled from future mischief by bodily mutilation, or else made to carry always a warning of what he was by marking him with some ineffaceable sign of ignominy.

The softening influences of Christian civilization have taught us to discard most of the penalties which criminal justice formerly imposed. The whipping-post, whether wisely or unwisely, has almost everywhere been abandoned,[1] and except for a steadily diminishing number of crimes called capital, the only sentences left to be imposed are those of fine or of imprisonment.

A fine is a slight penalty to the habitual criminal.

[1] A French convict, quoted by Lauvergne (*Les Forçats*, etc. 216), when sentenced to fifty lashes said: "Mais c'est plus douloureux que cinquante coups de guillotine; on souffre pendant et après."

If he can pay it, he at once returns to the society where he is out of place; if he is too poor for that, it is at most but equivalent to a term in jail.

The subject is one which was not overlooked by our first great American writer on systematic criminal procedure, Edward Livingston. In his "Code of Crimes and Punishments," reported to the legislature of Louisiana in 1824, we find a provision for an increased punishment in all cases on a second conviction, followed by this article: —

"Art. 53. And if any person, having been twice previously convicted of crimes, no matter of what nature, shall a third time be convicted of any crime afterwards committed, he shall be considered as unfit for society, and be imprisoned at hard labor for life."

Mr. Livingston was almost a sentimentalist in his views of penology. He would have abolished capital punishment, and the foundation-stone of his whole system is the proposition that "the sole object of punishment is to prevent the commission of crime." In the Reports accompanying his code he argued at length all points that seemed to him worthy of discussion, yet his only allusion to the life-sentence for the habitual criminal is the remark that it "seems so necessary and reasonable that it may pass without observation."

So far as I am aware, Virginia was the first of our States to adopt the plan thus proposed. In her code, framed shortly before the Civil War, she declared that every person sentenced to the penitentiary must be sentenced for life, if he had before been twice sentenced to the penitentiary by any court held within the United States.[1]

In Maine a similar punishment may be imposed for a second conviction. The provision is, that any person convicted of a State's prison offence, who has been previously sentenced to the State's prison by any court of the United States, or any State, may be imprisoned for life or any term of years.[2] It will be observed that this statute is permissive; not, like the others, mandatory. The court may, but is not bound to inflict the life-sentence. And, on the other hand, Maine requires but two convictions to justify this remedy, while Livingston's code and that of Virginia demand three.

In 1885, Ohio followed the lead of Virginia, but tempered the sentence by giving a chance of regaining a qualified liberty. Her statute reads thus: —

"Every person who, after having been twice convicted, sentenced and imprisoned in some penal institution for felony, whether committed heretofore or hereafter, and whether committed in this State or elsewhere within the limits of the United States of America, shall be convicted, sentenced, and imprisoned in the Ohio penitentiary for felony, hereafter committed, shall be deemed and taken to be an habitual criminal, and on the expiration of the term for which he shall be so sentenced, he shall not be discharged from imprisonment in the penitentiary, but shall be detained therein, for and during his natural life, unless pardoned by the Governor, and the liability to be so detained

[1] Virginia Code of 1860, p. 814, sec. 26.
[2] Maine Revised Statutes of 1871, p. 891, sec. 3.

shall be and constitute a part of every sentence to imprisonment in the penitentiary; provided, however, that after the expiration of the term for which he was so sentenced, he may, in the discretion of the board of managers, be allowed to go upon parole outside of the buildings and enclosures, but to remain, while on parole, in the legal custody and under the control of said board, and subject at any time to be taken back within the inclosure of said institution; and the power is hereby conferred upon said board to establish rules and regulations, under which such habitual criminals who are prisoners may so go out upon parole, and full power to enforce such rules and regulations, and to retake and re-imprison any such convict so going out on parole, is hereby conferred upon said board, whose written order, certified by its secretary, shall be sufficient warrant to authorize any police officer to return to actual custody any such conditionally released or paroled prisoner."[1]

We observe here, as an alternative of the life-sentence, or rather as a provisional and temporary substitute for it, something like the English ticket-of-leave system. The board of managers of the penitentiary have the powers which the Act of 16 & 17 Vict. ch. 99, sections 9-11, gave in 1853 to the State Department. The convict may be put under watch outside the prison, instead of within it, — under the watch of the police, instead of the jailer. This is a necessary incident of the power to establish rules for his control, after his provisional liberation.

In 1882, the American Bar Association instructed its committee on jurisprudence and law reform to " re-

[1] Ohio Session Laws for 1885, p. 237, sec. 2.

port a proper method and criterion, for discriminating between professional and non-professional criminals, and for the protection of society against the former, when so ascertained." Such a report was presented to the Association in 1885, and the following resolutions recommended for adoption: —

" 1. Resolved, That provision should be made by law in every State, for keeping a record of the name, age, personal appearance, residence, occupation, and general antecedents of every person who may be convicted in its courts of felony, or who may have been twice sentenced to imprisonment for any crime or misdemeanor; and for printing such records annually, for distribution to its courts and police authorities, and for exchange for similar publications of other States; and that photographs of convicts deemed specially dangerous should also be taken, to be used in a similar manner.

" 2. Resolved, That provision should be made by law in every State, for subjecting all persons who have been twice sentenced to imprisonment for any crime or misdemeanor, to police supervision for life, or such shorter term, not less than five years after the expiration of their second term of imprisonment, as the court may order; and also to perpetual deprivation of the right to vote or hold public office."

This report was the subject of full discussion, and at the succeeding annual meeting, in 1886, the resolutions were adopted. Since then, legislation similar in many respects to that of Ohio has been had in Massachusetts, Connecticut, Rhode Island, and Utah, and the Bertillon system has been adopted by the police authorities in Illinois, Michigan, Wisconsin, Massachusetts, Rhode Island, and New York city. In some of the States mentioned Livingston's rule is followed, and a third conviction of felony deemed absolute proof that the offender is incorrigible, his sentence being to confinement for life, with no hope of release on parole, however he may subsequently seem to have become reformed.[1]

These statutes and the course of legislation recommended by the American Bar Association both rest on the assumption that habitual criminals are an especially dangerous class, against which it is proper to guard by unusual laws. They agree, also, in making repeated convictions the criterion for determining the members of this class. The plan of the Bar Association differs from that of most of the statutes in imposing a liability to police supervision after a second sentence to imprisonment, even for simple misdemeanors, has been served out. It also differs in emphasizing the necessity of instituting in every State an exact system of registration for convicted criminals, to be made useful throughout the country, by suitable arrangements for exchange of information.

This first became possible through the invention of Bertillon.

The line of policy upon which a few of the States have thus tentatively entered, and which has the support of the only body which assumes to represent the lawyers of the country, is not a novel one. It

[1] Connecticut, after first extending the benefit of the parole to this class (Gen. Stat., § 1644), withdrew it in 1897.

applies to habitual criminals rules which the leading nations of the world have long applied not only to them, but to those generally who have committed grave, though single crimes.

It may be said that its spirit is un-American. It is. During most of our history we were content, when a convict's term of imprisonment ended and we saw him pass out of the jail door, to say with Dogberry, " Thank God, we are well rid of the knave." But we found, as our prisons improved, and the stocks and the whipping-post disappeared, that he generally came back. Then Prisoners' Aid Societies were tried, which are really a form of supervision by the executive agent of a charitable organization, though with the immediate design of supplying good influences and help to find work, rather than of watching against new crime. The State, in some instances, has contributed to the support of these organizations, and their supervision has then become, in a measure, that of a public officer, but in a measure only.

We have tried, too, Lynch-law, very vigorously. It is effectual against horse-thieves and stage-robbers in new States. It is a thoroughly American remedy. It aims, in a rough way, at the same end that England aimed at by law when our ancestors left it, — the extermination by death of the flagrant criminal, before he has an opportunity to become an habitual one. But its existence, even in the South, where the conditions of society, so exceptional as respects temptation and opportunity for one crime, would excuse it, if anywhere, is a national disgrace.

We cannot return to the severity of our early codes. We cannot tolerate the swift vengeance that anticipates the law or goes beyond it. Those who have studied the course of Prisoners' Aid Societies know how little they can do to make honest men of rogues. Their watch over the discharged convict who accepts their good offices is of value, so far as it goes, but it cannot go as far as if maintained or seconded, as in European fashion, by the police.

The Penal Code[1] of France put every convict sentenced to imprisonment at hard labor, or for long terms, under police supervision for life. Before his discharge he had to declare where he wished to reside. The government might grant his wish, or might refuse it, in which case he must select another place for its approbation. He received a sort of passport to the place appointed, specifying how long he might take for the journey, and what stops he might make on the way. Within twenty-four hours from his arrival he had to report to the mayor of the place, and he could not leave it without a new passport, after three days' notice. Five years' imprisonment might be the punishment of any infraction of these rules. Those twice convicted of petty offences might be put under similar supervision for from five to ten years. In 1885[2] there was substituted for these provisions a system of transportation for all habitual criminals.

The general registration law of France, also, assigns every man a legal domicile, which he can only change by a formal notification to the public

---

[1] Art. 11, 44 *et seq.*   [2] Law of May 27.

authorities, and where the main events of his life are recorded.

In England,[1] on a second conviction of one previously sentenced to imprisonment for the same offence, the criminal may be put under police supervision for seven years, after the expiration of his second term. And though not sentenced to such supervision, yet if within seven years after his second term, any proper court finds reasonable grounds for believing that he is getting his living by dishonest means, or "if he is found in any place, whether public or private, under such circumstances as to satisfy the Court that he was about to commit, or aid in the commission of, any offence punishable on indictment or summary conviction;" or if he be found in any house, shop, or yard, "without being able to account to the satisfaction of the Court, before whom he is brought, for his being found on said premises," he may be sentenced, without further evidence, to a year's imprisonment.

This system of police supervision obviously cannot be made fully effective here, without exacter methods than we have yet pursued for the registration and description of known criminals. The photograph gives a cheap and easy, though far from certain, way of identifying them, and it has come into general use in the police offices of our larger cities, without any authority of law. A "rogues' gallery" of photographic portraits ought to be found in every State prison, and a sufficient number of each likeness

---

[1] By Act of 1871 (34 & 35 Vict., ch. 112).

should be printed, in case of habitual criminals, to distribute in all the great centres of population in the United States. England, in 1876 (39 & 40 Vict., ch. 23), formally adopted this policy. The State department is to fix from time to time the classes of convicts to which it shall apply, and each member of every such class shall be photographed in any style of dress the authorities may prescribe. A record is also to be made of his name, age, personal description, offence, occupation, residence, etc., and the information thus gained is tabulated, and registered in London for English, in Edinburgh for Scotch, and in Dublin for Irish convicts. The result has been that while at the date of the adoption of this system the average number confined in British prisons every day in the year was over twenty thousand, it fell to less than thirteen thousand four hundred in 1893, and it is generally agreed that there has been a reduction of crime to the extent of twenty-five per cent during this period, without counting the very considerable increase of population.[1]

If similar records were kept in each of our States, and printed for exchange with other States, as well as for use by its own local authorities, a long step would be taken towards suppressing the habitual criminal, who now finds it easy to flit, under an *alias*, beyond the shadow of his local reputation, without going farther than the State line. Massachusetts has made provision for gathering information of this general

[1] Report of the United States Delegates to the Fifth International Prison Congress, 91.

character, as part of her "probation officer" system in regard to all persons arrested for every offence; but it is not gathered for dissemination and has no relation to the mischief now under consideration. It looks to probation in lieu of imprisonment, not after and in addition to it.

It is my belief that the best way to deal with the habitual criminal lies in the direction suggested by the American Bar Association. Let there be a full record kept under the Bertillon system of the description and general history of every convicted felon, and of every man twice sentenced to imprisonment for any offence. These should be made available for the information of the public authorities of every State. Put all persons twice sentenced to imprisonment for any offence under police supervision for life, or such shorter term as the court may fix. Let them also be forever deprived of the right to vote or hold office.

The habitual criminal is not likely ever to hold public office, but he ought not to vote for those who do. A single conviction of felony, and a second conviction for any offence for which imprisonment has been inflicted, also indicate generally a depravation of character which should work a forfeiture of the elective franchise. In exceptional cases this may be too great a penalty. For such, there is an adequate remedy by a resort to executive pardon, or legislative clemency. But in ninety-nine cases out of a hundred, the forfeiture is right, and the great interests of society demand its exaction.

In several of our States, constitutional or legislative provisions disqualify from voting or from holding office those who come from other States, where they had been disqualified by conviction for crime. Such an exclusion evinces a spirit of comity which, it would seem, should be universal, in respect to offences involving moral turpitude, and which are regarded by each of the States concerned as equally criminal.[1]

It is not altogether creditable to the United States that we have thus far made so limited a use of this mode of punishment. It was familiar to the ancients: it is familiar to every nation in Europe. For all grave crimes and for many minor ones the French Code imposes it.[2] Italy and Belgium do the same. Germany, Holland, and Sweden allow the courts to impose it, in their discretion, within certain limits. "Civic degradation" for habitual criminals seems the natural badge of their condition; and it is a badge, in our land of frequent and close-fought elections, which is sure to attract public attention, and therefore to put the public on their guard.

While few would object to the other requirements of registration, photographing, and police supervision, in the case of the hardened and professional criminal, they may be thought by some to be harsh measures to apply upon a first conviction for felony, or a second sentence to jail for any offence.

But we must try to prevent any one from becoming a habitual criminal. The convicted felon has gone a

---

[1] See Code of Georgia, Rev. of 1882, § 129.
[2] *Code Pénal*, Art. 28, 34; Law of February 2d, 1852.

long way towards joining their ranks. He has attacked the good order of society with violence and effect. He ought not to complain if the State makes a full record of the affair, and gives it to the police of his country. And is it too much to keep under police supervision those who have been twice imprisoned, though only for a misdemeanor? Who is there familiar with jails who does not know that the cases are rare when two such sentences are not rapidly followed by a third, and a fourth? For their own sake, such men need to feel that the eye of the police is upon them. To know that they are watched is a real terror and a real deterrent to evil-doers. The common punishment for petty offences is a fine. If imprisonment is imposed, it is a pretty sure sign of some circumstance of aggravation; if it is imposed twice, though only for drunkenness or assault, it indicates a very bad opinion of the prisoner by the court.

The term " police supervision " also is an elastic one. It would mean one thing for the professional bank-robber, and another thing for the twice convicted chicken-thief. From the hardened felon who expects to make his living by acts of violence or fraud, it might require monthly reports of his occupation, instant notice of a change of residence, and submission to frequent domiciliary visits of inspection. To the man who although twice imprisoned for minor offences, follows some regular business, and has not irrevocably lost his good name, it might take no formal shape, beyond keeping up the record of his life in the police register, from such information as could be obtained from outside sources, without

AS A CLASS TO BE TREATED BY ITSELF 309

giving him any personal annoyance, or attracting any public attention to his history.

A man who is known to the police to belong to the class of habitual criminals, who is publicly registered as such, and has twice served out a term in prison, has but a poor chance, no doubt, of gaining an honest living. But no man is wholly bad, and the poorest chance is better than none.

It will be both for his interest, and that of the State where his crimes were committed, to better his prospects by removal to new scenes. But if the State assumes the responsibility of his release and the possibility of his removal, she ought to give those among whom he may go the means of knowing what he has been. The registration of these criminals in one State would do little except drive them to some other, unless each State which desires it can have the benefit of the registers kept elsewhere. When France adopted the Bertillon system, there was a general exodus of the habitual criminals to the next rich French-speaking country,—Belgium. Belgium then put it into use against them, and they began to migrate to Switzerland. The Swiss armed themselves in the same way, and with the same success. The whole class, as door after door was thus closed against those who belonged to it, was lessened as well as scattered.

An exchange system in the United States between the public authorities of the different States, under which the records of each are made accessible to all, would be an easy matter to arrange. For many years, the "rogues' gallery" of photographs in the city of New York, and the police record that accompanied them, begun without the requirements of law, were, by the courtesy of her authorities, often the means of following and identifying the criminals who had gone into other jurisdictions. Each State might, at slight expense, publish annually descriptive registers of all its habitual misdemeanants, proved such by a second conviction; send copies to the authorities of every considerable place within its limits, and to each of its criminal tribunals; and exchange others with any or all of its sister States. Each name would have its number, and in the graver cases at least photographs should be taken, and copies furnished to any public officer on payment of the necessary expense.

It would be also desirable to have a sort of clearing house at Washington to which all the States should report, and where each could gain early information as to the last advices from any convict of the dangerous class. This was one of the recommendations made to the Department of State by the delegates to the Fifth International Prison Congress held at Paris in 1895. In their official report it is thus mentioned: —

"As an efficient agent for the repression of crime, the Bertillon system is of the highest value, and it ought to be in operation all over the United States, with a central bureau at Washington, under the support and direction of the General Government."[1]

Ten minutes now suffices for running through the Bertillon files, in the Paris police offices (in which

[1] Report, Washington, 1896, pp. 75, 95.

are already the descriptions of many thousands of criminals), and picking out, if it is among them, that which identifies a new-comer. They are so classified and arranged that by a simple process of repeated exclusions, the result can be infallibly attained in every case.

The measurements required are readily taken with the aid of a head caliper and common rulers fitted with a sliding block. If a man were arrested under an *alias* in California, and his description, ascertained by the Bertillon method, telegraphed to such a central bureau of registration at Washington, a reply could be received in half an hour which would state his previous history.

Any system of dealing with habitual criminals as a separate class must, in a country like ours, be necessarily more complex than in one of the nations of Europe.

Criminal justice is administered with us by nearly fifty different sovereignties, yet so bound together that every peaceable citizen of one has an indefeasible right to travel into and do business in every other. Unless, then, convictions in one State or Territory, in considering previous sentences to imprisonment, are given equal weight in every other State with those had there, it will be easy to evade the force of any laws regarding habitual criminals, by merely crossing the imaginary line which divides one of these jurisdictions from the next. A number of our States have passed statutes to meet this difficulty. Mr. Livingston introduced in his Code of Crimes and

Punishments (art. 54) the provision that a previous conviction in any of our States should be as effectual for such purposes as a previous conviction in Louisiana. Missouri and Georgia have made this their law, and Maine, Virginia, and Ohio include also convictions before any United States court.

It may also be necessary for Congress to make further provision for the reclamation of prisoners released on parole or under surveillance in one State, who have fled into another. Where, in such a case, the release is conditional upon a continued residence within the State by which they were imprisoned, it may be regarded as merely a temporary enlargement of the jail limits, and extradition may be granted under the existing law.[1] But where, as may often be desirable, the convict is released with a view to his employment in another State, that theory may prove inadequate to justify his surrender, if he violate his parole.

Livingston may have been right in his day in laying down the peremptory rule of confining for life all who have been thrice sentenced to the penitentiary. Since the invention of the Bertillon system, I cannot believe that it is as well calculated to serve the community, or even to deal fairly with the convict, as that of intrusting the proper authorities with a discretionary power of conditional release.

The objections to confining the habitual criminal within four walls until death, are indeed many. It shuts him out from any chance of beginning a new

[1] Drinkall *v.* Spiegel, 68 Connecticut Reports, 441.

life as an honest man. It throws him as a perpetual burden on the public treasury. It tends to dissuade juries from conviction by the rigor of the penalty. It makes the criminal reckless how far he goes, since for any crime short of murder, there is the same length of imprisonment. It may sometimes give him the very thing he wants, a free bed and a free table.

Our prisons are already too full. In 1890 the census told us that 1315 out of every million of our population were imprisoned for crime. Ten years before, this number was 1169 to the million; in 1870 only 853. I do not think that this increase of numbers is simply due to the increase of crime, nor at all to any increased efficiency in criminal prosecutions. It is referable largely to the fact that our prisons are becoming boarding-schools for the young, and shelters for the aged. They are really attractive to not a few, and those to whom they are attractive are often these very habitual criminals. They feel at home there. The jail gives them better food, cleaner beds, purer air, an easier life, than they generally find outside. Not a few are vagabonds during the open season of the year, and count on regularly returning to prison for their winter residence.

On the other hand, police supervision for life, or for a term of years, leaves the convict free to build up a new character, and to earn his bread in his own way.

He is, no doubt, a constant object of suspicion. He is sensible that he is being continually watched. His neighbors will not be unlikely to know it too.

But with all these disadvantages, he is still breathing the open air, living in the home of his own choice, surrounded, if he will, by family ties, free from arrest unless he deserves it.

The fact that most of those who enter the class of habitual criminals seem almost fated to it from their birth by their physical constitution does not lessen the right of society to hold them in this way responsible for their misdeeds so far as is necessary for its own protection. The wolf is not to be blamed for ferocity, but we shoot him at sight. A man, the community cannot put to death, unless in absolute self-defence. Then it may, and it can with equal right, where the danger is less, do any less damage to him which self-preservation demands.

Such a system might require for its efficacy the multiplication of our police, but it would be likely to reduce the expenses of our jails and penitentiaries. Shorter sentences would be given if release meant freedom from confinement, not from supervision; and a second offence, for which imprisonment might be inflicted, would be less readily committed.

But to circumscribe and reduce the class of habitual criminals is an end which, if attained, justifies any outlay of money. Every member of that class is a perpetual drain on the community, by day and night. He must be put at a disadvantage, and kept there at whatever cost, and whatever inconvenience to society or himself. He gives no quarter, and he must expect none.

AS A CLASS TO BE TREATED BY ITSELF

We speak of criminals in a proverbial phrase, as to be kept "under watch and ward," and we have assumed that when the ward is relaxed, the watch may cease also. It may in many, in most cases; but habitual crime requires, if not both, then at least habitual watch. The worst enemies of the law ought never, for a moment, to be beyond its sight and reach.

The criterion proposed for distinguishing the professional from the ordinary criminal — that of repeated convictions and sentences to imprisonment — is but a rude one. There are notorious rogues who are never fairly caught but once; there are men who may be found guilty of two or three offences grave enough to send them to jail, and yet have no thought or power of making a livelihood of crime. But to take any other rule of discrimination would leave too much to *ex parte* human judgment. It must be exercised *ex parte*, unless there is a charge and a hearing, and if these are to be required, it seems proper to leave them to come only in the common course of criminal procedure, and let the record of the court determine the result. The test is also a familiar one, already provided for analogous purposes in the statutes of every State. If it had even less merits of its own, this general sanction by long use would seem sufficient to justify, if not to require, our reliance on it.

CHAPTER X

THE DEFENCE BY THE STATE OF SUITS ATTACKING TESTAMENTARY CHARITIES [1]

A CHARITABLE bequest is seldom relished by heirs. In most wills, the executor is himself an heir. If, then, the charitable intentions of the testator are to be carried out, it must often, if not ordinarily, be done by unfriendly hands.

As every will is a departure from the usual rules of succession established or approved by the law, it is also a kind of challenge to the community. It asserts that the testator can dispose of his property better than they can; that he can make a law for himself better than the law of the land. Our American States have adhered to the ancient principle of Roman law, as found in the Twelve Tables, that for every citizen "*uti legassit super pecunia, tutelave suæ rei, ita jus esto,*" more closely than did Rome herself. In most of them there is no statutory restriction on the right to disinherit. Precisely for this reason an American will is peculiarly open to attack. The sympathies of the people are with the heir, who has been stripped of everything, when they might not be

[1] The greater part of this chapter is taken from a paper read by the author in the Judicial section of the Congress of Jurisprudence, held at Chicago in connection with the Columbian Exposition, in 1893.

DEFENCE OF TESTAMENTARY CHARITIES 317

aroused if some Falcidian law guaranteed him a certain share of the inheritance. The validity of the will must be determined by a jury, and the jury will be a fair representative of popular sentiment.

Charitable bequests would be in less danger, also, had we a form of action such as is familiar to most countries, by which wills can be attacked directly and openly, when the heir is passed over without due cause. But, so far as I am aware, there is no remedy for a mere undutiful will, except in Louisiana. Elsewhere the heir can gain what the community are apt to regard as his rights against such an instrument only by breaking it altogether, as the act of one without testamentary capacity, or unduly influenced, or by maintaining some legal objection to particular provisions adverse to his interest.

Where the devisees or legatees are natural persons, taking a beneficial estate in their own right, they can be trusted to protect themselves. If minors, a guardian *ad litem* will maintain their interests, and, if necessary, even against their parents.

So provisions for charities may be adequately defended, if made in trust to corporations having funds with which to employ proper counsel. But it is not so when the trustees, whether natural persons or corporations, are without funds, or, if corporations, are not under efficient management. They can then hardly be expected to present their claims in the most effective way.

The executor, indeed, represents the dead, but if he be one of the heirs who would otherwise succeed, his adverse interest will be likely to make his defence perfunctory. He may, indeed, virtually lead the attack, by bringing an equitable action, after the probate of the will, to determine its proper construction and effect, where these are doubtful. The doubt may be so stated as to exaggerate its importance. Considerations and authorities tending to defeat the will may be brought to the attention of the court, and others left unnoticed which go to support it.

It is true that the court, in such a suit, may often, perhaps ordinarily, be trusted to recall the law, and apply the proper rule; but a decision upon a case that has been but half argued is seldom quite satisfactory, nor is it the true office of a judge to supply the want of counsel for the absent or undefended. This is a duty not to be disregarded, when it is forced upon the bench, but the rarer the occasions for its exercise, the better will be the administration of justice. It is a duty of the State, but one which the State can best discharge through its executive officers.

The French Code of Civil Procedure (article 83), provides that notice of every suit concerning public corporations and establishments, and gifts and legacies for the benefit of the poor, shall be given to the principal law officer of the State (*procureur de la république*), and bestows upon him authority to intervene in any other cause in which he may deem his participation necessary.

England makes it the duty of her Attorney-General to institute all proceedings necessary to secure the due application and administration of charitable endowments. A similar function has been cast upon the

Attorney-General of many of our States. I believe that this should be the practice in all, and that the French law might well be followed, by requiring service of process upon the Attorney-General in every suit affecting either the validity or the administration of a charitable gift.

It would not be difficult for him to ascertain whether, among the other parties to the controversy, were any who would adequately present the cause of the charity. His function in this respect would be somewhat analogous to that of the Queen's Proctor in England, in uncontested divorce suits. He would be bound to see that all the material facts were placed before the court; that there was nothing savoring of collusion; and that the leading authorities in support of the bequest, if its validity were questioned, were fairly presented. Should he find that others stood ready to do this, his active intervention would be unnecessary; but otherwise it would be vital to the attainment of justice.

The appearance of the Attorney-General in proceedings for the probate of a will may seem more like an intrusion into matters of private concern than his participation in suits arising as to the meaning and effect of the instrument. But where the executor is adversely interested, it is never safe to trust him implicitly. A very little inattention or neglect on his part will suffice to defeat the probate. The charitable provisions may be inconsiderable, as compared with the other bequests, but, be they great or small, the State which has, for its own good, given the testator power to make them, has an interest in their preservation, not only for what they are in themselves, but for their effect on the community. A government under which charitable wills are generally set aside will soon come to have few of them.

The object and effect of every charitable bequest is to confer a public benefit; else it is no charity. I say its effect, for on this point the opinion of the community, as manifested in its laws, must be decisive. Turgot did not speak for any century but his own when he declared that all permanent endowments were permanent evils. The tendencies of Christian civilization are all towards altruism. As the range of superstitious uses has been narrowed, that of public uses has been enlarged. We understand better the duties of man to man, and if the performance of some of them is too often deferred until after death, there is all the more reason why the State should see to it that the will by which it permits this to be done should have its full effect.

Capital is accumulated for a few by the labors of many. Charity returns it to the many. The individual, under the forces of civilization, is yielding to the masses by daily necessity. In charity, he yields from a better motive. It is the stream flowing to the sea. It is the gift coming back to the giver. In no country has this process gone on so rapidly as in the United States of the nineteenth century. The example in this, as in so much else, was set

ATTACKING TESTAMENTARY CHARITIES

by Franklin; and the richer among his countrymen, gaining wealth in the same way as he, as the easy reward of honest and intelligent industry under favorable circumstances, have followed him in leaving part of it behind them for the service of their fellow-citizens. With us it is a subject of remark when a rich man's will contains no charitable bequests. With us, therefore, it is peculiarly the duty of the State to guard this tribute from the dead which public opinion almost demands, and no surer safeguard can be found than the intervention of the principal law officers of the government from whose statutes the will derives its force.

CHAPTER XI

SALARIES FOR MEMBERS OF THE LEGISLATURE.

IT is one of the oldest of English political traditions that the member of a legislative body should serve without reward. He occupies a representative position. He is an agent for others, and the original conception of the nature of agency made it always a gratuitous contract. He is a spokesman for others, and an advocate in most countries has been considered as occupying a position of trust and honor, which he would degrade by demanding compensation.

Of the three departments of government established under the familiar though somewhat unpractical division of power which has found its way into most of our American Constitutions, the legislative is the only one whose principal members have not always been paid for their time.

The King, and his successors under republican institutions in independent States, have necessarily been subjected to large expense in maintaining such an establishment as the courtesies of official life require. They have been forced to live, to entertain, to travel, in a certain style, were it only to maintain the dignity of the people for whom they stand, in the eyes of foreign powers. Their appointments, therefore, have been on a liberal scale, and in case of Presidents of republics some regard has often been paid to the future by giving them a salary from which something can be saved towards their support on retirement to private life. In the United States this has been done in part by indirect and generally unnoticed means, through a gradually increasing number of items in the appropriation bills for horses and carriages, furniture, hot-houses, conservatories, fuel, light, and attendance at the executive mansion, books and stationery, and other "contingent expenses," and according to the President a tacit right to call on the navy to furnish the music for his state dinners, or the steamer for his summer vacation trips.

Judges, as they must devote their entire time to their official duties, have everywhere been salaried officers, and often received, when superannuated or otherwise withdrawn from service, a retiring pension.

From the days of the Roman republic, however, until the adoption of the Constitution of the United States, it was otherwise with members of legislative bodies. To pay them was deemed not only to degrade their office, but to present a temptation for its abuse. The natural measure of compensation, were any offered, would be the time spent in their public duties. But most nations have been content with the maxim that the fewest laws were the best, and therefore solicitous that legislative sessions should be short. Wherever any allowance was made to the law makers, it was by way of indemnity, not compensation. Their expenses only were defrayed.

This was the English practice when parliaments there first took shape. The King's writ of summons not only directed the election of knights, citizens, and burgesses, but ordered the sheriff to levy upon the landholders (who were electors of the shire), for the benefit of their representatives, such sums as would meet their "reasonable expenses" in travelling to and from parliament and while attending its sessions. Later, these sums were made certain, and the levy was to be for a specified number of days, at the rate of four shillings a day for each knight of the shire, and half that sum for a citizen or burgess.[1] The members, at this period, came to parliament with a commission in the fashion of a general letter of attorney, by which "*plena potestas*" was given to act for their constituents.[2]

Service upon such a footing was obviously incompatible with the character which the House of Commons soon came to assume. The members were under an implied obligation to keep the particular interests of those who sent and paid them in view, and to obey any directions which they might see fit to give. They could not act the free part of representatives of the English people and of all the people. As soon as this conception of a member's duty to his country at large began to prevail, the writs ceased to call for any levy for their use, and they became, for the first time, independent of local dictation.

By this time also the landed interest had found how valuable parliamentary representation was, and

[1] Blackstone's "Commentaries," Cooley's ed. i. *174, and note.
[2] Taylor's "Origin and Growth of the English Constitution," i. 476.

there was no trouble in filling the House of Commons with those who were willing to serve at their own charges.

The first English settlements were made in the United States before this change had been fully accomplished, and our colonial legislatures generally provided for the expenses of their members, but at the cost, not of the counties or towns from which they came, but of the general treasury.

When the Continental Congress came into existence, each State paid in the same way for the expenses of its delegation. In some of the Southern States a liberal allowance for this purpose was made. That of Virginia, Jefferson, in his "Notes on Virginia," estimates as averaging $7,000 a year in gold. The representatives of the Northern States, in which there were fewer independent fortunes, were men accustomed to live more simply, and generally received much less. Connecticut was in the habit of electing six delegates, but providing that not more than three at any one time should be in attendance at Congress at the expense of the State. The others might lend their presence, if they chose, at their own charges, but not otherwise.[1]

When the Convention that framed the Constitution of the United States met, this subject was discussed at great length and on several occasions. The Virginia resolutions, which constituted the original basis of their work, proposed that senators and representatives should "receive liberal stipends by which they may be compensated for the devotion of their time to the public service."

[1] Connecticut State Records, i. 10.

It was urged that under the system prevailing as to the existing Congress, the best men often declined to serve, on account of pecuniary inability;[1] and the reply was that the best men were seldom the poorest, and honor counted for more than pay. The word "liberal" was finally struck out, and after some hesitation as to whether or not to replace it by either "adequate" or "fixed,"[2] the article was put in the shape finally adopted, by which the rule was established (Art. I. Sec. 6) that "the senators and representatives shall receive a compensation for their services, to be ascertained by law and paid out of the treasury of the United States."

This was, I believe, the first declaration in history by any government that representatives in a legislative body should be paid for their services. It was carried against strong opposition. Gov. Gerry stated it as one of the reasons why he could not concur in behalf of Massachusetts, in signing the Constitution.[3]

Attempts were made, in the course of the discussions, to agree on some rate of compensation which should be definitely fixed in the Constitution itself. One delegate advocated $5 a day, and another $4, but the general opinion was that any sum which could be named would appear so extravagant to many of the people that the ratification of the Constitution might be imperilled. There were some of the Southern members also who opposed the grant of any compensation, on the ground that the want of it was the best way to fill Congress with men of property, and

---

[1] Madison's Journal, Scott's ed., 153.
[2] *Ibid.*, 153, 160, 220, 248, 445.   [3] *Ibid.*, 740.

that only if so constituted could it be depended on to guard the different interests to be committed to its keeping.[1]

The power thus intrusted by the Constitution to Congress was certainly not abused at first. A law was passéd giving each member six dollars for each day of actual attendance, and six dollars more for every twenty miles of distance by the usual route to and from his home. The senators in the first Congress asked and secured a dollar a day more, in view of their superior dignity, but the house insisted, in 1796, that its members should be put upon an equality with them.

Twenty years later an annual salary of $1,500 was substituted for the *per diem* allowance, and the measure made to apply to the Congress which passed the law. This retroactive feature of the bill made it exceedingly unpopular throughout the country. The first Congress had proposed an amendment to the Constitution prohibiting any such action, which received the approval of a majority of the States which voted on the question of ratification, though not of the necessary two thirds.[2] The people were indignant that a rule of propriety which had come so near to finding a place in the Constitution had been violated. The legislature of Massachusetts adopted a formal protest. Many of the representatives who had supported the law lost their seats; and before the session closed it was repealed. The next Con-

[1] Madison's Journal, Scott's ed., 247, 284, 494.
[2] Annual Report of the Am. Hist. Association for 1896, vol. ii. pp. 34, 317.

gress replaced it by one which returned to the *per diem* plan, but made the rate eight dollars instead of six dollars. This stood until 1856, when a bill prospective in its terms, established the compensation of members of both houses upon the footing of a salary. The amount was made $3,000, which was raised in 1866, when gold was at a considerable premium, to $5,000, and in 1873 to $7,500. This last measure was again a retrospective one, and with the same results for its promoters as in 1816.[1] There was a general cry of "back-pay grab" which defeated the re-election of most of the representatives who had taken advantage of its provisions, and led to the restoration, during the next year, of the former rate. Since then the only substantial change has been to give each member a clerk at the public expense.

The first European nation to follow the American lead in this matter was Belgium. Under her Con-

[1] It is an assuring indication of the good sense of the American people that so little has been seriously attempted in the line of constitutional amendments, and that the few which have been proposed by Congress have generally demonstrated their fitness by securing prompt ratification. This makes the more remarkable the rejection of that forbidding retrospective laws to increase the pay of members of Congress. Only nineteen amendments have ever been thus proposed, and of these but four failed to secure the approval of a majority of the States.

One of the four was that of 1789 which has been described; another that of 1789, regulating the apportionment of representatives; another that of 1810, disfranchising any citizen of the United States who might accept any title of nobility or honor, or without consent of Congress accept any emolument from any foreign power; and the last that of 1861, to prevent any future amendment of the Constitution for the abolition of slavery.

stitution of 1831 the deputies in the lower house of her legislative assembly received eighty dollars for each month of the session. This sum was fixed as a mode of reimbursement for money paid out, not remuneration for services rendered, and the members from Brussels could not claim it, they not being necessarily subjected to anything more than their ordinary expenses. To the senators nothing was given. No one was eligible to that office who was not a large taxpayer, and they therefore presumably had no occasion to look to the public treasury.

Our States have generally adhered to the practice of paying a daily allowance, which is often limited to a fixed number of days, or reduced after a fixed number of days has elapsed. In the few which have substituted salaries, the amount is not greater than would pay the board and incidental expenses of the member during the continuance of the session.

The absence of an hereditary aristocracy, or anything in the nature of a leisured class in this country made it necessary at least to indemnify our legislators against the actual cost of their temporary residence at the capital. The growing length of Congressional sessions has probably justified the change of policy by the United States. They have come to take most of the time of their senators and representatives, and it is proper that they should pay something, at least, towards the support of their families.

Soon after the passage of the Reform Bill in England, the leaders of the working people there began to advocate the introduction of salaries for members of the House of Commons, as well as the repeal of the statute which imposed a property qualification for their election. Of the six points in the People's Charter of 1838, these were two.[1]

The latter only met with any general favor. That, after a few years, was carried, but the other both the great parties have always hitherto refused to support. Nor has it received the adhesion of those who may be called the philosophical reformers. John Stuart Mill, Hare, and Bryce have pronounced strongly against it.[2] Justin McCarthy, no doubt, fairly represented the state of public opinion, on the part of the liberal school of politics, not less than the conservative side, when he spoke of it in his " History of Our Own Times " as decidedly objectionable."[3]

The revolutionary movements of 1848, though they did little to advance the cause of Chartism in England, left lasting effects on the Continent. The Constitution adopted in November of that year by the French Republic contained an article (chap. v., Art. 38) providing that " every representative of the people is to receive a remuneration which he is not at liberty to renounce."[4] It was a natural complement to two of the preceding articles (34 and 35) in the

[1] Jephson, on " The Platform," ii. 171.
[2] Mill's " Dissertations and Discussions," iv. 96; Bryce's " American Commonwealth," i. 191.   [3] Vol. i. p. 80.
[4] Denmark at about the same time adopted the rule of compensation, and has always adhered to it. It also took root in Norway. Prussia put the French provision into her Constitution of 1850, in almost the same words, as to members of the lower house.

same chapter, which declared that "the members of the national assembly are the representatives, not of the department which nominates them, but of the whole of France: they cannot receive imperative instructions." Three years later, all were swept away by the Constitution of 1851, framed by Louis Napoleon, in which any payment, either to senators or deputies, was prohibited (chap. iv., Art. 22; chap. v., Art. 37). He too was consistent with himself. De Tocqueville had written with a prophetic instinct a few years before, that when a democratic republic renders offices, which had formerly been remunerated, gratuitous, it may safely be believed that that State is advancing to monarchical institutions."[1]

During the brief life of the Constitution of 1848 a law was passed under which the deputies received a salary of $1,800. Immediately after the fall of the second empire, it was restored, and senators and deputies were, in 1875, placed upon the same footing.[2] That of the former has recently been raised to $3,000.

The French national assembly is not ordinarily in session for more than five months of the year. Its members come to the capital from a distance but little greater than that travelled by members of the British House of Commons, and there is no other reason why one nation should give and the other deny compensation to the representatives of its people, except that found in the more aristocratic character of

---

[1] Democracy in America, i. 224, Langley's ed.
[2] *Codes Français et Lois Usuelles*, Rivière's ed., pp. 8, 11. Laws of Aug. 2 and Nov. 30, 1875.

the older government This is steadily waning. The lowering of English rents has been a severe blow to the county family. The extension of the parliamentary franchise has brought new men, and new kinds of men, into positions of political influence. The very system of primogeniture, with the traditions which have grown up to strengthen its hold on English society, is continually driving more and more of the titled and landed class to seek their fortunes in trade, and make a name and place for themselves by their own exertions. If such men can no longer be sent to parliament by family interest; if the only way to gain a seat is to commend themselves to the mass of the people; if they have nothing to live on, should they secure an election, but a slender allowance charged on a diminishing estate, — they are not unlikely to come to view this question of payment for parliamentary service in a new light.

The House of Commons has undergone a greater change within the last thirty years than most English writers are willing to acknowledge. It does not yet fairly represent in its composition the people at large, but it is fast losing its ancient character as a body of landlords or dependents of landlords.

Were it not for the want of salaries, this change would be much more rapid. As things stand, if the workingmen wish to send John Burns there, they must provide for his support out of their own pockets. If Ireland desires a representation that really represents her, her hundred delegates must, almost to a man, be maintained at London by public subscriptions, and largely by American money.

There is something unseemly and incongruous in the dependence which such a system, in its practical working, entails on the legislator who looks to private charity for the payment of his board bill. Particularly is this true where the funds come in great part from a foreign country, and are contributed by those whose motive is the hope of effecting a fundamental change in the British Constitution. The American Irishman aids in keeping the Irish parliamentary delegation full, because he thinks it will further a repeal of the Act of Union of a hundred years ago. The very fact that their support is provided for from such a source puts the Irish members under a certain obligation to work towards that end. They would probably do so without the motive; but that they are placed in such a situation is, of itself, a reproach to the laws which make it possible, if not necessary.

Germany, with her popular assembly elected by universal suffrage and continuing for a five years' term, is faced by a similar demand. There, as in England, the influence of an aristocracy joined to the fears of capital is in steady opposition to any change, and there is a constitutional provision that " the members of the Reichstag shall not be allowed to draw any salary or be compensated, as such." If the representatives of the people were to be paid from the treasury, and paid enough to justify a workingman in laying down his tools with the certainty that his family would be well provided for while he was at the capital, the ranks of the socialist members would soon increase.

In Italy custom has relieved the government from any serious difficulty in dealing with this question. The saying there is that the senate is at Rome, but not the senators. Most of them, like the peers in the British House of Lords, though for different causes, are only occasionally at the capital. No compensation is paid to the members of either house. They have, however, a free pass to and from Rome over the railways, and it is freely used.

Bazin, in his "Italians of To-day," mentions a conversation on this subject with a senator from Vicenza who had been twenty years in office. It was seldom, he was told, that a majority of senators were in attendance. Most of them were to be found at their homes, engaged in ordinary business pursuits. The physician was visiting his patients, the lawyer advising his clients, the professor meeting his classes. Few senators or deputies were men of large fortune, but all had either some independent means, or an assured income from their own industry. They felt that under such a system, as representatives of the people, they were more vitally in touch with them than could be the case were each expected to remain at the capital through the entire legislative session.

Somewhat similar results follow in those States of the United States where free railroad passes are a perquisite of legislative membership. The representative generally spends his Sundays at home, and often the day before and the day after. He is, however, seldom absent from the legislative sessions. Public sentiment is against it, and the legal provision for his expenses makes constant attendance possible for the poorest.

Of the lesser American republics, several have followed the example of the United States.

Mexico, in her Constitution of 1859 (Tit. VI., Art. 120), provides that the members of the Chamber of Deputies shall receive a compensation for their services, which they may not renounce. It is to be fixed by law, prospectively only, and paid from the federal treasury.[1] Senators are to be paid, if at all, by the States which send them.

The practice in the British colonies differs widely.

In Australia a salary of $1,500 is allowed by the leading provinces to members of the lower house; those of the upper are sometimes paid less, because they need it less.[2] Canada confines herself to allowing a "sessional indemnity." In the Bahamas no compensation is allowed, but citizens of New Providence may be chosen as the representatives of other islands, and often are; the result of which has been greatly to strengthen the predominance of Nassau in the affairs of the government.

Sweden has adopted the Belgian system; paying the members of her lower house of Parliament, but not those of the upper house.

---

[1] Annals of the American Academy of Political and Social Science, ii. 44. Colombia, in her Constitution of 1886 (Art. 112), repeats the provision against retrospective increases of salaries.

[2] New Zealand pays £240 a year to those of the lower house, and only £150 to those of the upper.

The Swiss Federal Assembly, while leaving each canton to pay its own representatives in the Council of States, follows the general rule of our American States, by giving each delegate to the lower house a certain sum ($4) for each day's attendance, together with a mileage allowance for his travelling expenses.[1]

This is probably sufficient for any legislative assembly, under a republican form of government, whose annual session is short, and whose members are not too distant from their homes to prevent them from making frequent visits there, and so retaining some real hold upon their private affairs. It has worked well in this country, and will in any where the honor and the opportunity which office gives are its main attractions.

These are at their best in the United States. Here is the only land in which a civilized and educated people are building up new political institutions to suit themselves. Australia comes near it; but Australia is subject to the British Empire, and to a parliament in which she has no representation. Japan comes near it; but Japan is still subject to a sovereign who has, in theory and form at least, most of the powers of the Roman Emperor.

Every American citizen is engaged in a grand experiment — that for which Washington declared it was his main purpose in accepting the Presidency to secure a fair trial, — to determine " with what dose of

[1] Moses, on "Federal Government of Switzerland," 113. Until 1874, it was only $2.40 a day. A day's pay is docked for every day's absence without excuse. Winchester's "Swiss Republic," 68.

OF THE LEGISLATURE

liberty man can be trusted for his own good." The authoritative leaders in this work are our public officers and, most of all, our legislators. Much of the best of it, no doubt, is done by private individuals, in the press and on the platform, or in drawing and urging bills for legislatures to pass. But such men are laboring for others to reap. Nor at most can they do more than propose the form of laws and institutions. They must pass them over to others for the final touch and the last word. Seldom can they link their names to them in history. Often must they see them fail for want of intelligent support, or turned to folly by some hasty amendment.

The American legislator is tied down to no theory of political administration. His constituents expect him to add and to improve; not so much to hold fast to what is good as to make what is good better, and to state it better. The growing tendency towards codification necessarily increases his work and also his possibilities of personal distinction. He is a builder, and what he builds may set the fashion for other States and other times.

The architect who planned the cathedral of Cologne, though he might die before the foundations were fully laid, could count on the completion of the great structure in some distant age, in exact accordance with his original design, for he dealt with the immutable principles of an ideal science. But in government no principles are immutable, — none, at least, which men have thus far put in form. Gothic architecture can be stated in stone, but political science must be stated in the changing speech of men, and political institutions shaped by ever-moving national characteristics. To one whose station puts it in his power, without abandoning his ordinary means of livelihood, to share and direct in such a work, no reward ought to be needed that ambition does not supply.

No doubt there are enough who seek a seat in the legislature from motives very different, and make the want of a salary an excuse for selling their vote or petty pilfering from the public treasury. There have been representatives of this description both at Washington and our State capitals, who have trafficked in public documents, and carried home enough of pens and paper, inkstands and portfolios, twine and pocket-knives, from their desks to stock a country store. It is not long since a Western congressman declared that he had been able to save his entire salary by selling his stationery supplies to pay part of his board bill, and meeting the rest from the difference between his mileage and his actual travelling expenses.

There are, on the other hand, many of our best citizens who have no time that they can afford to give to the public, and are thus shut out of our legislatures, to make room for richer and weaker men. The description of the Senate of the United States as a club of millionaires has enough truth in it to make the jest a bitter one. The salary of a senator is inadequate to meet the expense of housekeeping at Washington in the style usual in the higher official circles to which he belongs. Nor, if he is content to live at a boarding-house or hotel, can he lay by enough to help him materially after his term of office has expired, in gaining a proper start in whatever business he may find open to him. One of the seven senators who saved the nation from a grave reproach by defeating the conviction of President Johnson, when impeached for defending what he deemed the constitutional prerogatives of the executive against congressional encroachment, and who lost his re-election by it, was, a few years ago, supporting himself as a compositor in a printing-office. [1]

But this is a difficulty inherent in the practical administration of republican government in a country without the traditions of a court. What salaries are given will not be very far above what is commonly earned in an ordinary business pursuit. In most of the States, even these salaries for the higher executive and judicial officers are felt to be a considerable burden on the treasury, and the inferior ones are largely compensated by fees paid by those for whom they are called upon to render service. This system often leads to absurd results. A clerk of court or the sheriff in attendance may thus receive twice, and sometimes ten times, the salary of the judge. But the foundation on which it rests, that a man's pay should be proportioned to his work and come from his work, is in accordance with American ideas. For legislation no fees can be safely paid to the legislators, and if there were no other reason for denying them a salary in the ordinary State, their number would be a sufficient one. Any salary that could be deemed an adequate remuneration for the

---

[1] This was Senator Ross of Kansas. President Cleveland came to his relief by giving him an appointment as a territorial governor.

time spent, when multiplied by one, two, or three hundred, would amount to a sum too large to be added to the annual budget without the strongest protest from those on whom the new burden would fall.

The rule of confining salaries to an indemnity for the expenses ordinarily incurred rests, therefore, upon solid foundations. The extension of the principle of federal government will tend to relax it in the case of the great powers, as it has already in the case of the United States. The influence of the large capitalists and corporations, on the other hand, will be exerted towards restricting salaries or excluding them altogether. The absence of remuneration is the least objectionable form of a property qualification for office; and the rich prefer to be governed by the rich.

I venture the prediction that half of the twentieth century will not pass away before England provides for the expenses of the members of her House of Commons. She would have done so before France, had her civil war not been before that of France. Governments are like railroads: they must all, in course of time, pass through a process of foreclosure and reorganization. The old management is set aside, and the plant put in new hands to be worked by new methods. The Stuart management was foreclosed by the English people a century before the French Revolution. The Hanoverian line came in before the theory of modern government had been evolved. Its quiet rule can be adapted to the new form which society is assuming, without a new foreclosure; but the process, though slower, will be not less sure.

CHAPTER XII

PERMANENT COURTS OF INTERNATIONAL ARBITRATION

IT was one of Matthew Arnold's fine sayings that two things govern the world, Force and Right, — Force till Right is ready.

Right has already displaced force as the real basis and criterion of authority in the government of every civilized country. If the sovereign power is in the hands of an absolute monarch, he claims it only by "hereditary right," or popular choice, and appeals to law as its source and sanction. The principles of jurisprudence, also, recognized as governing the relations of private citizens to each other, are substantially the same in all the leading nations of the world; and they are the same because they are derived from the conception of the equality of right. Altruism has become an accepted standard of human conduct. Some still deny the fatherhood of God, but no one disputes the brotherhood of man. That selfish spirit which once made every nation call all foreigners either enemies or barbarians has shrunk away to the furthest outskirts of civilization.

These upward tendencies of the human race may be said to have become first discernible as world forces in the control of social movements shortly after the era of the Reformation.

The Roman Catholic church had before interposed a power between God and man, and between nation and nation, which had been necessarily antagonistic to the development of such ideas. Ecclesiastical power had often had little to do with right; and men knew it. God was the God of the Catholic, as Jehovah had been called the God of Israel; not the father and lover of all. It was not until 1537 that the papal bull was published which declared the natives of America to be rational beings. The sixteenth century began with the attacks of Luther on the usurped position of the church as the central power on earth, and of Copernicus on the usurped position of the earth as the centre of the universe. It was a logical consequence of these new views of things that nations should begin to assume new relations to each other. The foundations of human philosophy had been moved. The only form of ecumenical human authority had been swept away. Something must be brought forward to replace what had been thrown aside, something better and higher.

The seventeenth century responded with the proposition of Henry IV. of France, made in 1609, to establish the Christian Republic of Europe. It was to consist of fifteen States, each to be of as nearly the same size and power as the others, or, should Russia accede to it, of sixteen. The Turks were to be driven back into Asia. A diet of four representatives from each State, to be constituted by the name of the Senate of the Christian Republic, was to regulate the relations between the constituent powers, raise a sufficient military force to preserve the peace of

Europe, and make an equitable apportionment of the necessary expense.

The death of Henry during the following year, and the accession of a child to the throne as his successor, left France in no position to press this scheme; but it was, no doubt, one of the things that led Grotius to prepare his work on the " Law of War and Peace," which was the real beginning of international law. This was published in 1625, soon after Louis XIII. had come of age; and in an elaborate dedication of the treatise to the young king, Grotius declares that all Christian peoples demand of him no less than that, under his lead, wars may be everywhere extinguished, and peace return to States and to the Church alike. On the foundations thus laid there has been since built up by slow degrees, during a period of nearly three centuries, a new science.

It is a science that it would have been impossible for men to comprehend prior to the Reformation. Until Christianity took possession of the Roman Empire and of the thought of the world, nations occupied a position of entire estrangement from, if not of hostility to each other. After the Roman church rose into power and the papacy was developed, it assumed the position of the universal lawgiver and judge. A general council of the church was, in truth, a council of the world, and spoke with a world-wide authority.

That international law which has taken the place in Christendom of the will of the church, does not profess to have, of itself, any original and binding force. It is not law, in any sense in which that term is ordinarily used in civil government; but it rests on the same foundations as municipal law, — the consent of the governed. The people in every community make their own law; and most of it they make from day to day by their habits of life and business usages. So have civilized nations generally come, as a result of their ordinary intercourse, to agree on certain rules of conduct to govern their mutual relations. Here, however, we must stop to mark a point of essential difference. Each community can enforce its own laws on its own people, and on all who are found within its territory. It may and does adopt international law as a part of its municipal law, and enforce it in the same way. But there is no common authority to compel the observance of international law by or between independent nations.

The decisions of courts of justice in rude ages, and in uncivilized countries in our own time, are little regarded, except as obedience is exacted by the strong hand. Under such governments, however, as those to which we are subject, the judgments of courts are commonly executed without any resort to compulsory process. Public opinion demands that they be respected, and the services of the sheriff are not required.

If, then, there is such a thing as a public opinion common to several independent nations, why may it not have, for all practical purposes, the same effect, in producing acquiescence in results reached by international tribunals on principles of international law?

The phrase "republic of letters" has long been a familiar one. It recognizes no local or national boundaries; it expresses the community of thought and feeling which exists between all educated men. Has there not come to be, is there at least not coming to be, a similar unity of conviction among the leading nations of the world as to standards of national duty?

Grotius said [1] that there was no room for decisive and final arbitration between kings or peoples, because there could be no superior power to create or to dissolve an obligation under such conditions. There was none in his day; but he has helped to make one in ours. His discussions and propositions have not only led to something like a systematic code of international law, but to a certain *consensus* as to international morals. Plain dealing is now recognized as the best mode of diplomatic negotiation. No Machiavelli, and, we may even say, no Talleyrand would now be tolerated at the head of any English, French, or German Cabinet. The greater participation of the people in the government, the publicity given to ministerial despatches and parliamentary debates by the press and the ocean cable, have changed the face of international politics within fifty years. They are unifying mankind. As we read our morning newspapers, we feel the pulse beat of the world; and it is one and the same.

What is now so well known as international arbitration is largely of American origin. It has hitherto

[1] *De Jure Belli et Pacis*, 3: 20, 46.

consisted of proceedings before tribunals organized to settle a controversy after it has arisen. Over a hundred matters of difference between nations have been thus adjusted during the nineteenth century, each of which might otherwise have been an occasion of war.

We have been parties to so many of these hearings that we are in a position to judge with some degree of assurance as to their merits and their defects. Both are great. No arbitration agreement, made after a particular matter of dispute has arisen, can be drawn quite as unreservedly in the interests of justice as one made before. The mere words used to state the question give an opportunity for equivocation. In the selection of arbitrators each party is certain to favor those whom it may think most likely to concur in its own views. In the choice of the place for the hearing there will be some thought of the state of public sentiment there, in circles into which the arbitrators may be thrown. On the other hand, the best men to decide a question of compensation for property unjustly seized might not be the best to pass upon a disputed boundary, nor at all fit to decide upon such a matter as the proper limits of the right of search, or the true meaning of some expression in a treaty.

A permanent international court would have several obvious advantages over any board of arbitration, so constituted for a single occasion.

As it would precede, so it would tend to prevent the occurrence, of any serious controversy. The knowledge of each party to the treaty, by which it was established, that it was in existence and would have jurisdiction to settle the dispute, if it were not settled by the nations concerned, for themselves, would be a strong incentive toward a voluntary adjustment.

In the absence of such a court there would be always a right to reject any offer of arbitration; and it would be a right often exercised, particularly by the party in the wrong. And even if there were a treaty providing for the reference of any controversies that might arise to arbitrators to be chosen for the purpose, it would be a far less manifest breach of duty to refuse to join in selecting arbitrators, or to postpone action in that direction until it became too late to avoid a conflict of arms, than it would be to refuse to respect the summons of a tribunal already constituted for the disposition of precisely such a case.

There was a treaty between Prussia and Denmark, in 1863, which provided for the settlement by arbitration of such disputes as might arise between those powers. One did arise in relation to the Schleswig-Holstein succession, but Prussia found war more to her purpose than arbitration. War followed, and the weaker power lost everything that was at stake.

Permanent judges would also have a position entitling their decisions to far more respect than that likely to be accorded to any temporary arbitrators. There would be a certain unity to their mode of procedure, a certain consistency in their application of legal principles. They would be driven by the strongest motives of ambition as well as of duty to give the closest study and attention to whatever came before them, and to set forth the reasons of their judgments in a way to carry conviction at least to unprejudiced minds. They must thus gradually develop a true system of international jurisprudence, each rule of which would rest upon the general approval of civilized nations; for without that no rule they framed could have any enduring vitality.

Will the time ever come when it will be possible to establish such a tribunal? I believe that it has come, so far as Great Britain and the United States are concerned.

The project of constituting an international court with jurisdiction of differences between all the great powers of Europe received the countenance of Leibnitz, Kant, Lamartine, and Bentham; but no great and general revolution in methods of government has ever been accomplished in a sudden way. Mankind advances only step by step, and irregularly at that. The successful experiment in politics is that which is made under the most favorable conditions. The welfare of the race is too deeply concerned in any attempt to substitute judicial decision for military power in international disputes, to justify taking any risk not absolutely necessary.

The courts of England and the United States already occupy, in respect to almost all matters of municipal and of private international law, the same positions. As was said by the Supreme Court of Errors of Connecticut, in a recent decision,[1] which affirmed the conclusiveness in an American court of

[1] Fisher *v.* Fielding, vol. 67, Connecticut Law Reports, 91.

a judgment against an American, fairly obtained in an English court: —

"They are engaged in administering the same system of jurisprudence, and are bound together by common institutions and modes of thought, no less than by sharing the same language and the same history."

The forms of judicial procedure now in use at Chicago are more like those of England in the seventeenth century than those that are at present followed at London; and on the other hand, the simplification of legal pleadings which now obtains in the English courts had an American origin. The decisions of English courts and the works of English jurists are constantly cited as authorities before our tribunals, and similar respect is paid by their judges to the opinions of Marshall, Story, and Kent.

In both countries, also, the general attitude of the people towards the judicial tribunals is the same. They recognize and confide in them as courts of their own making, and their best defences against any act of executive or legislative injustice. They are prepared in advance to acquiesce in the decisions of those of last resort, and to believe that they are such as law and right demand. For nearly three generations these two nations have been at peace with each other, and engaged in the closest commercial intercourse, not only by sea, but across a frontier stretching for three thousand miles or more across the continent. No two powers in the world have ever before been in so fair a position to try this experiment of an international court.

The Pan-American Congress, held at Washington in 1890, formulated a project for a general treaty of arbitration between all the republics upon the Western continent. Its first article declared that arbitration was adopted as a principle of American International Law, and it proceeded to make a resort to it compulsory as to every question of difference between any of these powers, save such that the decision, in the judgment of one of the parties involved, might imperil its independence. In that case arbitration was to be optional as to that party, but obligatory as to the other. The choice of arbitrators was to be made for each particular controversy as it might arise. Any nation in the world was to have the absolute right to become a party to the treaty, at any time, by simply signing a copy of it, and depositing this instrument with the government of the United States.

This measure was obviously ill-considered and premature. It failed to receive the approval of any of the republics in the Congress, and has been laid upon the shelf as another example of the folly of endeavoring to bring different forms of civilization, and different types of national character, into permanent political union, upon an equal footing.

While this Congress was in session, the Congress of the United States, by concurrent resolution, requested the President " to invite from time to time, as fit occasions may arise, negotiations with any government with which the United States has or may have diplomatic relations, to the end that any differences or disputes arising between the two governments which cannot be adjusted by diplomatic agency may be referred to arbitration, and be peaceably adjusted by such means."

Three years later, the British House of Commons passed a resolution declaring its sympathy with the purpose of this overture, and its hope that it might be accepted by Great Britain. The Olney-Pauncefote treaty followed in 1896. As compared with the pretentious generalizations of the Pan-American project, it shows the difference between political speculation and practical statesmanship. Its failure, from the action of our Senate, is of less significance in the history of nations than the fact that the executive powers of both nations were able to agree upon it.

Had it stated in terms what perhaps may be read between the lines, that a court of permanent judges was contemplated, its fate might possibly have been different, for many of the objections urged against the scheme of procedure would then have fallen to the ground. Had it gone farther and provided for a court all whose judges should be either English or Americans, one vital amendment upon which the Senate insisted would certainly have been avoided.

There were obvious reasons for questioning the wisdom of resorting to a foreign sovereign for the appointment of an umpire. He would certainly not select either a subject of Great Britain or a citizen of the United States, and the umpire would therefore be one trained under different legal and political institutions, and out of tune, so to speak, with his fellow judges in respect to habits of weighing evidence and determining methods of procedure. It is to be regretted that the framers of the treaty did not rely exclusively, as a means of securing impartial judgments, on the plan of which they made so large and wise a use, that of requiring on matters of grave importance the concurrence of more than a majority, say five-sixths, of the members of the tribunal.

Were such a court of arbitration to be constituted, under an appropriate treaty, once for all, to decide future controversies as they might arise, there would be good reason to expect that unanimity in rulings upon minor matters would generally be attained, and to hope that the required majority would often concur in a final award.

I venture to add these further suggestions, as contributions to a working plan.

The presiding judge, under these circumstances, might be chosen from among themselves by the members of the court, either for a term of years or for life, and, should they be unable to agree, might be appointed by lot from the two having the most votes. He should have in all matters of procedure two votes, in case of a tie, as is the common practice in ordinary courts of justice. His successor should be selected in like manner, but from the other nation.

The number of judges ought to be about ten or twelve. With so large a number it would be less apt to divide on national lines, and their oath of office should bind them to act without favor or partiality. Every judge should be commissioned by his government for a term of not less than ten years, and per-

INTERNATIONAL ARBITRATION 353

haps better for life, but should be removable by the Executive, on the address of two-thirds of each house of the national legislature.

Among the American judges there should always be two Justices of the Supreme Court of the United States, and two of the English judges should, in like manner, be taken from the High Court of Justice of England. A larger number could hardly be spared from either bench during the months which might be occupied by an international trial.

It would tend to give dignity to the court, if, so far as there were any vacancies to fill, every ex-President of the United States and every ex-Lord High Chancellor of England were *ex officio* a member of it, so long as he occupied no other public office. While such a provision would bring a certain political element into the composition of the tribunal, the eminence of the men and their more than national reputation could hardly fail to strengthen public confidence in the ability of the court to deal with the largest questions of State. The remaining members it would probably be safer to select from those in each country already holding some judicial office. Great Britain could thus resort, if she pleased, to Scotland, Ireland, Canada, or Australia, while the United States could choose either from the Circuit or District Judges or the State judiciary.

There would, undoubtedly, be many questions that might come before the court upon which the judgment of an experienced diplomatist, a professor of international law, or a great geographer might be worth more than that of those who had had only a legal and judicial training. But the English and American people are accustomed to see their judges decide controversies of every nature, and have found that they are generally competent for the task. No questions of an international character could be presented more difficult or more important than those passed upon by the Supreme Court of the United States in respect to the right of President Lincoln to proclaim a blockade of the Southern ports in 1861,[1] or that disposed of by the English Court of Criminal Appeal in determining the distance from its shores within which it could exercise criminal jurisdiction over those on board a foreign ship.[2]

Trials should take place, unless the court otherwise ordered, in the country against which its jurisdiction was invoked, following the maxim, " *Actor sequitur forum rei.*" If the matter were one submitted by the joint action of both countries, the hearing should be had, in the absence of an agreement between them, wherever the court might direct.

All cases heard should be made the subject of a brief official report, published under the direction of the court in such a form as to be one of a series of similar reports, uniform in style and character. This series should be, in its general features, similar to the sets of reports of cases decided in courts of last resort in England and the United States, with which the bar and bench of each country are familiar. The genius of Anglo-American jurisprudence is respect for pre-

[1] Prize Cases, 2 Black's Reports, 635.
[2] Regina *v.* Keyn, 13 Cox Cr. Cases, 403; Law Reports, 2 Exch. Div. 63.

cedent, and every volume of the description indicated would furnish it new standing ground of that description.

The universal science of international law would be an immense gainer by the growth of such a body of orderly jurisprudence, proceeding from the application of its own principles by trained judges acting with the weight of public authority. For the expression of that common consent of civilized nations upon which the science has been built up, the world has thus far been forced to look to the treatises of jurists, and official documents put forth by particular nations for particular purposes and for their own purposes. A set of international law reports of a judicial character, if at all worthy of the place it filled, though the product of but two nations, could hardly fail, in course of time, to receive general acceptance and to be quoted as of universal authority.

The ordinary court of justice prevents more lawsuits than it decides. Those who know that if they engage in controversy, its determination will belong to another, proceeding under judicial authority, are apt to prefer an amicable settlement. An international court of standing jurisdiction, before which either of the powers for which it acts can always summon the other, must, as has been already said, have in some degree a like deterring effect. We may be sure that all the arts and arguments of diplomacy would be exhausted before any question in dispute was submitted to it for final adjudication.

It is doubtless true that cases would occur in which

anything approaching unanimity in the conclusions of such a tribunal could hardly be anticipated. Especially would this be so, when the experiment was first on trial, and there were no precedents of their own making, to which the attention of the judges could be turned. But they would still have filled an important function. " The law's delays " would have been attained. The nations at difference would have accustomed themselves to the thought that their dispute was to be peacefully adjusted. Any outbreak of a war spirit, incident to the original wrong or misunderstanding, would have spent its force, and the way would be smoothed towards a diplomatic settlement.

Had Spain responded favorably to the overtures of the United States in 1890, and a general treaty of arbitration then been concluded, providing for such a court as has been the subject of consideration, the events of 1898 must have taken a very different shape. The question of responsibility for the destruction of the *Maine*, so far as it might turn on the exercise of due diligence by the Spanish authorities in protecting the ship of a friendly power, would probably have fallen within the stipulated jurisdiction of such a tribunal. If there was room for a difference of opinion upon this point, long diplomatic negotiations would have followed, and however it might have been determined, the principal controversy, under those circumstances, could have had comparatively slight effect in fanning the flames of war.

The incidents of the Cuban revolution of 1895–8

show also the necessary limitations of all arbitration procedure between independent nations. Questions of national policy and national morals must be decided in other ways. Perhaps they indicate with equal force that the time is yet far distant when any permanent court of international arbitration could be wisely established between powers so far apart in their modes of thought and standards of conduct, and so impeded by differences of language and laws from coming to a common understanding on any point, as Spain and the United States. Courts can seldom do complete justice between parties who are not accustomed to the same general course of legal procedure.

In stating the subject of this chapter I have not hesitated to employ a term which, of late years, has been often used, though it is certainly subject to grave objections of form. It may be truly said that to call any tribunal of the character which has been sketched a court of arbitration is a misnomer, since it is of the essence of arbitration that it rest on a voluntary agreement. The objection is technically sound; but what better name can be suggested? We are attempting to describe a new agency of government, and it is not surprising that we find no terms of usage exactly fitted to the occasion. It is not, in strictness, a court, for every true court has inherent power to enforce its own decrees. It is not, in strictness, a board of arbitration, because, once established, either of the nations from whose joint action it derives its powers, becomes, so far as treaty obligations can avail, subject to its jurisdiction. Under these circumstances, while it must be conceded that, taking words in their accepted signification, there is no such thing as compulsory arbitration, it is no less true that there are no known terms that come nearer to the expression of this new idea than those that make up the phrase Permanent Court of International Arbitration. It is permanent as distinguished from a tribunal *ad hoc*. It is a court as distinguished from a board of arbitrators proceeding by their own sense of what is reasonable and fair. It is international, so far as two nations are concerned. It is a proceeding of arbitration, in so far as it can result in no judgment which the judges who render it can enforce.

CHAPTER XIII

THE MONROE DOCTRINE IN 1898

ONE of the weakest of American Presidents will be among those who are longest remembered in the history of the world. A few words in the annual presidential message sent to Congress in 1823, written by John Quincy Adams, the Secretary of State, and inspired by George Canning, the British Secretary of Foreign Affairs, have linked the name of President Monroe forever to what has become one of the fundamental rules of American public law.

A strong man who finds himself in a company which but for himself is composed wholly of children, has a certain responsibility, from the mere fact of their presence. Should their safety be menaced, they would naturally look to him for protection. In somewhat this position the United States found themselves in the first quarter of this century. They were the leading power on the American continent. Greater powers had had territorial possessions here, but only one of them continued to retain them. Revolutions had wrested those of the others from their hands, and at the same time and by the same cause there had been changes in the form of government. Royal authority had given place to republican institutions. The interests of the Roman Catholic church had suffered by these occurrences. They tended to weaken the foundations of monarchical institutions throughout the world. It was a time when matters of sentiment exerted a particularly strong influence in public affairs. Napoleon had recognized this force in politics, and had used it with skill. Upon his fall, the Czar of Russia, a mystic in religion, had brought all the powers of Europe except Great Britain, Turkey, and the Pope of Rome, to unite in a solemn covenant that in dealing with their subjects and with other nations alike, they would be governed by the rules of Christian justice and charity. This agreement, knitting so many great nations together into "the Holy Alliance," lent new weight to the position of Spain in South America. In 1822 the United States had recognized the independence of her revolted colonies there. Were she to attempt to reduce them to subjection again, and receive in this the aid of the Holy Alliance, success in South America might well lead her to think of reasserting some of her ancient rights in North America.

The Monroe doctrine, as originally promulgated, had immediate reference to this condition of things, and this alone. But it does not follow that it means no more now. Every doctrine of public law which has any vitality in it is subject to the law of growth. The United States were a third-rate power in 1823. They are one of the great powers of the world in 1898. The other American States meanwhile have gained little in importance. They are feeble republics, and we are a strong one.

Europe has always recognized the right of her great powers to intervene in any controversy between other States, or in other States, for the protection of those interests which are common to all. Their primacy in the "European concert" is acknowledged. A narrower right of intervention is conceded by the principles of international law to every nation in the affairs of any other, when their course is such as vitally to endanger the tranquillity or prosperity of the intervening power.

Whatever rights of either of these descriptions belong to one or all of the powers of Europe in respect to what passes on that continent, may fairly be claimed by the United States in respect to what passes on this hemisphere. Our Federal union is a stronger bond of connection than any European concert can be between independent States. Peace, under our republican institutions, imposing on us, as our Constitution does, serious obstacles to waging effective war, can be best secured by the absence from this continent of any monarchical powers.

Great Britain, since the Monroe doctrine was formulated, has become substantially a republic, and Canada has a form of government differing little from our own. If we have anything to fear from the influence of monarchical institutions, it will come from the lands that lie south of us.

At the time when the Monroe doctrine was announced, a proposition was made for the convocation of a Pan-American Congress to construct a continental system. Colombia and Chili had already acceded to it. Clay was its foremost advocate in the United States. Jefferson gave it his countenance. "Our first and fundamental maxim," he wrote when consulted by President Monroe as to the propriety of following the suggestion of Canning, "should be, never to entangle ourselves in the broils of Europe. Our second never to suffer Europe to intermeddle with cisatlantic affairs. America, North and South, has certain interests distinct from those of Europe, and peculiarly her own. She should therefore have a system of her own, separate and apart from that of Europe. While the last is laboring to become the domicile of despotism, our endeavors should surely be to make our hemisphere that of freedom."

The Congress was called to meet at Panama early in 1826. The United States sent delegates to represent them, but it had adjourned before their arrival, and though the adjournment was intended to be a temporary one, it proved to be final. It had, however, by putting upon its programme, as a subject for deliberation, the emancipation of Cuba from Spanish control, stiffened the attitude of our government in relation to it so far that Clay, now Secretary of State, wrote, in 1825, to our minister at St. Petersburg, that we would not permit Cuba to pass from the hands of Spain into those of any other European power. And why not? Simply because, in

THE MONROE DOCTRINE IN 1898 363

the language of Monroe's message, we should consider any attempt of such a power to extend its system of government " to any portion of this hemisphere as dangerous to our peace and safety."

Forty years later, Austria and France undertook to set up an empire in Mexico. We affected, until the civil war was over, to believe that they were simply endeavoring to collect from Mexico certain claims for injuries to their subjects which they believed to be justly due; but as soon as our own affairs were composed, we assumed a different tone, and, under the stress of the Monroe doctrine, Maximilian's forces were withdrawn and he came to his end.

Thirty years more passed, and then we found another European power setting up pretensions to sovereignty over a large area of territory which the maps of the world gave to Venezuela. These two countries had come to a point in their controversy when their diplomatic relations had been broken off. There was no one at London to represent the interests of Venezuela at the foreign office. The Monroe doctrine seemed to President Cleveland to require him to proffer the mediation of the United States, and his action, as to matters of substance at least, was well received by the country as a whole. No better proof can be asked than the almost unanimous action taken upon his recommendation by a Congress controlled by a political party to which he did not belong. Territorial encroachments by a European power on an American republic, by the right of the stronger, without a declaration of war, violate the Monroe doctrine as much as if they were effected by military conquest. If sufficiently extensive, they might destroy the independence of the weaker power; and whether great or small, they tend directly, if not resisted, to degrade its character and with it that of republican government.

There were grave objections of form to the terms in which the dissatisfaction of the United States was expressed in the earlier State papers of the Venezuelan controversy; but the spirit of the Monroe doctrine, as that doctrine in course of time had come to be generally understood, here and abroad, was, it seems to me, a full justification for the American position.

Our immense increase in territory, wealth, and population since 1823 has not only given us new weight in American politics, but greater responsibilities to our weaker neighbors. More than ever since the Pan-American Congress of Washington have they looked upon us as holding, in some sort, an American protectorate. The Monroe doctrine, in its original terms, was couched in phrases of diplomatic reserve. And what was thus reserved? I should say the right of emphasizing our position as the natural guardian of republican institutions then or thereafter existing on this continent or on the islands in either ocean whose control may nearly affect our interests, as far and as fast as circumstances would admit.

The "London Spectator" said, in 1896, that "thirty or fifty years hence Europe, pressed almost to madness by inability to feed overcrowded peoples, will want to swarm into South America under its own flags. To deny them will mean attempting to crush the combined fleets and armies of Europe."

The Monroe doctrine has come to assume proportions that make it impossible that anticipations like those of the "Spectator" can ever be fulfilled; and it is quite as well that the world should know it. The Venezuelan incident was the occasion of official action on the part of the United States that will never be retraced, for it voiced (though perhaps in too *brusque* a way) the general sentiment of the American people. "Nothing succeeds like success." If the course of President Cleveland in that matter did not command universal approval in 1896, its results have secured it in 1898.

It is too early to pronounce as to what will be the final verdict of the world on the special message of President McKinley, as to intervention in Cuban affairs, sent in on April 11th, 1898, and the action which it led Congress to take. Not the least significant feature of that message was the absence of any allusion to the collective note of the great powers, addressed to him a few days before, in which they made a "pressing appeal" for the maintenance of peace. The reception of that note, and the reply which was given to it, certainly cannot be fairly considered as in any way in derogation of the Monroe doctrine. That, as we originally stated and have always maintained it, protests against European interposition in American affairs for the purpose of controlling the destiny of any government which we have recognized as free and independent, or of establishing any colony on either of our continents. It coupled with this, however, when first announced, the statement that "with the existing colonies or dependencies of any European power we have not interfered and shall not interfere."

The powers were fully warranted by this avowal in taking the action now in question. Nor if the expression of our intention not to interfere with existing European colonies in America can be regarded as the legal consideration, so to speak, of our demand that no more of them should be planted in the future, could that expression have been understood to qualify our right to complain of any wrong which might be thereafter done to us or to the people of neighboring countries, and to take such action in regard to it as might be justified by the general rules of international law.

Indeed, in regard to Cuban insurrections and Cuban misrule, we had, more than twenty years before, taken the initiative ourselves in procuring a friendly representation to Spain on the part of the same powers, in support of our views of the necessity of an immediate pacification of the island.[1] The propriety of this action on our part was challenged in some quarters, and our Department of State took occasion to vindicate it in a despatch to our minister at Berlin, in 1876. "The expression to Spain," wrote Mr. Fish, then our Secretary of State, "by the United States, in connection with other powers, of a desire that the civil war in Cuba should be brought

[1] Wharton's International Law Digest, § 60, pp. 403, 409.

to a close, without, however, taking any decided steps of interference, it being understood that the United States ' neither sought nor desired any physical force or pressure, but simply the moral influence of concurrence of opinion as to the protraction of the contest,' is not inconsistent with the traditions of the United States." [1]

The only difference between the concerted representation to Spain procured by us under President Grant's administration, and the concerted representation to us made by the same powers (with the addition of Austria-Hungary) under President McKinley's administration, was that the latter action took the shape of a collective note, and the former that of separate despatches. This made the action taken more impressive, and to that extent added to its weight, but it did not vary its essential character. Indeed the studied moderation of the note may fairly be considered to strengthen any claims we have or may have to influence the general course of American government.

[1] Wharton's International Law Digest, § 60, p. 410.

Index

ABSOLUTISM, political, 80; follows centralization, 85; in the U. S., 83, 84, 112; in Russia, 84; executive, 80; fruit of Collectivism, 113; a necessity in republics, 116; in modern business, 218.
Academic degrees, 196–198.
Act, and intent, 270.
Adams, John, 241.
——, John Quincy, 359.
Administration, judicial, 257.
Administrative functions, 198, 214, 257.
Admiralty, jurisdiction, 250, 251.
Advocates, 322.
Africa, 229.
African Company, 166, 168, 176.
Agency, a gratuitous contract, 322.
Agricultural Bank, 202.
Aktiengesellschaft, 208.
Alexander Severus, 152.
Allegiance, right to transfer, 43, 241.
Altruism, 320, 341.
Amendments, constitutional, how made, 45–47; to State Constitutions, 45, 51.
—— to United States Constitution, possible range of, 81; proposed, 21, 327, 328, note; proclamation of, 114; first, 21; first ten, 41, 110; fifth, 117, 137; eleventh, 110; twelfth, 110; thirteenth, 111; fourteenth, 65, 111, 112, 113, 115; fifteenth, 111, 112, 115.

American Bar Association, resolutions as to habitual criminals, 299.
Americans, national type, 240; a composite race, 240, 264.
Amicable Insurance Co., 171.
Anarchy, 116.
Anglo-Saxons, 286.
Annapolis, charter, 184.
Anthropology, criminal, 290.
Anthropometry, 291.
Antiquity, reverence for, 288.
Apollonius, 153.
Appeals, in criminal proceedings, 138.
Apprentices, 176, note, 190.
Aragon, justiciary of, 30.
Arbitration, international, 345–358; beginnings of, 345; want of sanction, 345; limitations of subjects, 357; as to parties, 357; procedure in, 346; selection of arbitrators, 346; recommended by Pan-American Congress, 350; overture from the United States, 350, 351; permanent courts of, 346–358; between England and the United States, 348–354; permanent judges, 351; procedure, 352–355.
Aristotle, 108.
Arnold, Matthew, 341.
Arts, improvements in, 216.
Aryans, 240.
Asia, 229.
Assassination, 109.

Assault, 278.
Associations, unincorporated, 145, 146; English, 170, 187; French, 181; of workingmen, 230.
Associative spirit, 220; a necessity of modern life, 221–224; a source of corporate life, 222.
Attorney-General, 318.
Australia, experiments in legislation, 194; legislative salaries, 335; political characteristics, 336.
Australian ballot, 28.
Austria, policy towards corporations, 210; municipal government in, 214.
Austrian Bank, 170.

BACKUS, Isaac, 20.
Bacon, Lord, on antiquity, 288; criminal procedure, 123–125; revenge, 278.
Bahamas, 335.
Balance of power, 31.
Ballot, Australian, 28; English, 27, 71; Roman, 28; extension of, 27, 28; numbering, 71.
Baltimore, Lord, 184.
Banks, incorporated, 191; earliest, 170; State, 54; free, 195, 196; Defoe's plan, 171; land banks, 171, 185; American, constitutional restrictions, 67, 200; English, 200, 205; Brazilian, 208; English joint-stock, 202; Irish, 201; national, in United States, 199; Bank of Amsterdam, 170, note; of England, 170; of Ireland, 201; of the Manhattan Co., 189; of North America, 188; of Scotland, 170; of St. George, 170; of the United States, 96, 97, 188; of Venice, 170.
Bar, work in developing law, 260, 261; American, 260.

Barbarians, former use of term, 341; mediæval codes, 160.
Baring Brothers, 237.
Bathurst, Lord, 190.
Bazin, 334.
Beavers, 190.
Beccaria, 264.
Belcher, Governor, 187.
Belgium, incorporation laws, 207; legislative salaries, 328; socialism in, 213; criminal procedure in, 307, 309.
Benefit societies, 213, 231.
Berlin, 227.
Bertillon system, 291, 300, 306, 309–311.
Bill of Rights, American, 40.
Biology, law of, 268, 296.
Blockade of 1861 by U. S., 354.
Body, human, 291.
Borgeaud, on American Constitutions, 48.
Bracton, 118.
Bram's Case, 126.
Brazil, free incorporation law, 207.
Brewer, Mr. Justice, 138.
Bristol, 166.
British Linen Company, 206.
Britton, on torture, 118.
Brotherhood of St. Thomas Becket, 165.
Brown, Mr. Justice, 249.
Brown University, 184.
Bubble Act, 178, 187, 200.
Burgundy, 165.
Burlingame treaty, 66.
Burr, Aaron, 92, 189.

CABINET, President's, 32, 88.
California, anti-Chinese laws, 65; taxation in, 68.
Canada, general incorporation law, 210; power of Governor-General, 63; legislative salaries, 335.

INDEX

Canals, 191, 213.
Canning, George, 359.
Capital, altruistic use of, 320; Collectivism as to, 237; combination with labor, 217, 229; of fraternal societies, 220, 231; these discourage individual accumulation, 231, 232; pressure for investment, 170, 200.
Capital crimes, 242.
Capitalists, among workingmen, 231, 232; leaning towards corporations, 218.
Carlyle, on heroes, 34; on national history, 42.
Carnot, President, 10, 11.
Carolina Charter, 167, 168.
Castellum, 159, note.
Castrum, 159, note.
Cato, 145.
Caucus, 38.
Charitable, bequests, 274, 316, 320; gifts, 320; corporations, 206.
Charles I., 285.
Charters, as contracts, 121; colonial, 166, 167, 169, 185; proposed revocation, 169; monopolistic, 169; municipal, 212; royal, 185, 202; special, 146, 150, 193, 224, 227.
Chartists, 330.
Chinese labor, 65.
Christian Church, at first unfavorable to patriotism, 13; position as affected by the Reformation, 342; alliance with the State, 15.
Christian Republic of Europe, 342.
Christianity, catholicity of, 15; altruistic, 320; its international influences, 343.
Church, ancient functions, 21; interpretation of Pentateuch, 283; confiscation of property by Henry VIII., 173; libraries, 24; registers, 24; support of morals, 24.
Church and State, ancient union, 15; separation of, 15, 16, 246.
Church of England, 19.
Cicero, 147, 240.
Cincinnati, 240.
Cities, decay of power in middle ages, 164; early charters, 160, note; growth of, 35, 294; in the United States, 293; dangers from, 293, 294; modern functions, 213; trade-city, 162.
Citizens, of the United States, 253; of the State, 65, 253; corporations as, 65; rights against State, 247.
City-State, 141.
Civil Law, as to corporations, 145–158; as to partnerships, 181.
Civil Procedure, 247.
Civil Rights Bill, 76.
Civil Service Examinations, 39.
Civil War, American, results, 50.
Civilization, altruistic, 320; irregular advance, 348.
Class, criminal, 292, 293; distinctions of, 26; of wage earners, 232; political aims, 212.
Clay, Henry, 362.
Clergy, American, favor religious liberty, 19.
Cleveland, President, 105.
Clodian law, 148.
Code pleading, 57, 247.
Codes, Austrian, 280; barbarian, 160; Louisiana, 297; of international law, 43; of Napoleon, 207, 280, 281; Theodosian, 154, note.
Codification, 256, 257.
Coke, Sir Edward, 118, 206.
Colbert, 168, 179.
Coleridge, S. T., 113.

Collectivism, gain of, 113, 114, 237; Roman, 142.
College, Stephen, 243.
Colleges, colonial charters, 185; degrees from, 196-198; incorporation under general laws, 196.
Collegium, 145, 151, 157.
Cologne, 158.
Colombia, 258, 335, note.
Colonia, 158, 159, note.
Colonial government, charters, 166, 169, 184; early, 263; in New England, 8.
Columbia College, 185.
Combinations, of labor, 220; of labor and capital, 217.
Comes civitatis, 160.
Comity, 307.
Commerce, 164, 234.
Common Recovery, 269.
Communauté, 161.
Commune, 214.
Compagnie, 182.
Companies Act, 205, 225.
Company, joint-stock, 154, 164; "regulated," 164, 166, note; trading, 165, 169.
Competition, 164, 233.
Compte en participation, 182.
Conciliabulum, 159, note.
Confederate States of America, 90, 95.
Confessions, extorting, 118, 125; extra-judicial, 125, 126.
Congress, Continental, 325; of the United States, 326-328.
Connecticut, admission of interested witnesses, 249; colonial charters by, 184, note, 185; colonial Constitution, 48, 258; corporations in, 226; taxation of, 236, note; delegates to Continental Congress, 325; first State Constitution, 46; copied largely from that of Mississippi,

47; initiates the *referendum*, 47; parole of prisoners, 301, note; *referendum* in, 260.
Conservatism, 286.
Constitution of the United States, first ten amendments, 41; last five amendments, 110, 111; remade by XIVth Amendment, 113; unwillingness to alter, 328, note. See "Amendments, Constitutional."
Constitutional Conventions, 47, 259; national, 82; of United States in 1787, 10, 18.
Constitutional law, 31, 101, 252, 257, 258.
Constitutions, executive construction of, 101, 252, 253, 257, 258; expansion by necessity, 93; historical development of, 87, 120; judicial construction of, 31; proper scope, 78; State, changes in, 45, 51; State, general incorporation laws, 199; State, modes of change, 47; State, popular ratification of, 46; style and form, 37, 75; written, 30.
Consuls of trading companies, 166, note.
Contempt of court, 56.
Continental Congress, 325.
Contracts, obligation of, 121, 253; liability to make, 248.
Convention, constitutional, 47, 259.
Convention of 1787, 10, 18; debates on the executive, 87, 88; debates on legislative salaries, 325, 326; debates on chartering corporations, 188.
Convicts, police supervision of, 301-306; paroles to, 299; recidivists, 297, 298.
Co-operative associations, 209, 226, 233.
Copernican system, 283, 342.

INDEX 373

Coroners' inquests, 270, 274.
Corporations, municipal, American and English laws of, compared, 211, 212; general incorporation laws, 198-200, 210-212; German conception, 162; home rule in, 142, 158, 214; in American colonies, 184; in dark ages, 159; mayor, 85, 160; origin, 34, 35, 141; personality, 142; political control, 212; powers, 73, 211; Roman, 157, 158; State supervision, 214.
——, private, American and English laws of, contrasted, 206, 207, 251, 252; American legislation as to, 63, 64; as masters, 229; by-laws, 165; cumulative vote, 70; Dartmouth College Case, 121, 253; directors of, 173, 219, 251; distrust of, in 18th century, 190; failures and re-organizations, 228; fictitious capitalization, 68; general incorporation laws, 64, 146, 150, 173, 183, 193-198, 200-207, 220, 225, 248; history in England, 170, 173, 175, 200-207; history in Germany, 208, 209; history in France, 179-183; history in modern Europe, 170, 192, 207; history in Rome, 141, 145, 155; history in United States, 63, 184-189, 193-198; how far citizens, 65; individual liability, 157, 204; influence on legislation, 64; legislative control of, 65; limitations of power, 196; moneyed, essential elements, 173; personality, 142, 143, 206; relations to socialism, 236-238; results of, 225; taxation, 234; trust-fund doctrine, 252; unity of management, 217; watered stock, 64, 176.
Corporation Act, English, 19.

Corpus, 143, 154, 164, 233.
Countess of Shrewsbury's Case, 119, 123, 124.
Courts, American canons of decision, 251; resemblance to English, 348; as interpreters of Constitutions, 258; constitutional functions, 30; despatch of business in, 56; inherent powers, 357; international, 346, 357; jury trials, 249; legal fictions in, 268-289; litigation with foreigners, 357; local, 262; popular regard for, 349; preventive effect, 355; respect to precedent, 250; respect to truth, 283; sanction of decisions, 344.
Coxe, Brinton, 31.
Crime, as a profession, 294; causes, 290; decline in England, 305.
Criminal anthropology, 290; personal responsibility for crime, 314.
Criminal law, English, 278.
Criminal procedure, allowing defendant to testify, 127; his cross-examination, 129; American system, 242; appeals, 138, 244; extenuating circumstances, 280; Austrian, 280; Bavarian, 132; Beccaria's influence, 264; Bertillon system, 291, 300, 306, 309, 311; branding, 281, note; British, 132, 243, 295, 299, 304, 305; conclusive proof demanded, 131; defence of insanity, 270, 277-282; discretion of trial judge, 278; early modes, 296; exemption of accused from examination, 117, 123, 134, 243; *ex post facto* laws, 246, 253; favoring the accused, 129, 130; fine, 296; French, 134, 280, 303; functions of committing magistrate,

124, 133; habitual criminals, 290; legislation needed, 136; life sentences, 297, 312; parole system, 298; penitentiaries, 242; pleadings, 130; probationers, 242, 306; public prosecutors, 133, 244, 247; Sir John Jervis' Act, 123; ticket of leave, 299; torture, 121, 132, 135; uncertainties of American, 130; use of jury in, 132; whipping, 296.
Criminals, habitual, 290-315; police supervision of, 301-306, 313; registration of, 301, 309, 310.
Cuba, 357, 362, 365, 366.
Cummings v. Missouri, 253.
Cumulative vote, 70.
Cuq, on Roman Institutions, 142.
Currency, colonial, 187; paper, 185.

D'AGUESSEAU, 286.
Darien, Scotch settlement of, 177.
Dartmouth College, 185.
Dartmouth College Case, 121, 253.
Davis, Jefferson, 95.
Death, civil action for causing, 66.
Debtors, laws to favor, 73; imprisonment of, 248.
Debts, collection of, 73.
Declaration of Independence, 241.
Deeds, record of, 247, 262; disentailing, 269.
De Foe, 168, 171.
Degradation, civic, 307.
Degrees, academic, 196-198.
Denmark, salaried legislatures, 330; treaty with Prussia, 347.
Departments of government, three, 31, 322; executive functions, 87, 88; judicial functions, 198, 257; legislative functions, 49, 55; administrative functions, 198, 214.
Despotism, in democracies, 109.

De Tocqueville, views on taxation, 234; views on judicial power, 257; views on official salaries, 331.
Diploma, college, 198.
Diplomacy, modern methods, 345.
Directors, of corporations, 219.
Disestablishment, church, 17.
Disfranchisement, 306, 307.
Divorce, restrictive laws, 75; attitude of church, 254; at Rome, 254; procedure in, 255.
Domicile, registry of, 303; as a test of jurisdiction, 255.
Dorr's Rebellion, 91.
Duane, Wm. J., 115.
Duelling, 71.
Durham, bishop of, 211; University of, 197.

EAST INDIA COMPANY, English, 166, 168; Dutch, 167, 193, note; French, 168.
Eastland Company, 166.
Education, anciently in charge of church, 21; assumed by the State, 22, 72; religious, 23; importance attached to in colonial period, 53; in Southern States, 72; influence, internationally, 345.
Egypt, tradesmen in, 145, 150.
Eighteenth century, remoteness of, 83.
Elections, corruption in, 62; cumulative voting, 70; canvass of, 71; popular, 80.
Elective franchise, extension of, 25, 26; duty to use, 244; forfeiture of, 306, 307.
Electors, presidential, 85, 106, 107.
Elizabethan age, 263.
Eminent domain, 196.
England, cash system of trade, 233; changes in legal proced-

INDEX

ure, 349; decline of monarchy in, 88; fall of rents, 232; history of private corporations in, 170, 173, 175; American investments in, 227; now a republic, 107, 243; protection of charities, 318; the commonwealth, 340; trades unions in, 231. See "House of Commons," "House of Lords."
Entails, breaking, 269.
Epicurean philosophy, 232.
Equal rights, 221.
Equity, place in history, 267; procedure, 57.
European concert, 361.
Evidence, artificial rules of, 131; preponderance of, 131.
Evolution of institutions, 14.
Examination of criminals, 117, 128.
Exchange, stock, 169.
Exchequer bills, 171.
Executive, compensation of, 322; personal dignity, 33; term of office, 55.
Executive councils, 50, 88.
Executive power, checks in monarchies, 31; increase in our States, 55; its real nature, 87, 88; laws unexecuted by, 98; strength in republics, 31.
Executor, 317.
Exemptions from execution, 73.
Expatriation, voluntary, 43, 241.
Ex post facto law, 253.
Extradition of criminals, 312.

FACTORY, trading, 163; De Foe's project, 171.
Falcidian part, 272, 273, 274, 317.
Familia, 143, 144, 147, 155.
Family, Roman, 142, 144, 234; influence in American colonies, 53.
Farmers of the revenue, Roman, 147, 154.

Federalist, The, 86, 89.
Feltmakers, company of, 190.
Felton's Case, 122.
Feudalism, decay of, 164.
Fiction, legal, defined, 286; decadence of, 266; modern use, 266–289; nature, 267; origin, 266.
Field, David Dudley, 43, 248.
Finances, public, 54.
Finch's discourse on law, 120.
Fish, Hamilton, 366.
Fisher *v.* Fielding, 349.
Fletcher *v.* Peck, 252.
Force, governmental, 341, 344.
Foreign judgment, 348.
Foreigners, 341, 343, 357.
Fortescue, on judicial torture, 122.
Forum, 159, note.
France, influence on modern government, 9; influence on American thought, 264; Parliaments of Justice, 98; the States-General in 1789, 9, 10; the National Assembly, 10, 331; the revolution, 11, 83, 109, 162; religious liberty in, 21; first Constitution, 29; Constitution of 1848, 330; of 1851, 331; trade guilds, 161, 162; history of corporations in, 179–183, 226; criminal codes, 280, 281, 303, 307; socialism in, 213; the *Commune*, 214; trades unions in, 220, 231; State aid to co-operative production, 233; taxation in, 234; constitutional revision in, 259; registration in, 303; protection of charities, 318; salaried legislature, 330.
Franchise, elective, 306, 307; parliamentary, 332; corporate, 186, 207.
Franklin, Benjamin, 241, 321; his junto, 149; French ideas, 264.
Fraternities, religious, 160; Roman, 142; within a corpora-

tion, 186; of wage earners, 221;
mismanagement of, 232.
Freedmen, suffrage for, 26; apprentice laws, 26.
Frith-guild, 161.

GABINIAN law, 28.
Gambling Act, 179.
Garfield, assassination of, 110.
Gavelkind, 273.
Gellius, Aulus, 159, note.
Genesse Chief, The, 251.
Genossenschaften, 209.
George I., 340.
George II., 179.
George III., 285.
Georgia, constitutional changes in, 77.
Germans, ancient, 159, 259; in United States, 240.
Germany, free incorporation laws, 208, 209, 226; attract English capital, 227; journalism in, 38; socialism in, 333; State socialism in, 25; the Reichstag, 333; trades unions in, 220.
Gerry, Elbridge, 326.
Gladstone, 28.
God, ancient conception of, 342.
Goethe, on women, 27.
Government, ancient, its aims, 14; modern, began when, 6; its aims, 14; share of people in, 345; mutability of principles, 337; revolutions of form, 340; of methods, 348; sources of, 266.
Governor, State, term of office, 49, 55; veto power, 31, 55, 85; increase of power, 55; pardoning power, 85.
Grand jury, 56, 198, note.
Granger Cases, 65.
Grapeshot, Case of the, 103.
Gratuities, public, 62.
Great Britain, insecurity of property in, 40; now a democracy, 83, 361; responsible ministry in, 97; corporations in, 200-207, 225; labor associations in, 231; treaty of arbitration with, 348. See "England" and "House of Commons."
Grotius, 343, 345.
Guilds, Roman, 143, 150; mediæval, 160, 161; merchant, 161.

Habeas corpus, suspension in United States, 92, 95.
Habitual criminals, 290-315.
Hamburg, 162, note; Bank of, 170.
Hamburgh Company, 165, note.
Hamilton, Alexander, 189.
Hand in Hand Insurance Co., 171.
Hanoverian dynasty, 340.
Hanseatic league, 163.
Harvard College, 184.
Hatting trade, 190.
Hawaii, free incorporation law, 210.
Hayburn's Case, 31.
Heineccius, 149.
Heirs, cutting off by will, 316; legal protection of, 271, 272, 273, 274, 288; primogeniture, 262.
Hempstead, charter, 184, note.
Henry III., 161.
Henry IV. of France, 342.
Henry VIII., 173.
Hero worship, 33.
Holland, influence on American law, 239.
Holmes, Oliver Wendell, 261.
Holy Alliance, The, 360.
Home Rule, 35, 142.
Homicide, 139, 277, 280-282.
Honor, protection of, 277.
Hospitals, charitable, 174.
House of Commons, power of, 32; pay of members, 323-325, 329-333, 340; powers of members,

INDEX 377

324; functions of members, 324; landed interest in, 324; changes in composition, 332.
House of Lords, abolition of, 27; attendance in, 334.
Hudson, Henry, 167.
Hudson's Bay Company, 166, 168, 175.
Hume, 191.
Hungary, free incorporation law, 210.
Husband and wife, 254.

IDEAS of '89, 14, 29, 40, 42.
Identification, personal, 291.
Illinois, voting in, 29, 70.
Imprisonment, for debt, 73; for crime, 242, 296.
Incorporation, under general laws, 64, 199, 248.
India, Empress of, 83.
Indies, French Company of the, 180.
Individual, rights of, 40, 41; merger in corporations, 221, 237.
Individualism, effect of business corporations on, 237; effect of labor organizations on, 231, 232; French philosophy of, 13; in religious opinion, 17; loss of, 113, 114.
Infamy, 277, 306, 307.
Insanity, as a defence in criminal cases, 270, 277–282; as a legal fiction, 270–284; in suicides, 274–277; in testators, 271.
Inscriptions, Roman, 153.
Insolvent debtors, 248.
International Law, beginnings of, 343, 345; source and sanction, 343; part of municipal law, 343; American, 350; courts of arbitration between nations, 355.
Inter-State Commerce Act, 137.
Intervention, right of international, 361; by the United States in Cuban affairs, 365.
Iowa, general incorporation laws, 200.
Institutes of Justinian, 154.
Institutions, their characteristics, 2, 4, 82; legal, Taylor's definition, 3; modern political, beginning of, 1; list of, 3; growth of, 82; sentimental causes, 221, 224; national differences, 337, 338.
Insurance, companies, 170, 191, 196; taxation, 235; by Hudson's Bay Co., 176, note; compulsory, 25; benefit societies, 213, 231; endowment, 176, note; wagering, 178.
Intent, 270.
Ireland, results of the Union, 83; parliamentary delegation, 332, 333.
Irish, in the United States, 240.
Italians, New Orleans massacre, 244.
Italy, free incorporation law, 210, 227; trades unions in, 231; criminal punishments, 307; legislature, 334.

JACKSON, President, 99; foreign policy, 94; struggle with United States Bank, 96, 97; views of executive power, 101.
Jail, made too attractive, 313.
Japan, constitution of, 42; education in, 22; its political characteristics, 336; trades unions, 220.
Jardine, on torture, 122.
Jefferson, epitaph, 24; French ideas, 29, 264; influence in education, 23; influence in Virginia legislation, 17; Louisiana purchase, 96; on the Monroe Doc-

INDEX

trine, 362; views on expatriation, 241; views of power of President, 86, 99.
Jeffreys, Chief Justice, 119.
Johnson, President, 99, 101; impeachment of, 100, 115, 339.
Joint-Stock Companies Registration Act, 201, 203.
Joint-stock company, defined, 154, 164; beginnings of, 168; English laws as to, 203; limited liability in England, 204; in Germany, 209; consequences of failure, 227.
Journalism, influence on government, 37.
Judex, 160.
Judges, election, 50, 59; legislative appointment, 57; functions in jury trials, 249; in will cases, 318; salaries, 323; of international courts, 352, 353.
Judgment, foreign, 348.
Judiciary, interpreters of Constitutions, 30, 252, 258; judge-made law, 257; powers of, 257; elective, 50, 59, 250; term of office, 55; of the United States, 85; British, 132; executive protection of, 104; supervision of corporate organizations, 198.
Julius Cæsar, 148, 152.
Jurisdiction, admiralty, 251; in divorce suits, 255.
Jurisprudence, definition, 257; Roman definition, 246; universal principles, 341; American, 239, 257; its development, 260 263; a gauge of civilization, 239; leading decisions, 252, 253; outworn, 269; international, 347.
Jury, trial by, 56; issues before, 279; decadence of, 250; unanimity, 56; continental system, 279; American changes in trial by, 249; restricting powers of judge, 249; prosecutions for libel, 245.
Justice, natural, 253; through law, 282.
Justinian, Institutes, 154.

KENT, custom of, 273.
King, can do no wrong, 267, 285; appointments of, 322.
King, Rufus, 188.
Knights Templar, 160.
Kommanditgesellschaften auf Aktien, 208.
Kreisordnung, 210.

LABOR, individual skill now unimportant, 217; organized, 213, 217, 229, 231, 232; political representation, 332; protection of, 15; relations to capital, 217; Roman guilds, 143.
Land, modes of transfer, 269; registry of titles, 247.
Land Banks, English, 171; in Connecticut, 185.
Landgemeineordnung, 210, note.
Lanuvium, inscription, 151, note.
Latin, use in middle ages, 263.
Lauvergne, 292, 297.
Law, becoming institutional, 121; customary, 287, 288, 344; development of, 120, 260, 261, 266, 267; *ex post facto*, 253; general and equal, 221; rests on consent, 344; sanction, 344; Stoic conception of, 282; unconstitutional, 99; unjust, 279; unsuited to the community, 277-279; when ancient and settled, 285, 315. See "Criminal Procedure," "Constitutional Law," "International Law," "Roman Law."
Law, John, 179.
Law merchant, 219.

INDEX

Lawyers, duty in argument of causes, 250; work in developing law, 260, 261.
Legal fiction, see "Fiction, legal."
Legislation, American, 36, 337; effect on governments, 267; equality, 221; experiments in, 194; growth in modern times, 36; inconsiderate, 33; outside influence on, 337; progress in, 287; relation to unwritten law, 287; Roman, 46; special prohibited, 36, 57, 146, 200.
Legislative department, American checks on, 49, 53, 258; growing distrust of, 57, 224; inherent limitations, 253; judicial powers, 55.
Legislatures, appointment of members to office, 58; biennial sessions, 69; colonial in America, 325; control by agricultural interest, 236; executive sessions, 37; favoritism in, 224; popular representation in, 224; position of members, 322; power in free governments, 337; procedure in, 61, 62; rush of business in, 224; salaries for members, 69, 322-340.
Leipsic, church services in, 16.
Leon, charter of, 160, note.
Levant Company, 166.
Libel, 245.
Liberty, civil, 248; how affected by war, 253; of contract, 248; restraint for criminals, 295; religious, 15, 23.
Libraries, public, 24.
Lieber, Francis, 220.
Life insurance, early English, 176, note; gambling in, 178.
Limited companies, 205, 209, 218.
Lincoln, President, 92, 93, 99.

Liquor-selling, prohibition of, 75.
Literature, early colonial, 263; mediæval, 263; Revolutionary era, 264.
Liverpool Insurance Co., 202.
Livingston, Edward, 297.
Loan Association v. Topeka, 253.
Loans, public, 62.
Lobbying, 63.
Local Government Act, 211.
Lombroso, 290.
London, trade of, 165; livery companies, 162; guild-hall, 162; penny post, 168; water supply, 171; banking in, 202, 205.
Lotteries, 71.
Louis, Saint, 275.
Louis XIII., 168, 343.
Louis Napoleon, 331.
Louisiana, purchase of, 96; repudiation in, 74; penal code, 297, 311; lotteries in, 71; undutiful wills, 317; Provisional Court in, 103; general incorporation laws, 199.
Loyalty, 13.
Luther, 342.
Lynch law, 136, 139, 244, 302.
Lyons, 158, 229.

MACAULAY, T. B., 93.
Machiavelli, 345.
Machinery, political consequences, 216.
Madison, views on religious liberty, 16; on executive power, 88, 101; as to corporations, 188.
Magister, 147, 154.
Magna Charta, 14, 118.
Maine, criminal punishments in, 298.
———, Sir H. S., 89, 266, 269.
———, The, 356.
Maisons de Dieu, 174.
Majorities, influence of party

nominations on, 39; tyranny of, 33.
Man, brotherhood of, 341, 345; classes of mankind, 292; duties of, 320; evolution of, 292; rights of, 40; The Forgotten, 130.
Manchester, 211, 213, note, 229.
Manhattan Company, 189.
Manslaughter, 281, note.
Manufactures, household, 216; in American colonies, 190; modern characteristics, 217; public aid for, 213; overproduction, 229.
Marbury v. Madison, 31, 252.
Marcus Aurelius, 34, 149.
Marine Hospital Fund, 25.
Marriage as a sacrament, 284; divorce, 254.
Married women, 254.
Marshall, Chief Justice, 92, 121, 251, 252, 253.
Martial law, 92.
Maryland, colonial charters in, 184; early constitutional amendments, in, 47.
Marx, Karl, 238.
Mason, Jeremiah, 241.
Massachusetts, Constitution of 1780, 46, 51; forfeiture of charter, 184, note; patent, 166; probation system, 305; veto power in, 32; early incorporations in, 187.
Maxims, political, 267.
McCarthy, Justin, 330.
McCulloch, J. R., 218.
McCurdy, Charles J., 249, note.
McKinley, President, 95, 365.
Mechanical inventions, 35.
Merchant adventurers, 165, 167.
Merchant guilds, 161.
Merchants, London, 165.
Mexico, legislative salaries, 335; Maximilian, 363.

Michigan, free banking law, 195.
Militia of United States, 90.
Mill, J. S., on individualism, 14.
Milligan's Case, 92, 253.
Millionnaires, 237, 238.
Milton, on municipal government, 214–216.
Ministry, responsible, 32, 97, 267.
Minority, protection of, 70.
Minority representation, 29, 39; in England, 29; in Illinois, 29.
Mississippi, attack on reconstruction laws, 102.
Mississippi Company, 180.
Modern government, began when, 6, 16; its aims, 14; first centenary of, 42; flexibility, 42; share of people in, 345.
Modern society, preceded modern government, 6; Carnot's claim, 12; influence of the Church, 13.
Mommsen, Th., 149, 158, 163.
Monarchy, source of title, 341; hereditary succession, 108; decline of, 360; checks in, 31; in America, 361.
Monasteries, suppression of, 173.
Money, at Rome, 156.
Monopoly, 161, 165; Parliamentary protest, 175.
Monroe, President, 106, 359.
Monroe doctrine, 105, 359–367; origin, 359; scope of, 363, 364; limits of, 366; its acceptance by the great powers, 363; the collective note of 1898, 365, 367; applied to Mexico, 105; applied to Venezuela, 105.
Montesquieu, influence on modern government, 9, 31; in the United States, 18, 264.
Morellet, Abbé, 192.
Municipal corporations, origin, 34; Roman history, 157; home

INDEX

rule in, 35, 158, 214; general incorporation laws, 198, 200, 210–212; limitation on taxes, 73; State supervision, 214; mayor's power, 85; American and English laws of, contrasted, 211, 212; political control, 212.
Municipal Corporations Act, English, 27, 162.
Municipal Corporations (Consolidation) Act, 211.
Municipal Law, 344. See "Law."
Municipium, 158, 159, note.
Murder, 277, 280–282.
Museums, public, 25.

NAPOLEON, 277, 360.
National Assembly, of France, 110.
Nations, originally unfriendly, 343.
Natural selection, 222.
Navicularii, 156.
Neagle's Case, 104.
Nebraska, senatorial nominations in, 60.
Negro, education, 72; suffrage, 26, 50, 52, 111, 112.
Nemo tenetur, etc., 122.
Netherlands, English trade with, 165.
Netherlands Trading Company, 193, note.
Nevada, admission as a State, 112.
New Armsterdam, 167.
New England, colonial trade in, 190; farming in, 156; manufactures, 190.
New Hampshire, constitutional changes in, 20; constitutional ratification by people, 46; religious tests in, 47, 70.
New Jersey, criminal procedure in, 139; conservatism of, 139.

New London Society United, etc., 185.
New Netherlands, 167.
New Orleans, 244.
New York, ballot in, 28; code pleading in, 247; general incorporation laws, 194, 195; Revised Statutes, 256.
New York City, 167, 184; banking in, 189; foreign population, 240; rogues' gallery in, 309; water supply, 189.
New Zealand, legislative salaries, 335, note.
Newcastle, 211.
Newspapers, 37.
Nicholas I., 197.
Niebuhr, view of Roman corporations, 142.
Nineteenth century, characteristics, 289; international arbitration in, 346.
Nominations, for office, 244, 107; laws to protect, 38, 244.
Non-residents, suits against, 255.
Normans, influence on English law, 273.
North Carolina, charter, 166; vote on ratifying Constitution, 21; Reconstruction Constitution, 52.
Northern & Central Bank, 202.
Norway, salaried legislatures, 330.
Novalis, 130.
Novgorod, 163.

OATH, decisory, 248.
Obligation of contracts, 253.
Office, elective, 257; eligibility of women, 70; exclusion for crime, 306; legislative appointments to, 54, 58, 59; motives for seeking, 336; removals from, 59, 89; religious tests for, 19, 47, 70.
Officers, appointment, 257; removal, 257.

Ohio, habitual criminal law, 298.
Ohio Company, 188, note.
One man power, 218.
Oppidum, 159, note.
Ordinance of 1787, 78.
Oriental governments, 42.
Ortolan, on Roman law, 122.

PANAMA Congress, 362.
Pan-American Congress, of 1823, 362; of 1890, 349.
Panic, of 1836, 203; of 1837, 54.
Papacy, 343.
Pardoning power, 85; boards of pardons, 138.
Paris, trade in, 161; registration of criminals in, 310; university of, 197.
Parish, 160.
Parks, 25.
Parole to convicts, 298.
Partnerships, Anglo-American conception of, 181; civil law conception of, 181; *en commandite*, 179, 208, 226; in Germany, 209; Irish Act of 1782, 201; limited, 179; mining, 256; quasi-corporations, 170; yielding to corporations, 217.
Party, conventions, 107, 244; government, 38, 233, 244.
Patents, colonial, 166, 167.
Paterfamilias, 144.
Paternalism, 213.
Patriotism, revival of, 12.
Patterson, Wm., 139.
Pawn-shops, public, 213.
Payson, Phillips, 20.
Penal codes, Alabama, 77; Austria, 280; Belgium, 307; English, 119, 278; France, 280, 281, 303, 307; German, 307; Italian, 307; Louisiana, 297, 311.
Penn, Wm., 167, 168; heirs of, 169.

Pennsylvania, colonial charter, 167; constitution of 1873, 57; general incorporation laws, 194; judicial decisions, 241; penitentiary system, 242; University of, 184.
Penny-post, London, 168.
People, The, as legislators, 259, 260; of the United States, 80, 81, 84, 110.
People's charter, 330.
Perpetuities, 320.
Physical force, inextinguishable, 260.
Pinckney, Charles, 18, 19, 86, 101, 188.
Plato, Republic of, 22, 87.
Pleading, codes of, 57, 247; issues in, 279.
Pliny, 153.
Plymouth, colony of, 167.
Police, supervision of criminals by, 303, 304, 308, 313.
Police power, of State, 262; of the United States, 104.
Politics, experiments in, 348.
Pomeroy, J. N., 135.
Possession, adverse, 267; peaceable, 268.
Precedents, judicial, 250, 270, 285; reversal of, 251.
Prescription, 193, 267.
President of the United States, an elective king, 88; compensation and appointments of, 322, 323; diplomatic powers, 90, 104; his veto, 98; impeachment of, 100, 102; military power, 90–95; mode of election, 35, 85; powers, 84, 109; quasi-judicial power, 103; refusal to execute laws, 99; represents the people, 109; right of removal by, 89, 100; spokesman of the nation, 116; third term, 110; vacancy in office, 108.

Presumption, of guilt, 295, 304; judicial, 267.
Primaries, 38.
Primogeniture, 262, 333.
Princeton College, 184.
Printing, effect of discovery of, 263.
Prisoners, aid societies, 302, 303; examination of, 125; number in United States, 313.
Prisons, made too attractive, 313.
Probation officer, 306.
Procedure, civil, reform in, 247, 268, 283; criminal, see "Criminal Procedure;" English, 349; American, 349; law of evidence, 248; legal fictions, 268–289.
Process, imprisonment for debt, 248; legal fictions in, 268.
Progress, in jurisprudence, 287.
Prohibition of liquor selling, 78.
Property, constitutional guaranties, 39, 262; defence of, 277; private, foundation of, 267; State interference with, 262.
Prussia, country communities, 210; private corporations in, 226; salaried legislatures, 330, note; trades unions in, 231; treaty with Denmark, 347.
Ptolemaic system, 283.
Public, credit, loan of, 62; grants, revocation of, 252; inspection by, 247; law, development of, 360; opinion, force of, 344, international, 344, 367; prosecutors, 133, 247; schools, 22; supervision of private property, 262; uses, 320.
Puritanism, in New England, 8.
Puritans, debt to Holland, 239; notion of religious liberty, 15, 16.

QUASI-CORPORATIONS, 203, note.
Queen's Proctor, 319.

RAILROADS, regulation of charges on, 65, 262; taxation, 235; state regulation of, 262; free passes, 334.
Raleigh, Sir Walter, 166.
Real estate, transfers of titles, 247.
Recidivists, 292, 315.
Reconstruction laws, 52, 99.
Record offices, 24, 247.
Referendum, origin of, 48, 260; Swiss use of, 49.
Reform bill, English, 83, 162, 211, 243.
Reformation, of criminals, 78; Protestant, 341, 342, 343.
Regina *v*. Keyn, 354, note.
Registration, public, 24; of individual citizens, 303.
Religion, as a social force, 15.
Religious, establishments, 19, 20, 21; liberty, 15; test, 19; societies, incorporated, 185.
Reports, judicial, 250, 354.
Republic of letters, 196, 345.
Republics, executive power in, 31; weakness of, 30.
Responsibility, for crime, 314; of British ministry, 32, 97, 267.
Revenge, 278.
Revenue, farmers of, 147, 154; raised from corporations, 234, 235.
Reverence, 33, 288.
Revolution, American, influence on our literary ideas, 264.
Rheims, 158.
Rhode Island, toleration in, 15; constitutional law in, 31; first State Constitution, 46.
Richelieu, 168.
Right, as a governmental force, 341.
Rights, of the citizen, 247; equal, 341; of individual against State,

247, 253; of man, 40; of State against individual, 247.
Robertson, F. W., 7.
Rogers, Thorold, 228.
Rogues' Gallery, 304, 309.
Roman Catholic Church, attitude towards schools, 23; towards suicide, 276; before the Reformation, 342; canon law overruled by civil law, 246; ecumenical councils, 343; marriage as a sacrament, 254; the Holy Alliance, 360; the papacy, 343; Vatican Council, 10.
Roman Catholics, exclusion from office, 15, 70.
Roman law, as to undutiful wills, 271, 272, 316; decisory oath, 248; guilds, 143; in United States, 239; of corporations, 141, 145-158; of divorce, 254; of libel, 245; of pleadings, 279; special legislation, 146; Twelve Tables, 143, 146, 245, 316.
Rome, modern, 227; patriotism in, 12; source of the imperial power, 98; source of military power, 234; statute law in, 36. See "Roman Law."
Ross, Senator, 339, note.
Russia, absolutism in, 84; abolition of serfdom, 93; despotism in, 109; mediæval trade, 163; number of corporations, 226; policy towards corporations, 210; the Holy Alliance, 360.
Russian Company, 166.
Rutgers College, 184.

ST. MARY's City, 184.
Salaries, of executive officers, 322; of judicial, 323; of legislative, 322-340; the fee system, 339; capitalists favor low, 340.

Savigny, definition of corporation, 206, note.
Savings-banks, municipal, 213; taxation, 235.
Schleswig-Holstein difficulty, 347.
Schools, public, 72.
Schouler, James, 60.
Scotland, Act of Union, 177; trading charters, 168, 177; criminal verdicts, 279.
Secession, 52.
Secretary of State, 114.
Self-crimination, 137.
Selfishness of governments, 130.
Senators of United States, 60, 338; their pay, 325-328.
Senegal Company, 168.
Sentiment, as a social force, 221, 224; as a political force, 360.
Sentimentalism, 130.
Shaftesbury, Lord, 168.
Sherman, Roger, 87.
Shipowners, Roman, 148, note.
Shipping, American capital in foreign, 227.
Sigonius, 159.
Simian family, 292.
Skeleton, human, 291.
Slaughter House Cases, 253.
Slavery, Lincoln's Emancipation proclamation, 93.
Slaves, protection of freedmen, 111.
Slave-trade, 43.
Smith, Adam, influence on United States, 18; views on corporations, 191, 195.
Socialism, French philosophy of, 13; State, 25, 237; political influence, 212; its future, 238.
Societas, 143; *publica*, 154.
Société à responsabilité limitée, 183, note.
Société anonyme, 181, 201, 207, 226.
Société en commandite, 179, 226.
Société par actions, 181.

INDEX

Society, effect on government, 266, 267.
South America, relations of the United States to, 360; European colonization, 362, 364.
South Sea Co., English, 177, 190; French, 180.
Spain, free incorporation law, 210; in South America, 360; war with United States, 356.
Spectator, London, 364.
Spencer, Herbert, 240.
Staël, Madame de, 276.
State, relations to its citizens, 247; loan of credit, 62; police power, 262; sovereignty, 253.
State socialism, 25, 237.
State and Church, 15; separation, 16.
States, of the United States, 80; relation to the United States, 43, 80; constitutional changes in, 45; legislatures, 334.
States-General of France, 10.
Statutes, form, 337; unsettle law, 236; codification of, 256, 257; colonial, 256; revisions, 256; obsolete, 271, 287; unjust, 271, 279; repeal, 287. See "Legislation."
Stock Exchange, 169.
Stock-jobbing, 168, 178.
Stoic philosophy, 282.
Store, department, 163.
Story, Mr. Justice, 251.
Succession, to the dead, 287; intestate, 144; custom of Kent, 273; to land, 269.
Suffrage, early constitutional limitations, 47; broad, 25; universal, 26; qualifications, 25, 26, 47, 74; female, 27, 70; negro, 26, 50, 52, 112; educational, 78, 113; British, 27 : constitutional limitations in United States, 69.

Suicide, 270, 274-277.
Sumner, Wm. G., 129.
Susquehannah Company, 188, note.
Sweden, trading companies, 167; legislative salaries, 335.
Switzerland, *referendum* in, 49, 260; free incorporation law, 210; criminal laws, 309; legislative salaries, 336.

TACITUS, 259.
Talleyrand, 345.
Taney, chief-justice, 92; as secretary of the Treasury, 115.
Tax payers, voting by, 74.
Taxation, church exemptions, 24; constitutional provisions as to, 68; of corporations, 234; may lead to extravagance, 235; through municipalities, 234.
Tenement houses, unsanitary, 213.
Tennessee law, as to suicide, 275.
Tenure of Office Act, 99, 100.
Territories of United States, government of, 199.
Test, religious, 19.
Test Act, English, 19.
Teutons, 259.
Texas, constitutional changes in, 76.
Theodosian Code, 154, note.
Torture, in criminal cases, 118, 121.
Trade, American colonial, 190; guilds, 144; rapidity of modern, 220; Roman, 144.
Trade-city, 162.
Trade union, how produced, 221; legalized, 200, 220, 231; national, 199, 230; political ideas, 214; political influence, 212.
Trading companies, Dutch, 167; English, 162, 165-168; French,

168; Scotch, 168, 177; conflicting charters, 170; colonial, 186.
Trajan, 153.
Treaties, have force of law, in United States, 242; for arbitration, 346, 347; permanent and continental, 350.
Tredwell, Thomas, 41.
Truth, in judicial proceedings, 283.
Turgot, 320.
Turkey company, 166, note.

UMPIRE, 351.
United Provinces, 215.
United States, abrogation of Articles of Confederation, 12; absolutism in, 84; among the oldest of nations, 83; Articles of Confederation, 51; citizens of, 253; continental responsibilities, 359, 364; convention of 1787, 10; criminal statistics, 313; early weakness of, 86; growth of, 360; increasing city population, 293; nationalization of, 113, 116; police power of, 104; registration of criminals by, 310; relation to the States, 43, 80; reserved rights, 111; sovereignty over States, 109, 112, 114; the people of, 80, 81, 84, 110. See "Amendments, constitutional," and "Constitution."
Universitas, 144.
Universities, degrees from, 196–198; incorporation under general laws, 196; State, 23, 72.
University of Virginia, 23, 24.

VATICAN Council, 10.
Venezuela, 363, 366.
Vermont, general incorporation laws, 195.
Veto power, colonial, 31; English, 97; in States and United States, 32, 85, 98; use by President Jackson, 97.
Vice-President of United States, 108.
Vicus, 159, note.
Vienna, 170, 214.
Virginia, charter, 166; criminal punishments, 297; delegates to Continental Congress, 325; religious liberty in, 16.
Virginia Company, 166, 167.
Voting, ballot, 27, 28, 71; exclusion for crime, 306, 307.

WAGE earners, exemption from attachment, 73; mediæval craftguilds, 161.
Wages, combinations to raise, 213.
Waltzing, on Roman Corporations, 155.
War, constitutional impediments in United States, 361; effect of international arbitration courts, 355; effect on individual liberty, 253; progress towards extinction, 343; social effects, 50; Spanish of 1898, 356; supersedes courts, 103; suspension of *habeas corpus*, 92–95.
Washington, George, Genet's recall, 90; inaugural address, 44; influence on frame of Constitution, 106; influence on its ratification, 86, 336.
Waterworks, city, 171, 192, 195.
Wealth, influence in colonial politics, 53; men of, in United States, 47.
Webster, Daniel, 94.
West India Company, Dutch, 167; French, 168; Swedish, 167.
West Jersey, 168.
Whipping-post, 296.

INDEX

Wife, 253, 254.
William and Mary College, 185.
Wills, charitable bequests, 274; defence by State, 316; English statute of, 273; Falcidian part, 272; hard, 271, 288; Roman, 271, 272; suits to construe, 318; undutiful, 271, 317.
Wilson, James, on modern government, 7.
Wingate's "Maxims," 122, 123.
Winthrop, Governor John, 166; Governor John, Jr., 48.
Witchcraft, 34.
Witness, confidential communications, 56; decisory oath, 248; interested, 126, 127, 248.
Women, love of order, 27; eligibility to office, 70; suffrage for, 27, 70; married, 253, 254.
Words, want of apt, 357.
Workingmen, Roman guilds, 143, 150; trades unions, 200, 229-231; political influence, 233, 332; national trade unions, 199; individual qualities, 217; right to combine, 220, 231; decline in small capitalists, 232.

YALE College, 184, and note.

www.ingramcontent.com/pod-product-compliance
Lightning Source LLC
Chambersburg PA
CBHW032022220426
43664CB00006B/337